BLOODY HARVEST

The killing of Falun Gong for their organs

Other books by David Matas

Justice Delayed: Nazi War Criminals in Canada
with Susan Charendoff

Closing the Doors: The Failure of Refugee Protection
with Ilana Simon

No More: The Battle Against Human Rights Violations

Bloody Words: Hate and Free Speech

Aftershock: anti-Zionism and anti-Semitism

and co-editor of
The Machinery of Death

Other books by David Kilgour

Uneasy Patriots: Western Canadians in Confederation

Betrayal: The Spy Canada Abandoned

Uneasy Neighbours:
Canada, the USA and the Dynamics of
State, Industry and Culture
with David T. Jones

BLOODY HARVEST

The killing of Falun Gong for their organs

David Matas and David Kilgour

Seraphim
EDITIONS

Reproduced by Permission, the Royal Society of Medicine Press, London – Treasure, The Falun Gong, organ transplantation, the holocaust and ourselves. Mar 2007, 100; 119-121

The publisher gratefully acknowledges the financial assistance of the Canada Council for the Arts and the Ontario Arts Council.

 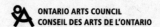

Library and Archives Canada Cataloguing in Publication

Matas, David
Bloody harvest : the killing of Falun Gong for their organs / David Matas and David Kilgour.

ISBN 978-0-9808879-7-6

1. Transplantation of organs, tissues, etc.–Corrupt practices–China.
2. Sale of organs, tissues, etc.–Corrupt practices–China. 3. Falun Gong (Organization). 4. Prisoners–Crimes against–China. 5. Political persecution–China. 6. Human rights–China. I. Kilgour, David, 1941- II. Title.

HV6627.M38 2009   364.1'322   C2009-906041-8

Editor: George Down
Cover Design and Typography: Julie McNeill, McNeill Design Arts

Published in 2009 by
Seraphim Editions
54 Bay Street
Woodstock, ON
Canada N4S 3K9

Fifth printing, 2012

Printed and bound in Canada

Table of Contents

Introduction

A woman using the pseudonym Annie told the newspaper *The Epoch Times* in a story published in its March 17, 2006 issue:

> "One of my family members was involved in the operation to harvest Falun Gong practitioners' organs. This brought great pain to our family."

Annie's interview led to a controversy about whether or not she was telling the truth. The Government of China denied everything. Others, who had begun some initial investigations based on what Annie said, asserted that Falun Gong practitioners were victims of live organ-harvesting throughout China.

Falun Gong is a set of exercises with a spiritual foundation which was banned in China in 1999. Those who did the exercises after 1999 were arrested and asked to denounce the practice. Those who did so were released. Those who did not were tortured. Those who still refused to recant after torture disappeared.

What happened to the disappeared? It was claimed by Annie and others that they were organ-harvested, that organ-pillaging was being inflicted on unwilling Falun Gong practitioners at a wide variety of locations, pursuant to a systematic policy, in large numbers.

Organ-harvesting is a step in organ transplants. The purpose is to provide organs for transplants. Transplants do not necessarily have to take place in the same place as the location of the organ-harvesting. The two locations are often different; organs harvested in one place are shipped to another place for transplanting.

The claim was further that the organs are harvested from the practitioners while they are still alive. The practitioners are killed in the course of the organ-harvesting operations or immediately thereafter. These operations are a form of murder.

Finally, it was claimed that the practitioners killed in this way are then cremated. There would be no corpse left to examine, to identify as the source of an organ transplant.

The Coalition to Investigate the Persecution of the Falun Gong in China (CIPFG) in May 2006 asked us to investigate these claims. In light of the seriousness of the claims, as well as our own commitment to respect for human rights, we accepted the request. Though the organization offered to pay our expenses, we never asked it to do so.

We first set out the results of our investigation in a report released in July 2006. A second version of the report was released in January 2007. Our conclusion was indeed that innocent Falun Gong practitioners were being killed for their organs.

This book presents our investigation in updated form. It secondly presents how we and others dealt with the evidence we accumulated. Because we are both human rights activists, we could not sit idly by once we concluded that innocents were being killed for their organs.

The book has two parts. The first part sets out the evidence. Our investigation did not end with the first version of our report, nor the second. We continued to receive new evidence after each version of the report came out, not only additional evidence of the sort we had already received, but whole new categories of evidence. The second part sets out the reactions we got to our report and the advocacy we undertook to end the abuse we identified.

Our advocacy and the investigation were mutually reinforcing. Because of our advocacy we continued to receive new evidence. And because the new evidence all pointed in the same direction, supporting our conclusions, the new evidence reinforced our advocacy.

Laws and practices have changed since the two versions of our report came out, possibly partly because of the report. This book attempts to look at the situation as it has evolved, addressing the question not only whether the abuse has occurred, but also whether it is still occurring.

Part I: The Evidence

Chapter One

Methods

The Coalition to Investigate the Persecution of Falun Gong in China by letter asked us to investigate the allegations of organ-harvesting of Falun Gong practitioners. This is the letter:

"May 24, 2006

To: Mr. David Matas and Mr. David Kilgour

The Coalition to Investigate the Persecution of the Falun Gong in China (CIPFG), a nongovernmental organization registered in Washington, D.C., U.S.A. with a branch in Ottawa, Ontario, Canada, respectfully asks for your assistance in investigating allegations that state institutions and employees of the government of People's Republic of China have been harvesting organs from live Falun Gong practitioners, killing the practitioners in the process. The Coalition has received evidence to substantiate these allegations, but also is aware that some people are unsure whether or not these allegations are true and that others deny them.

The Coalition understands that you will conduct your investigation independently from the Coalition or any other organization/government. You are free to report your findings or come to any conclusion based on the evidence collected.

The Coalition will pay for all your expenses upon presentation of receipts. We understand that you will not charge a fee for your work.

Your working methods are entirely of your own choosing. We understand that you will provide us with your report, at the latest, by June 30, 2006.

Thank you for agreeing to undertake this important task.

Sincerely,
John Jaw, Ph.D.
President, The Coalition to Investigate the Persecution of the Falun Gong
Address: 106 G St. SW, Washington, DC USA 20024
Web: www.cipfg.org.
Tel: (781) 710 4515. Fax: (202) 234 7113.
Email: info@cipfg.org"

Neither of us is a Falun Gong practitioner. The Coalition gave us no instructions; they did not tell us what to find, only to investigate.

As a refugee and human rights lawyer, David Matas had some awareness of Falun Gong victimization before we began our work. David Matas had spoken at some conferences on international human rights law organized by Falun Gong practitioners and had a few cases with clients who were Falun Gong practitioners.

As a political figure used to speaking out on human rights violations, David Kilgour had protested the violations inflicted on Falun Gong practitioners in much the same way as he had protested the violations inflicted on other victim communities. He too had no special, focused relationship with Falun Gong before he began our work. The sort of contact we had was no different from the contact we had with many other victim communities.

Both of us are lawyers. Because we are lawyers, we are aware of and attempt to follow legal principles. One principle is that past convictions (even if there is a pattern of past convictions) do not prove that the accused has committed a similar offence now. In law, evidence of past convictions is inadmissible in evidence at trial before conviction as prejudicial.

While we could not ignore the past history of the Chinese government human rights violations against Falun Gong practitioners, we knew that those violations could not prove these allegations. We knew to guard against the prejudice to the Chinese government position that those past violations would cause.

Our independence mattered because of the need to counter Chinese government propaganda. That propaganda portrayed Falun Gong practitioners as puppets, people who could not think independently.

The official Chinese government slogan about Falun Gong is that it is an "evil cult". The Falun Gong movement has been inspired by the writings of Li Hongzhi. According to the Government of China, they follow the secret orders of their "cult" leader, Li Hongzhi.

All Li's writings are public. There are no secret orders. But in the paranoic mind of the Chinese Communist Party, the very fact that there is no evidence of secret orders proves their secrecy.

Chinese government literature states: "Falun Gong practitioners, as if bound by a magic spell, blindly obeyed his [Li Hongzhi's] order." Their propaganda refers to Mr. Li as "trying to control the minds of Falun Gong practitioners, order them about ... Deceived and bewitched by him, Falun Gong practitioners ..."

Our doing the report, at least in theory, allowed for an avoidance of these propaganda-induced suspicions about Falun Gong. Whatever one may think of the influence of Li Hongzhi on Falun Gong practitioners, he certainly had and has no influence on us. We have never met him nor heard him speak. At the time we began our report, we had not read anything he had written.

In any case, our work stands on its own. The issue is what was said rather than who said it. Readers can reject or accept this work as they see fit. All our sources of evidence are set out and are independently verifiable. Any one who wants to do his or her own research to check our conclusions can do so. We are not asking people to believe us because of who we are. We ask only that people consider our work and make up their own minds.

When we began our work, we had no views whether the allegations were true or untrue. The allegations were so shocking that they are almost impossible to believe.

Our preference would have been to find the allegations to be untrue. The allegations, if true, represented a disgusting form of evil which, despite all the depravities humanity has seen, was new to this planet. The very horror made us reel back in disbelief. But disbelief did not mean that the allegations were untrue.

We were well aware of the statement of U.S. Supreme Court Justice Felix Frankfurter in 1943 to a Polish diplomat in reaction to being told by Jan Karski about the Holocaust. Frankfurter said:

"I did not say that this young man was lying. I said that I was unable to believe what he told me. There is a difference."

Since the Holocaust, it is impossible to rule out any form of depravity. Whether an alleged evil has been perpetrated can be determined only by considering the facts.

The allegations, by their very nature, are difficult either to prove or disprove. The best evidence for proving any allegation is eyewitness evidence. Yet for this alleged crime, there is unlikely to be any eyewitness evidence.

The people present at the scene of organ-harvesting of Falun Gong practitioners, if it does occur, are either perpetrators or victims. There are no bystanders. Because the victims, according to the allegations, are murdered and cremated, there is no body to be found, no autopsy to be conducted. There are no surviving victims to tell what happened to them. Perpetrators are unlikely to confess to what would be, if they occurred, crimes against humanity. Nonetheless, though we did not get full-scale confessions, we garnered a surprising number of admissions through investigator phone calls.

The scene of the crime, if the crime has occurred, leaves no traces. Once an organ-harvesting is completed, the operating room in which it takes place looks like any other empty operating room.

The clampdown on human rights reporting in China makes assessment of the allegations difficult. The Chinese government, regrettably, represses human rights reporters and defenders. There is no freedom of expression. Those reporting on human rights violations from within China are often jailed and sometimes charged with communicating state secrets. In this context, the silence of human rights nongovernmental organizations on organ-harvesting of unwilling Falun Gong practitioners tells us nothing.

The International Committee of the Red Cross (ICRC) is not allowed to visit prisoners in China. Nor is any other organization which is concerned with human rights of prisoners. That also cuts off a potential source of evidence.

We did seek to visit China for our investigation. Our efforts went nowhere. We asked in writing for a meeting with the Chinese embassy to discuss terms of entry. This is our letter to the embassy:

"May 31, 2006,
Chinese Embassy
515 St. Patrick Street,
Ottawa, Ontario, KIN 5H3

Dear Mr. Ambassador,

We wish to visit China within the next month to pursue an investigation into allegations that state institutions and employees of the Government of China have been harvesting organs from live Falun Gong practitioners, killing the practitioners in the process. Prior to submitting formal visa applications, we considered it appropriate in the circumstances to ask you if we could meet with you or one of your staff to discuss this possible visit and the terms according to which we might be allowed to pursue our investigation within China.

We enclose a letter from the Coalition to Investigate the Persecution of the Falun Gong asking us to investigate the allegations.

Sincerely yours,

David Matas and David Kilgour"

Our request for a meeting was accepted. But the person who met with David Kilgour was interested only in denying the allegations and not in arranging for our visit.

Proof can be either inductive or deductive. Criminal investigations normally work deductively, stringing together individual pieces of evidence into a coherent whole. The limitations our investigation faced placed severe constraints in this deductive method. Some elements from which we could deduce what was happening were, nonetheless, available, in particular the investigator phone calls.

We also used inductive reasoning, working backwards as well as forwards. If the allegations were not true, how would we know they were not true? If the allegations were true, what facts would be consistent with those allegations? What would explain the reality of the allegations, if the allegations were real? Answers to those sorts of questions helped us to form our conclusions.

We also considered prevention. What are the safeguards that would prevent this sort of activity from happening? If precautions are in place, we could conclude that it is less likely that the activity is happening. If they are not in place, then the possibility that the activity is happening increases.

Our conclusion is that there has been and continues today to be large-scale organ seizures from unwilling Falun Gong practitioners. We have concluded that the government of China and its agencies in numerous parts of the country, in particular hospitals but also detention centres and 'people's courts', since 1999 have put to death a large but unknown number of Falun Gong prisoners of conscience. Their vital organs, including kidneys, livers, corneas and hearts, were seized involuntarily for sale at high prices, sometimes to foreigners, who normally face long waits for voluntary donations of such organs in their home countries.

Our conclusion comes not from any single item of evidence, but rather the piecing together of all the evidence we have considered. Each portion of the evidence we have considered is, in itself, verifiable and, in most cases, incontestable. Put together, they paint a damning whole picture. It is their combination that has convinced us.

Before our report came out, the conventional wisdom among human rights organizations was that the sourcing of organs for transplants was prisoners sentenced to death. This conclusion goes back many years.

A Human Rights Watch Report from August 1994 provides a detailed analysis, coming to the conclusion that "the bodies of executed prisoners are the source for many, in fact most of the organ transplant operations performed in China". The report relies on some documents and "a large body of anecdotal material". The report then lists some of this anecdotal evidence from sources who for reasons of personal safety cannot be identified except in general terms.[1]

If one compares the methodology, the quality of evidence and the Chinese government response, there is not much difference between our work and these early reports which concluded that the sourcing of organs for transplants is prisoners sentenced to death. If evidence in the nineties pointing to the conclusion that organs were sourced from prisoners sentenced to death was found to be probative, evidence of that same quality pointing today to the conclusion that organs are sourced from Falun Gong practitioners should also be probative.

How many of the victims were first convicted of any offence, serious or otherwise, in legitimate courts, we are unable to estimate because such information appears to be unavailable both to Chinese nationals and foreigners. A set of peaceful, healthful exercises with a spiritual foundation was made illegal in 1999 by the Communist Party because of fear it might threaten the Party's dominance, and it appears to us that many human beings engaged in these exercises have been in effect executed for their organs by medical practitioners.

Chapter Two

Context

China's party state violates human rights in a variety of ways. These violations are chronic and serious. Besides Falun Gong, other prime targets of human rights violations are Tibetans, Christians, Uighurs, democracy activists and human rights defenders. Rule of law mechanisms in place to prevent human rights violations, such as an independent judiciary, access to counsel on detention, *habeas corpus,* and the right to public trial, are absent. China, according to its constitution, is ruled by the Communist Party. It is not ruled by law.

Communist China has had a history of massive, jaw-dropping cruelty towards its own citizens. Since 1949 the regime has killed more innocents than did Nazi Germany and Stalinist Russia combined.[2] Girl children are killed, abandoned and neglected in massive numbers. Torture is widespread. The death penalty is both extensive and arbitrary. China executes more people than all other countries combined. Religious belief is suppressed.[3]

This pattern of human rights violations, like many other factors, does not in itself prove the allegations. But it removes an element of disproof. It is impossible to say of these allegations that the situation they describe is out of step with an overall pattern of respect for human dignity in China. While the organ-harvesting allegations, in themselves, are surprising, they are less surprising with a country that has the human rights record China does than they would be for many other countries.

The overwhelming majority of prisoners of conscience in Chinese prisons are Falun Gong. The U.N. Special Rapporteur on Torture's 2006 report on his 2005 mission to China[4] noted:

"Since 2000, the Special Rapporteur and his predecessors have reported 314 cases of alleged torture to the Government of China. These cases represent well over 1,160 individuals ... In addition to this figure, it is to be noted that one case sent in 2003 detailed the alleged ill treatment and torture of thousands of Falun Gong practitioners."

Furthermore, the report indicated that 66% of the victims of alleged torture and ill-treatment in China were Falun Gong practitioners, with the remaining victims comprising Uighurs (11%), sex workers (8%), Tibetans (6%), human rights defenders (5%), political dissidents (2%), and others (persons infected with HIV/AIDS and members of religious groups 2%).[5]

The extremes of language the Chinese government uses against the Falun Gong are unparalleled, unmatched by the comparatively mild criticisms China has of the victims the West is accustomed to defending. The documented yearly arbitrary killings and disappearances of Falun Gong exceed by far the totals for any other victim group.

The standard regime refrain about the Falun Gong community is that it is an evil cult. Yet Falun Gong has none of the characteristics of a cult. It has no memberships, no offices and no officers. Falun Gong practitioners are not required to make financial contributions. They do not isolate themselves in communes or withdraw from the world. They remain within society and live with their families. They go to work and their children go to school.

There is no penalty for leaving the Falun Gong, since there is nothing to leave. Practitioners are free to practise Falun Gong as little or as much as they see fit. They can start and stop at any time. They can engage in their exercises in groups or singly.

Li Hongzhi, the author of the books which inspired Falun Gong practitioners, is not worshipped by practitioners. Nor does he receive funds from practitioners. He is a private person who meets rarely with practitioners. His advice to practitioners is publicly available information – conference lectures and published books.

The Chinese government labelling of the Falun Gong as an evil cult is a component of the repression of the Falun Gong, a pretext for that repression as well as a defamation, incitement to hatred, depersonalization, marginalization and dehumanization. But this labelling does not explain why the repression arose. The "evil cult" label is a manufactured tool of repression, but not its cause. The cause lies elsewhere.

In order to enforce conformity, Chinese exercise practices or qigong in all their variations were suppressed in 1949 after the Chinese Communist Party seized office. By the 1990s, the police state environment had become less oppressive for all forms of qigong, including Falun Gong.

Literally, the word "Gong" means "practice" or "set of exercises" and Falun means "the wheel of law". The phrase "wheel of the law" is a shorthand description of Falun Gong beliefs. So Falun Gong is a form or type of practice or exercises.

Falun Gong includes elements drawn from Buddhist and Taoist principles. In essence, it teaches methods of meditation through exercises intended to improve physical and spiritual health and fitness. The movement has no political platform; its followers seek to promote truth, tolerance and compassion across racial, national and cultural boundaries. Violence is anathema.

Li registered his movement with the government's Qigong Research Association. At a time when the movement was falling into official disfavour but before it was banned, in early 1998, Li moved to the United States. Falun Gong continued to flourish.

The Party, in April 1999, published an article in the Journal of the Tianjin Institute of Education, which defamed the practice of Falun Gong. A large number of Falun Gong adherents demonstrated against the contents of the piece outside the Tianjin editor's office. Arrests and police beatings resulted.

Falun Gong practitioners sought to petition the Government Petition Office in Beijing about these arrests. On April 25, 1999, 10,000–15,000 practitioners gathered from dawn until late at night outside the Party headquarters at Zhongnanhai next to Beijing's Forbidden City. The gathering was silent and without posters.[6]

On the same day, President Jiang Zemin wrote a letter to the standing members of the Political Bureau of Central Committee of the Chinese Communist Party about this gathering. Here is the letter in its entirety:

> "Today's event deserves our profound reflection. Without being noticed by humans or ghosts, more than 10,000

people gathered around the gate of the centre of the Party and State Power Centre for a whole day.

They are so strictly disciplined, and their transmission of information is so rapid. It is indeed rare.

However, our relevant departments had found nothing at all beforehand, even though from the Internet one can quickly find the local contacts of the Falun Gong organization. Isn't it thought-provoking?

The rapid development of information technology poses new subjects of studies. Our various departments have many computers. Has anyone noticed these new social trends? If yes, why isn't it reported to us? These issues require careful study.

After this incident occurred the Western media reported it immediately with seditious exaggeration. Is there any connection with the overseas, with the West? Is there a behind-the-scenes master in the planning command?

This is a new signal, and we should pay full attention to it. A sensitive period has arrived, and we must quickly take effective measures to prevent the recurrence of similar incidents.

This incident has had the most participants of all since the 1989 incident. I have repeatedly stressed the need to prevent the small from becoming large and to report all major events to us.

Since 1992, Falun Gong became involved in the activities of a considerable number of social groups of Party members and cadres, intellectuals, servicemen, workers and peasants. Yet it has not aroused our vigilance. I am deeply ashamed.

Two days ago there was an event of a Falun Gong group besieging the editorial department of a magazine in Tianjin. Prior to that, there were also other local incidents where Falun Gong besieged and sat in on governments. The relevant local departments didn't attach great importance to them or closely observe their movements.

This incident brings us experience and lessons. The relevant departments should conscientiously summarize and draw inferences from it so as to be able to deal with similar incidents.

The incident also indicates how weak is the ideological and political work and the work for the masses of some of our local governments and departments. [We] must use correct world-views, philosophy, and values to educate the cadres for the masses and the masses themselves.

Can't the Marxism our Communists have, the materialism, atheism we believe in really win over that suit of stuff aired by Falun Gong? If that were not the case, would it not be a thumping joke? Our leading cadres at all levels especially high-level officials should become sober now!"[7]

The official crackdown on Falun Gong was marked by several documents released around July 20, 1999. On July 19, the Central Committee issued a notice stating that Party members are not allowed to practise Falun Gong.[8] The Ministry of Civil Affairs decided on July 22 to ban the Falun Dafa Research Association.[9] On July 30, the Ministry of Public Security issued an arrest warrant for Falun Gong founder Mr. Li Hongzhi.[10] On July 22, the Ministry of Public Security stated that hanging or posting banners, posters, badges or other logos that advocate Falun Dafa (Falun Gong) was prohibited.[11]

The Government of China set up a dedicated bureaucracy assigned the task of repressing the Falun Gong. Because it was established on the tenth day of the six month of 1999, it is called, in shorthand, the 610 Office. The 610 Office has representatives in every province, city, county, university, government department and government-owned business in China.

Former president Jiang's mandate to the 610 Office was to "eradicate" Falun Gong. Here are quotes from a directive he issued June 7, 1999, three days before the establishment of the 610 Office:

"The central committee has already agreed to let comrade Li Lanqing be responsible for establishing a leadership group that will deal with problems of "FALUN GONG" specifically. Comrade Li Lanqing will be the director and comrades Ding Guangen and Luo Gan will be vice directors, comrades in charge of related departments will be the members of the group. [The group] will study the steps, methods and measures for solving the problem of "FALUN GONG" in a unified way. All CCP [Chinese Communist Party] central departments, administrative organs, all ministries, commissions, all provinces, self-governing districts, all cities directly under central government must cooperate with the group very closely. [...] After the leading group dealing with "FALUN GONG" problems has established at CCCCP [Central Committee of the Chinese Communist Party], it should immediately organize forces, find out the organization system nationwide of "FALUN GONG" ASAP, constitute the battling strategies, get fully prepared for the work of disintegrating [FALUN GONG], [we] should never launch a warfare without preparations. [...] The major responsible comrades in all areas, all departments must solidly take the responsibilities, carry out the tasks [of crushing Falun Gong] according to the CCCCP's requirements with the area's or department's actual situations taken into consideration."[12]

On November 30, the 610 Office called more than 3,000 officials to the Great Hall of the People in the capital to discuss the campaign against Falun Gong, which was then not going well. Demonstrations were continuing to occur at Tiananmen Square. The head of the 610 Office, Li Lanqing, announced the government's new policy on the movement: "Defame their reputations, bankrupt them financially and destroy them physically."[13]

The Falun Gong in China are dehumanized both in word and deed. Policy directives are matched by incitement to the population at large to justify the policy of persecution, to recruit participants, and to forestall opposition. This sort of vocabulary directed against a particular group has become both the precursor and the hallmark of gross human violations directed against the group.

According to Amnesty International, the Government adopted three strategies to crush Falun Gong: violence against practitioners who refuse to renounce their beliefs, "brainwashing" to force all known practitioners to abandon Falun Gong and renounce it, and a media campaign to turn public opinion against Falun Gong.[14] Local governments were authorized to implement Beijing's orders to repress the Falun Gong.

Implementation meant in part staged attempts to demonstrate to China's population that practitioners committed suicide by self-immolation, killed and mutilated family members and refused medical treatment. Over time this campaign had the desired effect and many Chinese came to accept the Party view about Falun Gong.

This incitement to hatred is most acute in China, but it exists worldwide. Chinese officials, wherever they are posted, engage in this incitement as part of their official duties. In Edmonton, Alberta, Canada, this behaviour became the subject of a police recommendation for prosecution of two Chinese consular officials in Calgary for wilful promotion of hatred against the Falun Gong. Investigator Constable Stephen Camp, approved by Staff Sergeant Clifford McCann, wrote:

> "It is my professional opinion that the literature being disseminated by the accused does constitute hate as indicated by the Supreme Court of Canada in the Keegstra decision and that a charge of wilful promotion of hatred under section 319(2) CCC [Criminal Code of Canada] is warranted."[15]

Incitement to hatred is not specific enough to indicate the form that persecution takes. But it promotes any and all violations of the worst sort. It is hard to imagine the allegations we have heard being true in the absence of this sort of hate propaganda. Once this sort of incitement exists, the fact that people would engage in such behaviour against the Falun Gong – harvesting their organs and killing them in the process – ceases to be implausible.

Deputy Health Minister Huang Jiefu, speaking at a conference of surgeons in the southern city of Guangzhou in mid-November 2006, acknowledged that executed prisoners sentenced to death are a source of organ transplants. He said: "Apart from a small portion of traffic victims, most of the organs from cadavers are from executed prisoners." *Asia News* wrote:

> "'Under-the-table business must be banned,' Mr Huang said cognizant that too often organs come from non consenting parties and are sold for high fees to foreigners."

China has the death penalty for a large number of offences, including strictly political and economic crimes where there is no suggestion that the accused has committed a violent act. To go from executing no one to killing Falun Gong practitioners for their organs without their consent is a large step. To go from executing prisoners sentenced to death for political or economic crimes and harvesting their organs without their consent to killing Falun Gong practitioners for their organs without their consent is a much smaller step.

There are many reasons why the death penalty is wrong. Not least is the desensitization of the executioners. When the state kills defenceless human beings already in detention for their crimes, it becomes all too easy to take the next step – harvesting their organs without their consent. This is a step the Chinese government undoubtedly took. When the state harvests the organs of executed prisoners without their consent, another step that becomes all too easy and tempting to take is to harvest the organs of other vilified, depersonalized, defenceless prisoners without their consent. This is especially so when there is big money to be made from it.

It would be difficult to believe that a state which killed no one, which had no death penalty, which harvested the organs of no one else without their consent would harvest the organs of Falun Gong practitioners without their consent. It is a good deal easier to believe that a state which executes prisoners sentenced to death for economic or political crimes and harvests their organs without their consent would also kill Falun Gong practitioners for their organs without their consent.

Falun Gong practitioners constitute a prison population whom the Chinese authorities vilify, dehumanize, depersonalize, and marginalize even more than executed prisoners sentenced to death for criminal offences. Indeed, if one considers only the official rhetoric directed against the two populations, it would seem that the Falun Gong would be a target for organ-harvesting even before prisoners sentenced to death.

Human rights organizations have condemned China's campaign against the practice of Falun Gong. Criticisms issued forth almost immediately after the campaign began. For example, Amnesty International in its Annual Report for the year 2000 wrote that 77 Falun Gong practitioners had "died in custody, or shortly after release, in suspicious circumstances since the crackdown began in July 1999". Many governments, including the Government of Canada, have expressed their concern.

Massive arrests of practitioners are a form of physical persecution which deserves separate attention because of its potential link to organ-harvesting. Any person organ-harvested against his or her will has to be detained first.

China engages systematically in forced labour in all forms of detention facilities – prisons which house sentenced criminals, administrative detention for those not yet charged, and re-education through labour camps. A 1998 declaration of the International Labour Organization (ILO) commits all member states, including China, to eliminate forced labour. The Government of China reported to the ILO that its constitution prohibits forced labour and that there is a national policy of eliminating all forms of forced labour.

Yet, forced labour in detention is not an abuse of Chinese law. It is the law. The Chinese Law on Prisons stipulates that prisons may punish a prisoner who is able-bodied but refuses to work.[16]

The United States signed a memorandum of understanding with China in 1992 committing the Government of China to ensure that prison labour products are not exported to the United States. The U.S. in 1994 signed a statement of co-operation which in principle allowed U.S. officials to gain access to Chinese production facilities suspected of exporting prison labour products. The U.S.-China Economic and Security Review Commission in its report to Congress for 2008 wrote that "the Chinese government has not complied with its commitments" under the 1992 and 1994 agreement, making it "impossible for U.S. officials to conduct complete and useful investigations of such allegations".

Speaking to US journalists in November 1993, in answer to a question about the desire by rights groups to inspect prisons, then Chinese Foreign Minister Qian Qichen said, "I believe that if the Red Cross does put forward such a request ... we would give positive consideration to that request." The Red Cross did put forward such a request, and there was no positive consideration.

Persons are routinely detained in China without charge or for long periods before a charge is laid. Forced labour occurs in administrative detention as well as in prisons where sentenced criminals are kept.

Repression of Falun Gong included sending thousands upon thousands of its practitioners to prisons and labour camps beginning in the summer of 1999. The U.S. State Department's 2005 country report on China[17] indicates that its police run hundreds of detention centres, with the 340 re-education-through-labour ones alone having a holding capacity of about 300,000 persons. The Department of State's Country Reports for 2008 state:

> "Some foreign observers estimated that Falun Gong adherents constituted at least half of the 250,000 officially recorded inmates in the country's re-education-through-labour camps ..."[18]

Hundreds of thousands of Falun Gong practitioners travelled to Beijing to protest or to unfold banners calling for the group's legalization. People came almost daily. Author Jennifer Zeng, formerly of Beijing and now living in Australia, told us that by the end of April 2001 there had been approximately 830,000 arrests in Beijing of Falun Gong adherents who had been identified. There are no statistics available of practitioners who were arrested but refused to self-identify. From our interviews with released Falun Gong practitioners, we know that the number of those who did not self-identify is large. But we do not know how large.

Large numbers of Falun Gong adherents in arbitrary indefinite secret detention do not alone prove the allegations. But the opposite, the absence of such a pool of detainees, would undermine the allegations. An extremely large group of people subject to the exercise of the whims and power of the state, without recourse to any form of protection of their rights, provides a potential source for organ-harvesting of the unwilling. These detention facilities are not just forced labour camps. They are also potential forced organ donor banks.

The United States Department of State Country Report for China in 2007 indicated that the number of Falun Gong practitioners who died in custody was estimated to be from a few hundred to a few thousand. As of December 22, 2006, the Falun Dafa Information Centre identified 3,006 named Falun Gong practitioners who died as a result of persecution.

These identified victims can be gathered into six groups. One is victims who died from stress-related causes precipitated by constant harassment and threats from the authorities. A second is those mistreated in detention and then released alive to their families, but who died subsequently of their mistreatment. The third group is the victims who died of torture in detention and whose bodies were released by the authorities to their families for cremation. The fourth is the victims who died in detention of mistreatment and were cremated while still detained, but whose families got to see the bodies in between death and cremation. The fifth is the victims who died in detention and were cremated without the families ever seeing the bodies. The sixth is the victims who died in detention but we do not have enough information to determine whether the families saw the bodies before cremation.

The bulk of the possible Falun Gong victims of organ-harvesting are, from what we can determine, those whose families were not notified of the deaths of their loved ones. This failure to notify had two causes. One was that the practitioners refused to identify themselves to the authorities. The other was that the authorities, though they knew who the practitioners were, refused to notify the families of their detention; as well, these practitioners were not allowed to contact their families before dying.

However, we cannot exclude the possibility that the fifth and sixth groups of the identified dead were also victims of organ-harvesting. This group numbers about 300. The fifth group in particular raises suspicions.

The large number of Falun Gong practitioners killed by the authorities through torture supports the allegation we are investigating. When the life of a Falun Gong practitioner is cheap, there is no particular reason to rule out one cause of death. If the Government of China is willing to kill large numbers of Falun Gong practitioners through torture, it is not that hard to believe they would be willing to do the same through organ-harvesting.

Chapter Three

Victims - The unidentified

Falun Gong detentions present an unusual feature. Falun Gong practitioners who came from all over the country to Tiananmen Square in Beijing to appeal or protest were systematically arrested. Those who revealed their identities to their captors would be shipped back to their home localities. Their families would be implicated in their Falun Gong activities and pressured to join in the effort to get the practitioners to renounce Falun Gong. Their workplace leaders, their co-workers, their local government leaders would be held responsible and penalized for the fact that these individuals had gone to Beijing to appeal or protest.

To protect their families and avoid the hostility of the people in their locality, many detained Falun Gong declined to identify themselves. The result was a large Falun Gong prison population whose identities the authorities did not know. As well, no one who knew them knew where they were.

Though this refusal to identify themselves was done for protection purposes, it may have had the opposite effect. It is easier to victimize a person whose whereabouts is unknown to family members than a person whose location the family knows. This population is a remarkably undefended group of people, even by Chinese standards.

Those who refused to self-identify were treated especially badly, and were moved around within the Chinese prison system for reasons not explained to the prisoners.

Was this a population which became a source of harvested Falun Gong organs? Obviously, the mere existence of this population does not tell us that this is so. Yet the existence of this population provides a ready explanation for the source of harvested organs, if the allegations are true. Members of this population could just disappear without anyone outside of the prison system being the wiser.

For us, the investigations which led to this work had many chilling moments. Because of the publicity surrounding the announcement that we were doing a report on organ-harvesting of Falun Gong practitioners, and then the publicity about the report itself, many Falun Gong practitioner victim/witnesses came forward. As we did the research for our report and travelled around the world to publicize it, we met many of these victim/witnesses whom we interviewed. With some of them, we shared public platforms where we talked about our report and they talked about what they lived. We asked those who came forward, those whom we interviewed and those whom we heard speak to e-mail us their stories. Practitioner after practitioner who eventually was released from detention spoke and wrote about this population of the unidentified. A collection of some of their statements is given below.

What these practitioners told us was that they personally met the unidentified in detention in significant numbers. We have met many Falun Gong practitioners who were released from Chinese detention. Except for those detained during the early days of Falun Gong repression, we have yet to meet or hear of a practitioner released from detention who refused to self-identify in detention from the beginning to the end of the detention period. What happened to these many practitioners? Where are they?

The problem of enforced disappearances is distinguishable from the problem of the unidentified because, in the case of enforced disappearances, families know that the state is involved. For the unidentified, all the families know is that they have lost track of a loved one. For those victims of enforced disappearances, the families or witnesses know more. They know that the person was at one time in the custody of the state. The state either refuses to acknowledge that the person was ever in its custody or conceals the fate or whereabouts of the person.[19]

There are some Falun Gong practitioners who have disappeared, abducted by the authorities. However, the only disappearance cases of which we know are people who were subsequently released and then spoke of their abduction. It is only after the fact – once they reappeared – that we know these victims were made to disappear. It is likely that there are other such practitioners who were never released.

When family members know only that they have lost contact with a loved one, they do not necessarily turn to the state to ask if the person has been detained. When the missing person is an adherent to a practice which is brutally repressed by the state, the tendency of the family to avoid the government is heightened. Nonetheless a few have sought out Chinese government help to find a missing Falun Gong practitioner family member.

Here are some witness statements:

1. Testimony of Shuang LUAN, Melbourne, Australia

My name is Shuang Luan, I am a Falun Dafa practitioner. I am from Shenzhen City, Guangdong Province, China. I am living in Melbourne now.

On the 1st of January 2001, I went to Beijing and appealed for Falun Gong, with the hope of stopping the persecution of Falun Gong. As a result, I was arrested by Beijing Police in Tian'anmen Square.

I found that lots of Falun Gong practitioners came to appeal that day. The police forced me into a police van, which was full of Falun Gong practitioners.

We were taken to a temporary detention place. There were about 200 Falun Gong practitioners detained there. Several hours later, the back door was opened. Four armed military men pushed us into police cars.

Then we were taken to No. 1 detention Centre in Chaoyang district of Beijing. We were forced to sit on the ground of the yard; there were several hundreds of practitioners sitting there. Then they divided us into small groups.

I was sent into a small cell, which held 27 people. Among us, 23 were Falun Gong practitioners. Later I heard that all the prisons and detention centres in Beijing were full because they have arrested too many Falun Gong practitioners during that period of time.

I was detained for 22 days in the No. 1 detention Centre in Chaoyang district of Beijing. The policemen kept asking where we were from. But we never told them.

The purpose of these policemen was to send us back to our original area, letting the local police continue the persecution, because they couldn't deal with too many practitioners in Beijing. We didn't do anything wrong of course; we didn't cooperate. Every day we were interrogated.

One policeman said, 'Why did so many practitioners came to Beijing? [Don't you know that] the video surveillance in Tian'anmen square recorded everything?' There were no results at all after 20 days' interrogation.

Then the police began their cruelty and summoned more police force. Those who still wouldn't tell names would be treated with tortures. Falun Gong practitioners in my cell were tortured severely and some of them had their fingers nipped by pincers, their faces were deformed by beating.

There was one practitioner who was badly beaten by 21 policemen. (She went back to cell just for a very short time and then was asked to go out again. The police worried that we might know her situation.)

Practitioners still kept mouths shut up in spite of the severe tortures. At one time a practitioner returned to our cell and told us that the police threatened her, 'If you still refuse to tell your names you will be sent to the North East.' (We did not know what the policeman meant then.)

It was about Chinese New Year's time, one night lots of practitioners were given number-codes and were taken away with their belongings. We still don't know where they were taken and their whereabouts now. Later I was deceived by police and disclosed my name. Then they told my local police, thus I was taken back for ongoing persecution.

2. Testimony of Mr. Baoqing LI, Sydney, Australia

On January 9, 2000, I went to the Standing Committee of The People's Congress, which is next to the Hall of People's Congress at Tiananmen Square, to deliver my letter of appeal to Li Peng, Chairman of the People's Congress of Mainland China, asking the People's Congress to stop persecuting Falun Gong. However, the gate guard called for the police who then took me to the Tiananmen Police Station and locked me up in an iron cage.

At the time, there were already over 10 Falun Gong practitioners detained there for the same reason. The room opposite the iron cage was for registration. The police at Tiananmen Square would bring those Falun Gong practitioners who came to Tiananmen Square to appeal to that room to register their names, occupations, age, addresses, their work units and their activities at Tiananmen, etc. Then, the police would do a body search before they (the prisoners) were thrown into the iron cage waiting for the Beijing Deputy Office of The Public Security Bureau from other provinces to detain them at their respective provinces. Since 10 o'clock in the morning when I was detained there, more and more Falun Gong practitioners were detained there.

Most of them were young male practitioners and some of them were elderly and children. I could often hear the police shouting questions to practitioners and the beating of them; most of the time it was to forcibly get their names and addresses.

We would then shout: 'Stop beating people.' As the number of detainees increased, the police's supervision was a bit loose. We could then talk to each other secretly and the main topic was whether we should provide our names and addresses.

I thought that as a practitioner, we should be dignified and we had nothing to hide, so why not report our names and addresses? Some other practitioners said that we came to Beijing to inform them of what is wrong and provide our opinion, so we should provide our real names and addresses.

As I was from Beijing and I am an elderly intellectual, everyone was willing to talk to me. A young man from Qinhuangdao City, Hebei Province said: 'Last time when I came to Beijing, I reported my name straight away when asked by the police. As a result, I was sent home before I could do anything. My whole family was also affected by this; adults were fired from work while children couldn't attend school, not to mention the fact that I was beaten up by the police. Nobody was happy with me. So, this time, I am determined not to provide my name and address.'

A teacher from Guansu province or Xinjiang said: 'It was not at all an easy thing for me to come to Beijing. I had to prepare for the long journey and had to go through various checkpoints at bus stations and train stations. So I wanted to do more when I arrived in Beijing, but I was arrested immediately at Tiananmen Square when I laid out the banner of "Falun Dafa is good". If I provided my name and address, I will be sent back straight away, that would be very bad. So I just insisted not to report my name and address. I did nothing wrong, and there will be a day of my release.'

One person with a Henan accent and a cadre-like appearance said: 'The Chinese Communist regime has linked Falun Gong with everything in society. If any city or province has been found with Falun Gong practitioners in Beijing, that city or province would be in trouble, so I wouldn't provide my name and address to any one for the sake of other people's safety.'

One person with a strong Shandong accent said: 'The fact that we don't provide our names and addresses is the result of the persecution. One man should be able to take full responsibility for his own action even if it means torture and beatings. If I report my name and address, it will definitely affect others. I have a strong accent; they would know where I come from once I opened my mouth, so I refuse to speak. I was able to maintain this despite the shouting and beatings; I just wouldn't co-operate with them.'

I was transferred to the police station of the Asia Games Village in Beijing at around 2:00 p.m. that day. There were still about 50 Falun Gong practitioners inside the iron cage, apart from those who were already transferred elsewhere. A lot of them didn't provide their names and addresses. I have witnessed many Falun Gong practitioners who went to Beijing to appeal without reporting their names and addresses.

3. Testimony of Ms. Junyan SHU, Perth, Australia

I was a Beijing local living in the Xu Wu District. I have been granted a protection visa by the Australian Government and am now living in Perth, Western Australia. In October 1999, I was detained with 4 or 5 other practitioners in an unknown detention centre in Beijing after being arrested for 'illegal gathering'.

I and those other practitioners refused to reveal our identities for fear of threats being made to our work units and family members by the CCP. However, one policeman from the detention facility said to us: 'If you don't report your identities, there will be places to send you.'

And another policeman said to us: 'If you don't report your names, you will never be able to get out here.' So eventually I reported my name.

However, a male practitioner who was not a Beijing local never revealed his identity when I was there and I do not know what happened to him. Also, prisoners in the same detention facility told me that Falun Gong practitioners from other regions (from outside of Beijing) who were detained in other cells also refused to reveal their identities.

I have been detained several other times but each time I was recognized readily as I was arrested for practising the exercises at my local practice sites. So local police knew me. In June 2000, I unfurled banners on Tiananmen Square with 4 or 5 other practitioners.

Before we went there, we all decided not to reveal our identities. After we were arrested and taken to the Tiananmen Police Station, one of the practitioners eventually revealed the group's identity and so I was transferred to my local police station.

But before I left, I was taken into a room where I witnessed a female practitioner being tortured into revealing her identity. Practitioners who refused to reveal their identities would be tortured at that facility with handcuffs (joining the two hands behind their back). It was very common for Falun Gong practitioners to refuse to reveal who we are. We often only reveal ourselves as 'Dafa Disciples' or 'Dafa Practitioners'.

4. Testimony of Ms. Hong CHEN, Canberra, Australia

I lived in Ninghe County of Tianjin, China before I came to Australia. Back in China I was arrested five times because of practising Falun Gong and on 25th April 2000, I was sentenced illegally to one year's forced education-through-labour by Ninghe Branch, Tianjin Public Security Bureau.

I also remember that one day a female practitioner was sent in to our labour camp. When I was talking with her, I found her palms were dark and asked what had happened.

She said that she was tortured with electric batons while being detained in an unknown place, where a lot of other practitioners were kept. In order not to get their family and workplaces implicated, a lot of practitioners refused to say their names, including her.

She was transferred to my labour camp because she couldn't tolerate the torture and gave her name. I am very worried about the safety of those practitioners detained in that unknown place.

5. Testimony of Ms. Jinghang LIU, Sydney, Australia

I am a former associate research fellow in the Remote Sensing Application Research Institute of the Chinese Science Academy. Because I practise Falun Dafa, I was arrested by the Communist regime six times.

I was sentenced to three years in jail and detained in as many as 10 different places, during which time I came to know a lot of Falun Dafa practitioners who were severely tortured because they refused to provide their names and addresses to the regime. From June to November 2000, I was illegally detained at the detention centre of the Xicheng District Police Department in Beijing.

During this period, a lot of Falun Gong practitioners were detained there, and most of them refused to report their names and addresses. Around July 20th 1999, as there were too many female practitioners detained inside the women's cell, the police temporarily used a larger male cell as a women's cell.

I was transferred into this cell. Over 20 female practitioners were detained there; most of them were from outside Beijing. They didn't provide their names and addresses.

In less than two weeks' time, I was transferred back into cell 107 because that temporary cell was removed, but I don't know the whereabouts of those practitioners who refused to give their names and addresses. The police numbered all the practitioners as 'Falun Gong # xxx'. After one or two weeks, they were all transferred out.

Then a new group of practitioners were sent to this place and given numbers. In October, three Falun Gong practitioners inside my cell (cell 107) had their name-number-label surpassing 200 as they also refused to provide their names and addresses.

They told me that the reason they didn't report their names and addresses was that the CCP will persecute everyone associated with Falun Gong practitioners, including their family members, relatives and colleagues. These people might be fired or forced to quit school.

As practitioners do not want to bring trouble to others, they refused to provide their names and addresses. This is completely due to the persecution.

I was greatly touched by their compassion. There was a 20-year-old female practitioner with fair skin and a long braid. She was a painter. Once an officer forced her to paint him a portrait of himself with her signature.

She did a quick cartoon sketch instead and refused to sign her name. This officer was very angry and shouted at her: 'How could you draw me like this and didn't provide your name?' The police beat and kicked her severely.

In order not to implicate her family members, she did not tell her name and address. One day, she was called out of the prison room and did not come back. I hoped she was released back home.

But a person who was detained at the detention centre and had the chance to work outside the room said, 'It is not possible. The police do not know her name and address. How could they send her back home? I saw the police handcuff her with another Falun Gong practitioner and take them away.'

Another young healthy practitioner with a Northeast accent was beaten and kicked by the police as she refused to provide her name and address. She did this to help protect her parents and her work unit so that they wouldn't get into trouble.

As there was no contact from her family, she couldn't receive any financial or material assistance from them. She had only one pair of thin trousers on in mid-October. One day when she was asked to pack her things up, I gave her a pair of innerwear.

A young practitioner was on hunger strike twice and refused to give her name and address.

From January 2001 to February 2003, I was detained at Beijing Juvenile Detention Centre. The centre was further divided into four prison divisions. I was locked up at the fourth division, ninth subdivision.

During my time there, the Xicheng District Police Department in Beijing continuously transfer Falun Gong practitioners into this juvenile centre to forcibly transform them. In winter 2001, another group of five practitioners in their twenties were transferred into the juvenile centre.

As they held hunger strikes for several days as a protest against such illegal arrest, they were in very poor health and couldn't walk. Other criminals in the prison had to carry them.

They were constantly harassed, tortured by a group of perpetrators every day for the purpose of transforming them. The police still tortured them when their health was very weak due to hunger strike.

The police named three of them according to the colour of their clothes. Little White often fainted every other day; the police said that she was sent to the police hospital – Binhe Hospital. Little Red and Little Black were also transferred elsewhere two days later, their whereabouts are unknown.

Groups after groups of Falun Gong practitioners were taken away to unknown places because they refused to report their names and addresses; their whereabouts and whether they are still alive or not are still not clear.

Notes:

(1.) One policewoman in the detention centre of the Xicheng District Police Department in Beijing was surnamed Zhao and the other one was Su during my time there.

(2.) During my time at Beijing Juvenile Detention Centre, the perpetrators responsible for persecuting Falun Gong practitioners were Deputy Director Jinhua, head of the fourth prison division Huang Qinghua, and Head of the Ninth Subdivision Zheng Yumei.

6. Testimony of Ms. Jennifer ZENG, Sydney, Australia

My name is Jennifer Zeng. I come from China. I graduated from Beijing University with a Master of Science.

I came to Australia in 2001 and was granted refugee status in 2003. I began to practise Falun Gong in 1997. After the crackdown on Falun Gong began, I was arrested four times and then sentenced without trial to one year's hard labour reform in 2000.

Inmates of the labour camp were not allowed to exchange contact details, so there was no way to trace each other after we were released. When anyone disappeared from the camp, I would assume that she was released and had gone home.

But in reality that cannot be confirmed, as I had no way to trace others after my release. When I was held in the detention house, unnamed Falun Gong practitioners would often arrive there, being detained for a few days and then subsequently disappearing.

On the day of May 11, 2000 alone, 20-plus unnamed Falun Gong practitioners were sent there. One of them was numbered D3. She was detained in the same cell as me.

Twelve or thirteen days later she died as a result of force-feeding. We didn't know her name until she died, aware only that she was 45 years old, and that she came from Heilongjiang province.

I equally have no knowledge of the fate of all the other unnamed Falun Gong practitioners. There were about 1,000 inmates in the camp. Ninety-five percent were Falun Gong practitioners.

Apart from long hours of forced labour, I suffered from inhumane physical torture and mental torture and insults. I was forced to squat motionlessly and continuously under the scorching sun when the temperature of the ground was over fifty degrees Celsius. The longest period lasted more than 15 hours.

I was beaten, dragged along the floor and shocked with two electric batons until I lost consciousness when I insisted on my right to ask for a review of my labour camp sentence. I was forced to stand motionless with my head bowed, looking at my feet for sixteen hours every day, while repeatedly reciting out loud the insulting labour camp regulations.

The police and criminal inmates would shock me, curse me or force me to squat at any moment if I failed to do so. As a Falun Gong practitioner, I was under endless pressure to sign a statement to denounce Falun Gong as soon as I arrived.

I was watched twenty-four hours a day by criminal inmates, who were given the power to do anything they liked to me in order to make me sign. I was also forced to watch and listen to slandering attacks and lies about Falun Gong almost every day.

I then had to write 'thought reports' to the police after each session. Because of instigation and anti-Falun Gong propaganda, Falun Gong practitioners have been demonized and alienated.

This also prevents us from gaining understanding from family members. Hostile attitudes toward Falun Gong practitioners exist everywhere in society.

7. Testimony of Shuqiang LI, Rome, Italy.

(I am) a Falun Gong practitioner from Shenzhen city, currently living in Italy. I went to Beijing Tiananmen Square to clarify the truth on December 25, 2000.

I told people Falun Dafa is good, and it is righteous Fa. I was arrested by Beijing public security. Many practitioners did not reveal their names to the police, including me.

We were numbered and sent to different detention centres. I was detained in Dongcheng Detention Centre in Beijing. On December 30 or 31, 2000, Falun Gong practitioners who didn't identify their names were sent to Liaoning (including practitioners who were detained in other detention centres). There were big bus, vans, and different kinds of cars, about 70 to 80 vehicles taking us.

All the roads were blocked along the way. At Jinzhou city, we were distributed to different areas in Liaoning province. About ten other practitioners and I were detained in a county detention centre administered by Panjin city.

About 500 practitioners were transferred at this time. It was said that before us, those who didn't report their names were sent to ShanXi.

I and practitioners that I knew all reported our names after being transported to Panjin. Then we were picked up by our local police and transferred to our local detentions.

I was the second-last one to leave the detention centre in Panjin. The last person had also revealed his name when I left. I was transferred to Shenzhen re-education centre (i.e. brainwashing class) and was detained there until September 2002.

8. Testimony of Ms. Xiaoyan ZHU, Germany

In the noon of October 11, 2001, thirty-four Falun Gong practitioners (including my mother and I) were transferred from Tiananmen Square Police Station to Mentougou Detention Centre located west of Beijing. After one afternoon's isolated interrogation, 34 Falun Gong practitioners were all detained in the detention centre; 13 of the female practitioners refused to tell their names and where they were from. These 13 people (including me and my mother) were detained in the same cell.

Within a month, my mother and I were taken back to (our) hometown, Shenyang city, by Shenyang city 610 Office staff in Beijing, and were continuously detained at Longshan Re-education Centre Brainwashing class in Shenyang city. My mother was taken back 10 days after me. I still have some impression of seven of the eleven Falun Gong practitioners who refused to tell their names.

1. From one's accent I can tell she was from Shandong, about 30 years old. I saw purple bruises on her two legs, which was caused by beating of the police at Tiananmen Square Police Station. According to her, her whole body was beaten really badly. During those days she was at Mentougou Detention Centre, she had high fever all along. After nine days of hunger strike, on October 20, she was recognized by her colleague (who came to Beijing to search for her) and was taken away.

2. One was from Siping city of Jilin province. I even remember she worked in medical affairs. She should be more than 40 years old. After five days of hunger strike, she was relocated to another cell. Until (the time) I left there I had never (again) seen her.

3. There was a person from Hainan province; she only said her name was 'Yani' and didn't say her last name. In the end she was separated from me and transferred to other cells after five days of hunger strike.

4. Two others were from Dalian, both of them were 29 years old. Later they were identified by Dalian city judicatory bureau in Beijing and were taken away at probably around 11:00 p.m.

5. I can also remember an old lady from Sichuan province, probably 60 years old. The elder and her son came to Beijing to appeal for Falun Gong. At Tiananmen Square Police Station, the police beat her son in front of her and later beat her as well, very heavily on her head. So she always had dizzy feeling. She was separated with her son by the police and didn't know where his son was. I cannot remember how the elder left Mentougou Detention Centre, it seemed that the police from her hometown picked her up.

6. There was another woman who had Henan accent; I don't quite remember where she went.

9. Testimony of Ms. Ying CHEN, Paris, France

Between February 2000 and March 2001 I was held at Chaoyang Detention Centre in Beijing three times. I met many Falun Gong practitioners from all parts of the country there.

They came to Beijing only to tell the government, 'Falun Dafa is good! Falun Dafa has brought countless benefits and has not done an ounce of harm to society. We hope the government can learn the truth and restore Falun Gong's good name!'

These practitioners refused to tell their names after being arrested. They had numbers put on their backs after being sent to the detention centre.

In the evening the guards called them out and interrogated them. It was obvious that they had been beaten. Those who told their names were kept in labour camps in Beijing, and many of those who didn't tell their names disappeared!

During that time, the guards frequently called the numbers of the practitioners late at night to ask them to pack up their things. We thought the practitioners being called were being released, but it didn't seem like that. The inmates said, 'It is better to bring all your things. It seems that people are being sent to a place far, far away.'

The practitioners were called again in the early morning at about 4:00 a.m. There was an emergency gathering in the yard. The guards were quite nervous and were fully armed.

The guards returned after a quiet few days. I heard that those practitioners were sent to a concentration camp that holds only Falun Gong practitioners.

I remember the guards having said to us, 'If you continue to practise, if you still don't tell your names, we will send you to an uninhabited desert that's isolated from the world. You will never be able to get out, and you can practise all you want over there!' The guards and the inmates talked about the Chinese Communist Party building bases (concentration camps) in Xinjiang, Hebei and Northeast China that were especially used to detain Falun Gong practitioners. They said, 'Don't be stubborn by clinging to your practice! Otherwise you'll face a terrible situation if you are sent over there ...'

10. Testimony of Ms. Na GAN, Toronto, Canada

My name is Na Gan and I'm a Falun Gong practitioner. For the past seven years, I've suffered much by the inhumane treatment of the Chinese communist authorities.

Just because I was persistent in defending my rights to have my belief, during the time when I was in China, I was arrested without warrant, detained several times and underwent unbearable torture both physically and mentally.

To give you some specific information, I am now sharing with you another disturbing experience. From 2001 to 2002, I was detained in a detention centre during the Chinese New Year.

During that period of time, the authorities detained lots of Falun Gong practitioners who went to Beijing to appeal. There were about nine cells; each has capacity of about 20 people, but actually overcrowded with 30-40 of female Falun Gong practitioners.

Many of them were not local practitioners. In order to escape from further persecution to them and their family members, many of them did not tell their real names and where they were from. They were numbered with four-digit numbers.

Each cell, over a dozen people got numbered. One night, I was waked up by some noises. All the Falun Gong practitioners who were numbered were dragged out of the prison cells, and then they never came back.

I have witnessed this scenario many times during my detention. Practitioners were arrested and sent to the detention centre continually. Numbered practitioners came and went like this.

In February 2000, during my detention, I started to know a Falun Gong practitioner from Xinjiang Province. She mentioned to me that her husband and child were also Falun Gong practitioners, but she did not know their whereabouts after they got arrested.

Two years later, I got in touch with her. I asked her if she had chance to contact her husband and son; she told me that she had not found them.

11. Testimony of Mr. Ming CHU, Hong Kong

I am a Hong Kong resident. I was secretly sentenced to five years' imprisonment for suing former leaders of the Communist regime, Jiang Zemin and Luo Gan for their illegal persecution of Falun Gong.

I was tortured by different means, including being shocked by nine electric batons simultaneously. Most of my teeth were knocked off. I have witnessed other practitioners were tortured to death or to disability, including Mr. Jie Wang, who had also sued Jiang Zemin and Luo Gan and later was persecuted to death.

Since the Jiang regime began to persecute Falun Gong, many practitioners from other provinces continuously went to Beijing Tiananmen Square, Appealing Office under the State Council, to appeal to the government. The majority of practitioners from other provinces didn't want to reveal their names and where they came from; some practitioner just said that his name was Dafa.

The reason behind it is that if practitioners from other provinces reported their names at Beijing, their local police stations would be penalized, their managers from their workplaces would be penalized, so would their family members; their everything including housing, jobs, and benefits would be all taken away, the impact would be tremendous. For practitioners who went to Beijing to appeal to the government and didn't reveal their identities, as I estimated, accounts for the majority. I don't know where they were sent away by police officers.

When I was detained at Beijing Haidian Detention Centre, I came across some Falun Gong practitioners, they didn't want to reveal their identities, and they said if they ever spoke about it, they would be in trouble. In addition, Beijing is the capital; at that time, every province has their liaison office set up in Beijing. When the persecution began, in order to arrest those Falun Gong practitioners, there were their local policemen sent to their own liaison office, then they had them wait in the office, and then asked them to identify Falun Gong practitioners from other provinces who were arrested at Tiananmen and other places, by listening to their accents.

Once those practitioners were identified, they were sent back the same time by their police officers, and then they were sent to their local detention centres to detain, and then sentenced. This is also a reason why practitioners from other provinces outside Beijing don't dare to tell their identities.

Most of those practitioners from other provinces didn't want to involve their families; many families didn't even know that practitioners went to Beijing. If their families went to ask local police officers about the whereabouts of the missing practitioners, they would incur a good cursing. What the police would say was that 'if we arrest your family member, we would notify you'. So practitioners' families had nothing to say.

12. Testimony of Ms. Jin CHEN, Malaysia

I am from Guangdong Province in China. I now have asylum under the United Nations. I was illegally sentenced to three-and-a-half years in prison by Chinese authorities because of my belief in and spreading the facts about Falun Gong.

After July 20, 1999, many people who had benefited from Falun Gong went to Beijing to appeal to the government on its behalf. From 1999 through 2002, every day a large number of people went to Tiananmen Square and the Appeals Bureau in Beijing to appeal to the authorities.

These practitioners, carrying nothing but a peaceful hope, were arrested and taken to the local police station. As a practitioner, I went to Tiananmen as well at the end of 1999.

At the time, plainclothes and uniformed police were everywhere. I was forced into a 10-person police van that was filled with practitioners, and we were taken to a local police station.

A few dozen practitioners were locked in a big cage, while more practitioners were being pushed in. The police interrogated them in small batches, mainly asking them their names and where they came from.

Most practitioners would not reveal their names because they thought they would be sentenced to prison or forced labour if they did. I do not know where those who refused to identify themselves were sent. I saw over a hundred practitioners that day who would not disclose their identities.

On April 17, 2001, I was arrested by the national security bureau and the local police because I was spreading the facts about Falun Gong. In jail I met a practitioner who would not disclose her name.

In September 2001, I was held in Hall #37 in Zhuhai City Jail. There were three female halls connected to each other. It had been peaceful until that day. I could hear cursing and shouting from the guards in Hall #35, followed by the sound of inmates being beaten. It was quite noisy. Listening closer, I knew that a practitioner who would not disclose her identity (later the police and other inmates all called her 'No-name') had arrived. I also knew that she was on a hunger strike in protest.

There were two other practitioners in the hall that I was in, one named Zhang Qingyun, the other Wang Zhijun. After a quick discussion among ourselves, we yelled: 'Stop persecuting Falun Gong practitioners!'

Things calmed down the next day. Two to three months later, an inmate named Ahong came to our hall. After we got more familiar with each other, she told me things about 'No-name'. She said: 'Since your yelling, the police moved her to Hall #14, lest she affect Li Chunyan (who was a student from Tsinghua University, also in Hall #35). She kept on with her hunger strike. The police tortured her with a method called "ride the airplane". I and a few others were asked to monitor her. After her hunger strike, the police opened another hall (Hall #34) and put her there to facilitate her administration.' This is what Ahong told me at that time.

During the Chinese New Year 2002, the guards sent me to post some pictures at each female hall, since I had been an art teacher. I went to Hall #34. At first I did not know which one was 'No-name'. A good-looking lady of about 30 brought me a chair. It was a very ordinary thing to do, but immediately a few inmates pushed her away, and the head of the inmates warned me not to talk to her. I sensed right away that she was 'No-name', so I watched her more closely and got an impression of her.

Around June 2002, I heard from other inmates that 'No-name' had been sent out. I thought that she had been released. In November 2002, I was sent to Shaoguan Prison in Guangdong Province. Because I refused to declare that I was a criminal, I was put in solitary confinement for a month.

Afterwards I was put in Team #14, where Ahong happened to be also. The shower facility in the prison was an open room big enough for over 100 people. It was a market-like atmosphere during shower time.

Because of our past relationship, Ahong always found opportunities to chat with me, and I asked her about 'No-name's' situation. I knew that Ahong's family was rather well-off financially and often bribed the guards, including one female guard named Ms. Wu. Ahong called Ms. Wu 'Aunt Wu' and was often called out by her for a chat. The guards often half-knowingly let Ahong in on some news.

I asked Ahong if 'No-name' had been released. Ahong said that because she did not disclose her name, they could not sentence her to forced labour or a prison term, and she was indeed sent out and not in jail anymore. But Aunt Wu was certain that 'No-name' was not sent home, but rather she was sent to a 'special place'.

Ahong said with a sympathetic tone: 'You are quite lucky. You will be released when your term is up. Aunt Wu told me that "No-name" probably would never get out of the place where she was sent.' I thought that the place she was referring to was the local brainwashing centre and therefore did not pay much attention.

I was released in October 2004. I was not allowed to go home because I had not been 'transformed'. The 610 Office in Zhuhai City sent me directly to the local brainwashing centre. I did not see 'No-name' there.

On December 25, Christmas Day, I was temporarily released to my family because I was awfully weak. At home 'No-name's' mother was introduced to us. She brought with her a photo, which I recognized right away.

Her mother told me: 'My daughter's name is Yuan Zheng. She came here to see me right after she was released from Masanjia Forced Labour Camp. She went to Tiananmen Square in September 2001 and has not returned since.' I told her that her daughter was brought to the jail in September 2001, and also shared with her the things that Ahong told me.

I told her to go to the 610 Office to ask for Yuan Zheng's release. Later I met her a few times. She wanted me to go and visit the 610 Office with her, but I was preparing to escape from China at the time and did not want to get into trouble, so I did not go.

I kept looking for information about Yuan Zheng after I came abroad, especially after the news about the CCP's organ-harvesting broke out. I kept contacting Falun Gong practitioners in China, but uncovered no news on Yuan Zheng. I am concerned about her safety.

Chapter Four

Victims – Blood testing and corpses

Blood testing and organ examination

Falun Gong practitioners in detention are systematically subjected to blood tests and organ examinations. Other prisoners, who are not practitioners, sitting side by side with practitioners, are not tested. This differential testing occurs in labour camps, prisons and detention centres. We have heard such a large number of testimonials concerning it, that this differential testing exists beyond a shadow of a doubt. The tests and examinations happen whether practitioners are held at labour camps, prisons or detention centres.

The practitioners themselves are not told the reason for the testing and examination. It is unlikely that the testing and examination serve a health purpose. For one thing, it is unnecessary to conduct blood tests and organ examinations systematically simply as a health precaution. For another, the health of the Falun Gong in detention is disregarded in so many other ways, it is implausible that the authorities would do blood tests and organ examinations on Falun Gong as a precautionary health measure.

Blood testing is a prerequisite for organ transplants. Donors need to be matched with recipients so that the antibodies of the recipients do not reject the organs of the donors.

The mere fact of blood testing and organ examination does not establish that organ-harvesting of Falun Gong practitioners is taking place. But the opposite is true. If there were no blood testing, the allegation would be disproved. The widespread blood testing of Falun Gong practitioners in detention cuts off this avenue of disproof.

Here are some witness statements:

Case 1: Testimony of Ms. Ying CHEN, Paris, France[20]

I was illegally detained three times and was forced to submit to a physical exam each time. I didn't understand why we had to have physicals done. The guard's answer was, 'It's a routine process.'

The way they conducted the exam made me feel that they were not doing it out of consideration for my health, but instead they wanted to get something specific from the results.

One week after I was detained the second time, the guards called me out and put heavy handcuffs and shackles on me. One practitioner who had also refused to tell her name was likewise handcuffed and shackled.

The guards put us into a car. Arriving at the destination, we saw a hospital. It was strange to me that the hospital was very quiet. The guards took us through a thorough examination, including heart, EKG, blood tests, and eye exam.

Case 2: Testimony of Mr. Xiaohua WANG, Montreal, Canada

In January 2002, while I was being persecuted at the 5th Brigade of Yunnan Labour Camp #2 (also named Yunnan Spring Wind School), the Camp Hospital (equivalent to a county hospital) unexpectedly conducted a comprehensive physical examination of every Falun Gong practitioner. The tests included electrocardiograms, whole body X-rays, liver and kidney checks, blood tests, etc. This kind of physical examination didn't ever happen to non-Falun-Gong-practitioners in the camp.

Case 3: Testimony of Ms. Na GAN, Toronto, Canada

From April 6 to September 6, 2001 I was illegally detained in XinAn Labour Camp where they specifically detain female Falun Gong practitioners. There were about seven 'teams' of practitioners. I was in the fifth team, which had about 125 Falun Gong practitioners and 5 or 6 non-practitioners.

During this five-month detention, I underwent a comprehensive physical examination, as did all other detained Falun Gong practitioners. We were taken to a nearby police hospital by armed guards. The physical examination included blood tests, X-Rays, urine tests, eye examination, etc.

This was not normal in the labour camp. I was wondering what they intended to do. We were treated so badly in the camp, why were they so suddenly interested in the state of our health?

Case 4: Testimony of Ms. Yuzhi WANG, Vancouver, Canada

Between 2000 and the end of 2001, the Chinese Communist regime abducted me three times. I spent most of that time in labour camps. In the labour camps 20 to 50 people were squeezed into a room of about 15 square metres. It was very crowded. We could sleep only on our sides, pressed together like sardines.

I went on a hunger strike after my request to be released unconditionally was refused. For this, I was brutally force-fed many times.

After more than 100 days of hunger strike and force-feeding, I felt dizzy even when lying down. I was tormented both mentally and physically and my eyesight was failing.

People from the '610 Office' – the government institution established on June 10, 1999, specifically to persecute Falun Gong practitioners – took me to four hospitals in Harbin City for comprehensive physical examinations between October 2001 and April 2002. The four hospitals were: Harbin Public Security Hospital, No. 2 Hospital of Heilongjiang Province, No. 1 Hospital of Harbin City, and No. 2 Hospital of Harbin City.

At each hospital, blood samples were taken. They told me my blood type was AB, which is quite rare. I was beaten severely because I resisted the examinations.

The police ordered the doctors to inject unknown substances into me, which caused me to lose consciousness. I waited for the final health exam results at Harbin No.1 College Hospital.

The doctor said all hospitals suspected that my organs had problems. It was decided that my body was 'useless'.

In order to treat my illness, the hospital demanded about 50,000 yuan from my family. However, the '610 Office' suddenly lost interest in me when the doctor said I would be a 'walking dead person' even if I recovered. Finally, I managed to escape from the hospital.

Case 5: Testimony of Ms. Huagui LI, St. Louis, United States

In 2001, starting from July, I was unlawfully imprisoned in Sanshui Women's Labour Camp in Guangdong Province for eight months, for no more than clarifying the truth to the public. There were four sections in the labour camp, and practitioners were detained in the No. 2 Section.

Around October 2001, Sanshui Women's Labour Camp carried out a full physical examination on all Falun Gong practitioners, including hearts, X-rays and ultrasound scans, etc. Not too long afterwards, some doctors came to the working area (where practitioners were used for slave labour) to examine the practitioners' blood pressure.

Practitioners who refused to take the checkups were cursed by the police, saying they did not recognize it as a privilege that inmates in other sections (non-practitioners) did not have. It means other inmates (non-practitioners) were not examined. But at that time, we did not think too much about it.

Case 6: Testimony of Xuefei ZHOU, Atlanta, United States[21]

In 2003 I was detained in Brigade Two of the Sanshui Women's Labour Camp in Guangdong Province. Brigade Two consisted of Falun Gong practitioners only. In spring, I and other Falun Gong practitioners were asked to go through a medical examination in the camp clinic.

I saw Tang Xiangping, deputy head of the Brigade Two, and several police officers standing there. Their faces had strange expressions.

That was my first time to see all Falun Gong practitioners taken to the medical clinic to do physicals. Non-Falun Gong practitioners were not asked to participate in the checkup.

There were several checkup items, including ECG and blood test. I do not remember all the items. After the examination was done, no one mentioned this matter any more, such as the written reports of the results. It looked more like a field test.

Corpses with missing organs

A number of family members of Falun Gong practitioners who died in detention reported seeing the corpses of their loved ones with surgical incisions and with body parts missing. The authorities gave no coherent explanation for these mutilated corpses.

We have only a few instances of such mutilated corpses. We have no official explanation why they were mutilated. Their mutilation is consistent with organ-harvesting.

Sample Cases:

Case 1: Bin WANG, male

Home Address: Daqing City, Heilongjiang Province
Location of Detention: Dongfeng Xinchun Labour Camp, Daqing City
Date of Death: October 4, 2000

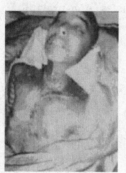

At the end of May 2000, Mr. Bin Wang went to Beijing to appeal to the Chinese government for the right to practise Falun Gong. He was arrested and taken to the Dongfeng Xinchun Labour Camp.[22] He died in detention.

After Mr. Wang died, two doctors removed his heart and brain without consent of his family. The picture shows the rough stitches he received after his body was cut open to remove his organs. As of late 2000, Bin Wang's corpse was stored at the morgue of the Daqing City's People's Hospital, but his heart and brain were missing.

The first version of our report had this picture. One comment we received back is that the stitches the photos show are consistent with an autopsy.

We observe that organs may indeed be removed for autopsies in order to determine the cause of death. A corpse which has been autopsied may well have stitches similar to those shown in the photo. Outside of China, except for organ donors, that is likely the reason why organs would be removed from a corpse.

Similarly, outside of China, when people are blood tested, typically the test is done for their own health. However, the suggestion that Falun Gong practitioners who are tortured to the point of death are blood tested for their health or that practitioners who are tortured to death are autopsied to determine the cause of death belies the torture experience.

Beatings caused the artery in Mr. Wang's neck, and other major blood vessels, to break. As a result, his tonsils were injured, his lymph nodes were crushed, and several bones were fractured. He had cigarette burns on the backs of his hands and inside his nostrils. There were bruises all over his body. Even though he was already close to death, he was tortured again at night. He finally lost consciousness. On the night of October 4, 2000, Mr. Wang died from his injuries.

The purpose of an autopsy report is to determine the cause of death when the cause is otherwise unknown. But in the case of Bin Wang, the cause of death was known before his organs were removed. The suggestion that Mr. Wang would be autopsied to determine the cause of death after he was tortured to death is not plausible. His family was not asked for consent before the organs of the victim were removed, nor was an autopsy report provided afterwards. The suggestion of an autopsy is not a tenable explanation for the stitches on Bin Wang's body.

Case 2: Zhongfang YANG, female

Home Address: Chengdu City, Sichuan Province
Location of Detention: Jiangong Police Station, Yanji City[23]
Date of Death: July 1, 2002

At 6:00 a.m. on July 1, 2002, officers from the Jiangong Police Station surrounded 37-year-old Zhongfang Yang's home and arrested her, her husband, son, and daughter. Zhongfang Yang was beaten to death that night.[24]

By the time Yang's family and relatives arrived at the police station, her internal organs had been removed and the body sent to a crematorium. When the test results finally came out, the officials claimed she had died from 'more than a dozen acute illnesses'. Zhongfang Yang was healthy, as shown in her annual physical examinations.

Case 3: Yanchao ZHANG, male

Home Address: Lalin Town, Wuchang City, Heilongjiang Province
Location of Detention: Division 7 of the Harbin City Police Department
Date of Death: April 30, 2002

In early April of 2002, Mr. Yanchao Zhang, a Falun Gong practitioner from Lalin Town, Wuchang City, Heilongjiang Province, was arrested and detained by agents from the Hongqi Township Police Station. Several days later, officers from Harbin City Police Department took Mr. Zhang away.[25]

On April 30, 2002, Mr. Zhang's family was notified that he had died in police custody. Police did not ask for any consent from the family regarding his body.

At the Huangshanzuizi Crematory in Harbin City, Mr. Zhang's family members saw his body, which had been brutalized beyond recognition and was appallingly disfigured. One of his legs was broken. One of his eyeballs was missing and the socket was caved in, leaving a gaping hole. There was virtually no skin on his head, face, and most parts of his body, and there was not a single tooth left in his lower jaw, which was shattered. His clothes were also gone. Bruises and wounds could be seen everywhere on his body. There was a long cut on his chest, which had obviously been sewn up later. His chest was also caved in, his skull was opened, and a part of his brain was removed. His internal organs were missing.

More than 60 armed policemen were present in the crematorium during the visit of Zhang's family. They declared that whoever appealed for Yanchao Zhang would be arrested immediately and handled as a 'counterrevolutionary'.

According to insiders, Yanchao Zhang was held in a torture chamber at Division 7 of the Harbin City Police Department where more than 40 torture tools were present. He died after one day and one night.

Case 4: Pengwu REN, male

Home Address: Harbin City, Heilongjiang Province
Location of Detention: Hulan County Second Detention Centre
Date of Death: February 21, 2001

On February 16, 2001, Mr. Ren was illegally arrested by the Hulan County police for giving out factual information about the alleged Falun Gong self-immolation incident. After his arrest he was detained in the Hulan County Second Detention Centre. Before dawn on February 21, he was tortured to death.[26] The officials declared that Mr. Ren died due to heart disease. Eyewitnesses confirmed that during his imprisonment, Pengwu Ren endured long, brutal beatings and cruel force-feeding by the police on many occasions. After he had suffered brutal, unrestrained beatings by the police, it became obvious before dawn on February 21, 2001 that Pengwu Ren's life was in danger. His cellmate saw that he was near death and immediately reported this to the police. The police didn't send Pengwu Ren to the hospital until four hours after receiving the report; as a result, he was dead on arrival at the hospital.

Police did not permit Mr. Ren's family members to take photographs of the disfigured body. Without obtaining the family's permission, at the order of the authorities all of Ren's organs were removed, from his pharynx and larynx to his penis. His body was then hastily cremated.

Case 5: Xianghe ZHU, male

Home Address: Wumutun Village, Suining County,
Jiangsu Province
Location of Detention: Sutang Brainwashing Centre in
Suining County[27]
Date of Death: April 20, 2005

While Mr. Zhu was working at home on April 1, 2005, officers from the village police station illegally arrested him
and took him to Sutang Brainwashing Centre in Suining
County, where he was beaten to death. A witness said that
Zhu's fingers and toes were completely black. The family
discovered that his eyes and internal organs had been
removed. To keep the family quiet, the county's 610 Office
and local police paid Zhu's family 15,000 yuan for the bur-
ial, and gave Zhu's wife a monthly allowance of 150 yuan.
Then, the 610 Office and police cremated the body.[28]

Chapter Five

Patients

Organ transplant surgery, as described by the recipients and their relatives, is conducted in almost total secrecy, as if it were a crime which needed cover-up. As much information as possible is withheld from the recipients and their families. They are not told the identity of the donors. They are never shown written consents from the donors or their families.

Some would-be recipients come to China with their own supporting medical personnel from their home countries. Neither accompanying friends nor relatives nor even medical personnel are allowed entry to the operating theatre.

The identities of the operating doctor and support staff are often not disclosed, despite requests for this information. Recipients and their families are commonly told the time of the operation only shortly before it occurs. Operations sometimes occur in the middle of the night. The whole procedure is done on a 'don't ask, don't tell' basis.

When people act as if they have something to hide, it is reasonable to conclude that they have something to hide. Since organ-sourcing from prisoners sentenced to death is widely known and even acknowledged by the Government of China, Chinese transplant hospitals cannot be trying to hide that. It must be something else. What is it?

Military involvement in organ-harvesting extends into civilian hospitals. Recipients often tell us that, even when they receive transplants in civilian hospitals, those conducting the operation are military personnel. They are told that only military hospitals or doctors working at the army hospitals can easily obtain organs.

The military have access to prisons and prisoners. Their operations are even more secretive than those of the civilian government. They are impervious to the rule of law.

Below are some statements from patients. (To protect organ recipients, their real names are not disclosed.)

Case 1: Ms. T, from Asia

Ms. T was diagnosed with chronic renal insufficiency in 2000 and started to have dialysis in July 2003. T got in touch with a local organ broker in November 2005. She had a pre-transplant and immunological evaluation at a local hospital and gave the evaluation documents to the broker in early December.

The broker asked her to prepare twenty-six thousand U.S. dollars, and told T that it usually took one week to find matching organs. The broker said that it was preferable for the patient to go to mainland China to wait for the matched organ. But T said that she would like to wait for a matched organ to be located before she left for mainland China.

T was informed on January 4, 2006 that an organ had been found and the air ticket was ready. On January 6, 2006, the broker took T and another organ transplant patient to Wuhan in Hubei province.

The same day (January 6, 2006), at 2:00 p.m. T arrived at Land Force General Hospital of Wuhan, a military hospital, and had a blood test immediately. She was sent into the operating room at 5:00 p.m. and got spinal anaesthesia. She was sent out of the operating room at about 8:00 p.m.

The doctor in charge of her case was Ligong Tang. There were three rooms for transplant patients and each room had three patients; there were nine beds in total. T was told by a doctor in the hospital that she got an HLA 3 matched organ.

No family members were allowed to go to visit the patients. T was out of the hospital on January 19, 2006 and went back to Taiwan.

T didn't know the source of the organ. The broker said it was from an executed prisoner.

Case 2: Ms. RZ

RZ was diagnosed as having chronic renal insufficiency in 1986. By December 2004, her situation deteriorated. She developed renal failure and required dialysis.

In early December of 2004, it was suggested that she go to mainland China for a transplant. She was told that many patients had travelled to China for transplants in recent years and were mostly doing well, including a patient who had received a kidney six months previously.

RZ was introduced to a broker. The broker took RZ's blood sample to mainland China on December 17, 2004. Two days later, RZ was notified that a matching organ had been found and that she could travel immediately to Guangzhou for the transplant.

As RZ had a bad cold at the time, she was not able to go to Guangzhou until December 24, on which date she travelled there with her husband and younger sister. The name of the hospital was the Economy and Technical Development Hospital of Guangzhou. It was situated far away from the city and was very desolate. There were not as many patients as in her home country. The transplant department was on the tenth floor and had 13 rooms with three beds each.

Each hospitalized patient could have his or her family members live in the room. The physician was Minzhuan Lin, chief of the transplant department. There were at least ten other patients waiting for transplants or recovering from operations. RZ saw that they were Taiwanese, Malaysian, Indonesian, etc.

The cost of the operation was U.S. $27,000 (including hospitalization, food and transportation). The money was paid in cash to Minzhuan Lin's younger brother (the chief administrator) right before the operation. No receipt was issued at the time the money changed hands, but at the request of RZ's husband a simple note was issued indicating that U.S. $27,000 was paid.

RZ entered the operating room at 5:00 p.m. on December 30, 2004. The hospital staff went to fetch the kidney for her in the morning that same day. The operation lasted approximately four hours under spinal anaesthesia.

There were four other patients receiving kidney transplants on the same day. RZ was told by a doctor in the hospital that she got an HLA 5 matched kidney.

During the next five days, she was hospitalized in an isolated care unit (the unit had six beds and was monitored by staff 24 hours a day, with only one staff person at night). After that, she lived in an ordinary room for seven days. She returned home after the stitches were removed on January 11, 2005.

A booklet was handed to her with some information about her transplant operation and what special attention was needed. The doctors in the hospital did not reveal the source of organ for her. The broker told RZ the organ supplier was an executed prisoner.

The Economy and Technical Development Hospital of Guangzhou where RZ had the transplant was not a military hospital. However, the physician-in-chief of the transplant department, Minzhuan Lin, also held positions at the Transplant Department of Zhujiang Hospital affiliated to the No. 1 Military Medical University.[29]

Case 3: Mr. HX, from Asia

In 1999, HX was found to have chronic renal insufficiency. In the year 2000 he went to several hospitals in Taiwan waiting to have a kidney transplant. In July or August 2003, he decided to go to mainland China.

At the time, a dialysis care-giver introduced HX to a broker for transplants in mainland China. In September 2003, the broker informed him that an HLA 3 matched kidney had been found for him. So he went to mainland China for a kidney transplant for the price of RMB 20,000 (20,000 Renminbi, the currency of the People's Republic of China) negotiated before his departure.

Accompanied by his wife, HX arrived in Shanghai. The Shanghai No.1 People's Hospital (also called Affiliated Hospital of Shanghai Jiaotong University) arranged to have him picked up, and he was hospitalized right away.

Once an organ arrived, a crossmatching would be performed. If the test result were positive the transplant operation would have to be cancelled, but if it were negative the operation would proceed.

HX was found to be crossmatch positive when the kidney was delivered, so he could not use this organ.

He continued to be hospitalized waiting for a matching organ for two weeks. During this period of time, fresh kidneys were transported to this hospital three more times. Every time, after the kidney arrived, an antibody crossmatching test was performed. Each time the test result was positive. Two weeks later, on October 1, HX went back home due to commitments at his workplace.

HX decided he was not in a hurry to do the transplant, and wanted to take some time to rest and recover. Not until March 2004 did he again seek to have a transplant. He was notified again that a matching organ had been found, and was asked to go to mainland China. Again he was hospitalized in Shanghai No.1 People's Hospital.

This time again the crossmatch test result was positive after the matching kidney had been delivered to the hospital and the test was done. HX continued to wait at the hospital. Two more matching organs were found and brought in for his transplant operation on two separate occasions, but again these kidneys could not be used due to an antibody crossmatch positive.

Not till late April was an HLA 4 matched kidney found for him. This time the antibody crossmatch was negative. HX underwent the transplant operation on April 23, 2004. The doctor in charge was Dr. Jianming Tan. Dr. Tan told the recipient that this kidney, the eighth, came from an unwilling executed prisoner.

After the operation, the patient stayed in an isolation ward for one week before he was transferred. He then stayed eight days at the Overseas Chinese Department of the No. 85 Hospital of the People's Liberation Army. He returned to Taiwan on May 8, 2004.

HX said that the Shanghai No. 1 People's Hospital mainly did organ transplants for wealthy people coming from Hong Kong, Macao and Taiwan. Local people and people coming from Malaysia and Indonesia would mainly go to the No. 85 Hospital of the People's Liberation Army for organ transplants. These two hospitals were also under the supervision of Dr. Tan's group; Tan came from Fuzhou General Hospital of the Nanjing Military Area.

HX's wife saw around 20 sheets of papers which Tan carried. They contained lists of prospective 'donors', based on various tissue and blood characteristics, from which he would select names. He was observed at various times leaving the hospital in uniform and returning two to three hours later with containers bearing kidneys.

Shanghai No. 1 People's Hospital, where HX had his transplant, is a civilian hospital. But the chief physician of the Transplant Department, Jianming Tan, was also director of the Organ Transplant Centre of the Whole Army, the director of Urinary Department and also the deputy head of Fuzhou General Hospital of the Nanjing Military Area.[30]

Case 4: Ms. RouZ, from Asia

RouZ was diagnosed as having chronic renal insufficiency in May 2000. After undergoing kidney dialysis, RouZ was recommended to go to mainland China for a kidney transplant.

On May 11, 2001, the broker obtained her health record and she was told to stay at home to await further notice. Approximately two weeks later, RouZ got a notice that a matched organ was located and that she could go to China for the transplant.

At that time, RouZ was not mentally prepared; she did not expect a matching organ to be found so quickly. So she gave up this opportunity.

After another two weeks the broker called again, saying that another matching organ had been found. This time RouZ agreed to travel to mainland China for the transplant, and an operation was scheduled in late June.

A group of seven patients went to China together for organ transplants. Everyone was asked to bring 200,000 HK$. The broker received them on June 25, 2001 at the airport and took them on a bus ride (approximately two hours long) to Humen, Dongguan City. They were hospitalized in the Taiping People's Hospital in Dongyuan (in Humen District, Dongyuan City). Health checkups were performed (blood test, X-ray and supersonic rays). The same day (June 25, 2001), hospital staff collected from each of them 140,000 to 150,000 Hong Kong dollars. (Patients with blood type O and those above 60 years old had to pay an extra 20,000 Hong Kong dollars.) A simple receipt was handed out.

The entire transplant centre was headed by Professor Wei Gao, but RouZ did not know who her surgeon was.

All seven had kidney transplant operations the second day (June 26, 2001). Three operating rooms were used simultaneously. Spinal anaesthesia was applied. RouZ was sent into the operating room at approximately 8:00 p.m. and the operation was completed at 12:00 midnight.

Ms. RouZ was told by a doctor in the hospital that she got an HLA 4 matched organ. Other patients who received transplant on the same day included an Indonesian, a French Chinese and a local Chinese. Deputy Chief Jiahua Xu of the hospital had told them earlier that as long as a patient performed kidney dialysis within the hospital for five years, the patient could get a free kidney transplant.

The seven patients stayed in the isolation room for seven days, and returned home on July 3. The doctors in the hospital did not disclose the source of Rouz's organ. The broker told her that the organ was from an executed prisoner.

Taiping People's Hospital of Dongyuan (in Humen District, Dongyuan City, Guangdong Province) was not a military hospital. However, the physician-in-chief of the transplant department, Wei Gao, was also a professor of and physician-in-chief at the Zhujiang Research Institute of No. 1 Military Medical University.[31] Other people in positions of authority of this transplant department were from military hospitals. Wei Gao and the others also did transplant operations at Guangdong Province Border Patrol Armed Police Central Hospital (as in Case 6, for example).

Case 5: Mr. C

C was from Asia. He died in China in the summer of 2005 after a failed liver transplant. C was hospitalized in the Sino-Japanese Friendship Hospital in Beijing in early August due to an abdominal ache when travelling with his wife and son in China. He was diagnosed as having a tumour in the liver. He was talked into having an operation by the hospital, and the operation proceeded on September 7, 2005.

C was in critical condition after the operation. The president of the hospital suggested to the patient that he transfer to the Beijing Armed Police Hospital and have a liver transplant.

Within 24 hours of C's admission to the Beijing Armed Police Hospital, a matched liver was found and the transplant operation was immediately performed. The patient died four days after that operation.

Case 6: Mr. JC

JC, in his fifties, had been diagnosed with chronic renal insufficiency. In January 2005, he suddenly had trouble breathing, and had rapid heartbeats. He was diagnosed with acute renal failure. A pre-transplant evaluation was done and he was found to have no hepatitis B antibodies. He had to have hepatitis B antibodies before a kidney transplant could be done, so he began to have hepatitis B vaccine injections in March and waited for the antibodies to generate. By September, the hepatitis B antibodies generated. He was then told he could have an organ transplant in mainland China.

JC received notification of an organ match on October 19. He attended a pre-trip seminar on October 20, 2005, at which he and other patients were informed of the cost involved. The patients were also informed that the organs had all been matched, so there was no need to worry.

On October 26 the group of eight patients arrived at the Guangdong Province Border Patrol Armed Police Central Hospital in Shenzhen at 4:10 p.m. Professor Wei Gao gave a pre-surgery seminar that evening. A surgery fee of 150,000 Hong Kong dollars in cash was collected from JC.

At the time, patients were asking how the condemned criminals were executed. Dr. Gao said they were not shot. They were given two injections – one was an anaesthetic, the second was a painkiller – and then the organs were taken.

JC paid 2,700 yuan for accommodation, plus 12,800 Hong Kong dollars for medicine and 700 yuan for haemodialysis. The entire operation cost was 169,019 Hong Kong dollars – about U.S. $29,000. All payment was cash in Hong Kong dollars through the middleman. The time in China was only three days.

According to JC, the transplant hospitals in mainland China do not issue receipts of payment for medical treatment. The hospital only gives out proof of medical treatment when deemed absolutely necessary. Hospital staff would provide proof of the last two dialyses done before surgery. This was done in order to allow patients to apply for public health insurance reimbursement once they returned to Taiwan.

Nurses, riding in an ambulance and carrying cooler boxes, brought eight harvested kidneys to the hospital at about 2:10 p.m. in the afternoon of October 28. JC entered the operating room at about 4:00 p.m. and came out of it at about 8:30 p.m.

After their operations, the eight transplant patients were hospitalized in the Supervision Unit, which family members were not allowed to enter. JC left the hospital on November 4, and went back home.

The doctors in the hospital were all military doctors. The medical certificate was given in the name of the Auxing Group Junhui Company (translated by sound of name), and the type of hospitalization was registered as self-paid locals. JC said that the group before them was from Indonesia. The day after they left, a group from Singapore came to the hospital for organ transplants.

Case 7: Mr. KZ

KZ was in his forties at the time of operation, and died. He suffered from diabetes. This patient started to have the symptoms of exhaustion and jaundice in June 2005, for two weeks. He was diagnosed as having acute hepatitis B and was hospitalized for treatment for three weeks.

On June 27, 2005, his condition deteriorated. As a result, KZ was transferred to the hospital attached to Taiwan University in Taipei for a liver transplant assessment and to await a liver transplant. He had to wait for a patient whose brain had already died. KZ waited until August and thought that there was little hope.

KZ's situation kept deteriorating, and several times he lost consciousness. As a result, his family members decided he should go to mainland China for a liver transplant.

KZ had a friend working in Shanghai who helped by sending his medical records to the hospitals in Shanghai. This friend told KZ that he should choose from three hospitals: Huashan Hospital affiliated with Fudan University in Shanghai, Changzheng Hospital in Shanghai, and Shanghai No.1 People's Hospital.

KZ and his family thought that the university hospital probably was better equipped, and decided to go to Huashan Hospital. The friend then made inquiries to the Huashan Hospital about doing a liver transplant and was told that, if KZ came right away, they had a liver for him.

KZ went to Shanghai on August 11, 2005. The doctor in charge of Huashan Hospital was chief physician Jianmin Qian. KZ was asked to pay a deposit of 200,000 RMB. After the deposit was paid, Mr. and Mrs. KZ were notified there was no liver at the moment.

Because he arrived at the hospital one day later than expected, the hospital told him that the type A liver had been used by someone else. So he had to wait for the arrival of a new liver.

KZ was told that August 13/14 were holidays and that he had to wait till Monday. At the same time, Dr. Qian told KZ that, according to the law and regulation at the time, they were not allowed to do organ transplants for people coming from Hong Kong, Macao and Taiwan, and other foreigners. Also, the Health Department would come to inspect the medical institutes and hospitals. So on the first day, instead of going through the procedure for getting hospitalized, KZ was requested to go to the hotel opposite the Huashan Hospital to meet with Director Qian.

Dr. Qian told KZ that he had to say that he was a Fujianese and that was why his family members spoke Taiwan dialect (the same as Minnan dialect). Secondly, KZ had to tell people that he came to be treated for hepatitis instead of telling people that he came for a liver transplant. Thirdly, all the details related to the liver transplant had to be discussed secretly. In fact, all the hospital staff and the other patients were aware that he came from Taiwan for a liver transplant.

Mr. and Mrs. KZ were informed by the hospital that they should be prepared to pay for the medical needs, including equipment. Every day, all kinds of unnecessary equipment were brought over. Yet this equipment had to be paid for, including a thermometer. Without money, there would be no medical action or treatment at all.

Doctors from various departments came to see KZ and every doctor seemed to want to get something out of him. But KZ did not have a doctor who was in charge of him.

There were numerous documents that KZ had to sign, and he was asked to pay fees immediately. As a result, Mrs. KZ always carried cash with her to pay the fees. Doctors from other hospitals (from Kunming and Guangdong province, etc.) asked him if he would like to be transferred to their hospitals if a matching liver could not be found at this facility.

Doctors told him that his kidney did not function well either, and, if he wanted, he could have a kidney transplant at the same time as he had his liver transplant. It was all a trading or moneymaking business, and Mr. and Mrs. KZ felt that they allowed themselves to be trampled upon because KZ wanted a transplant to save his life.

KZ waited till Monday. The hospital still could not find a liver. So chief physician Qian asked Mrs. KZ to discuss KZ's situation in the hotel across the street from the hospital. Director Qian told her that they could not find an organ and indicated that he needed money to open up a channel for obtaining one. So Mrs. KZ gave him 10,000 RMB.

Tuesday came; they still could not find an organ. Chief physician Qian suggested that KZ be transferred to a military hospital called Changzheng Hospital. They got in touch with Doctor Wang from Changzheng Hospital in Shanghai through a friend who was doing business on the mainland. The doctor told the friend that he could find an organ.

On Wednesday, KZ was transferred to Changzheng Hospital. When he and his wife arrived there, they realized that all the patients on the 9th floor were waiting for liver transplants. They also realized that it was military hospitals that could get organs easily.

The difference between the Changzheng Hospital and Huashan Hospital was that Changzheng Hospital didn't need to worry about inspection by the Health Department because, as an army hospital, it was allowed to do transplant operations for overseas people. At 2:00 p.m. on the same day, the organ arrived at the hospital (Type A liver). Right after that, KZ was operated on.

At midnight, Mrs. KZ was notified that KZ's situation had deteriorated and that he had died. She was further told that hepatitis B is infectious and the body had to be cremated. The ashes were taken back home.

The estimated total expense was about 800,000 RMB. None of the relevant documents and certificates regarding KZ's trip mentioned anything about the fact this trip was for a liver transplant.

Case 8: Mr. L – chronic kidney function failure

In January 2001, L indicated that he wanted to go to China for an organ transplant, and had a sample of his blood taken by a clinic. About four or five days later, he got a phone call from the clinic that a matching kidney had been located in China, and that he could start to prepare for his trip. L hesitated at the beginning, and wondered how a matching organ could be found so swiftly.

After discussions with his family members, he decided to go anyway and left for China on February 1. A delegation of nine people – five males and four females – went together. All nine were hospitalized in Taiping Hospital of Dongyuan. L paid 130,000 HK Dollars, and was given the details of the bill. The kidney transplants were done two days later, together with another four patients from southeastern Asia, for a total of 13 transplants.

All 13 transplants were finished within two days. L was hospitalized for seven days before returning home. There were patients hospitalized for 14 days before returning home. L didn't get to know who the doctor was who operated on him, and nobody mentioned the source of the organ.

Taiping People's Hospital of Dongyuan (in Humen District, Dongyuan City, Guangdong Province) was not a military hospital.

However, the physician-in-chief of the transplant department of this hospital, Wei Gao, was also a professor of and physician-in-chief at the Zhujiang Research Institute of No.1 Military Medical University.[32] Some other people responsible for this transplant department were likewise from military hospitals. Wei Gao and others involved also do transplant operations at Guangdong Province Border Patrol Armed Police Central Hospital (as in Case 6, for example).

Chapter Six

Hospitals

Chinese hospitals have been making big money from transplant surgery. They actively promote sales, touting short waiting times, and then boast about the money they make.

Corruption is a major problem across China. State institutions are often run for the benefit of those in charge of them rather than for the benefit of the people.

Occasionally, the Chinese government engages in "Strike Hard" against corruption. But in the absence of rule of law and democracy, where secrecy holds sway and public accounting of public funds is absent, anti-corruption campaigns are more power struggles than genuine anti-corruption drives. They are politicized public relations drives, attempts to placate public concern about corruption.

The sale of organs is money-driven. But that is different from saying that it is a corruption problem. The sale of organs from unwilling donors combines hatred with greed. A party/state policy of persecution is acted out in a financially profitable way.

When China moved from a socialist to a market economy, the health system was a major part of the shift. From 1980, the Government began withdrawing funds from the health sector, expecting the health system to make up the difference through charges to consumers of health services. Since 1980, government spending dropped from 36% of all health care expenditure to 17%, while patients' out-of-pocket spending rocketed up from 20% to 59%.[33] A World Bank study reports that reductions in public health coverage were worsened by increases in costs by the private sector.[34]

According to cardiovascular doctor Hu Weimin, the state funding for the hospital where he works is not enough even to cover staff salaries for one month. He stated: "Under the current system, hospitals have to chase profit to survive." Human Rights in China reports: "Rural hospitals [have had] to invent ways to make money to generate sufficient revenue."[35]

The most obvious source was organ transplants. There is global demand for organs because of shortages everywhere.

The sale of organs became for hospitals a source of funding, a way to keep their doors open, and a means by which other health services could be provided to the community. One could see how this dire need for funds might lead first to a rationalization that harvesting organs from prisoners who would be executed anyways was acceptable, and second to a desire not to question too closely whether the donors wheeled in by the authorities really were prisoners sentenced to death.

China began the organ trade by selling the organs of prisoners sentenced to death. But the global demand for organs and the health system need for money quickly outgrew the available death row supply. The depersonalization of the Falun Gong, their huge numbers in detention and their vulnerability as an unidentified population meant they became the next source. Falun Gong were killed in the tens of thousands so that their organs could be sold to foreigners, generating a billion-dollar business for China.

Profiteering hospitals take advantage of defenceless captive detention populations in their regions. The people are in detention without rights, at the disposition of the authorities. The incitement to hatred against prisoners and their dehumanization means that they can be butchered and killed without qualms by those who buy into this official hate propaganda.

China's military, like the health system, has gone from public financing to private enterprise. The military is a conglomerate business. Its business activity is not corruption, a deviation from state policy. It is state sanctioned, an approved means of raising money for military activities. In 1985, then President Deng Xiaoping issued a directive allowing the People's Liberation Army units to earn money to make up the shortfall in their declining budgets.

Many of the transplant centres and general hospitals in China are military institutions, financed by organ transplant recipients. Military hospitals operate independently from the Ministry of Health. The funds they earn from organ transplants do more than pay the costs of these facilities. The money is used to finance the overall military budget.

There is, for instance, the Organ Transplant Centre of the Armed Police General Hospital in Beijing. This hospital boldly states:

> "Our Organ Transplant Centre is our main department for making money. Its gross income in 2003 was 16,070,000 yuan. From January to June of 2004 income was 13,570,000 yuan. This year (2004) there is a chance to break through 30,000,000 yuan."[36]

The military have access to prisons and prisoners. Their operations are even more secretive than those of the civilian government. They are impervious to the reach of the rule of law.

Albert Einstein wrote: "The release of atom power has changed everything except our way of thinking ... the solution to this problem lies in the heart of mankind. If only I had known, I should have become a watchmaker."

Technological developments do not change human nature. But they do change the ability to inflict harm. The development of transplant surgery has done much to improve the ability of humanity to cope with failing organs. But these developments in transplant surgery have not changed our way of thinking.

There is a tendency to regard any new medical development as a benefit to humanity. That is certainly the intent of the developers. But medical research, no matter how far advanced, comes face to face with the same old capacity for good and evil.

More advanced techniques in transplant surgery do not mean a more advanced Chinese political system. The Communist system remains. Developments in transplant surgery in China fall prey to the cruelty, the corruption, the repression which pervades China. Advances in transplant surgery provide new means for old cadres to act out their venality and ideology.

We do not suggest that those who developed transplant surgery should instead have become watchmakers. We do suggest that we should not be so naive as to think that just because transplant surgery was developed to do good, it can do no harm. The allegation made against the development of transplant surgery in China, that it is being used to harvest organs from unwilling Falun Gong practitioners, would be just the acting out, in a new context, of the lesson Albert Einstein was teaching. We have seen before that modern technologies developed for the benefit of humanity have been perverted to inflict harm. We should not be surprised if this has also happened to transplant surgery.

Hospital websites in China advertise short waiting times for organ transplants. Transplants of long dead donors are not viable because of organ deterioration after death. If we take these hospitals' self-promotions at face value, they tell us that there are a large number of people now alive who are available on demand as sources of organs.

The waiting times for organ transplants for organ recipients in China are much lower than anywhere else. The China International Transplantation Assistant Centre website says, "It may take only one week to find out the suitable (kidney) donor, the maximum time being one month ..."[37] It goes further, "If something wrong with the donor's organ happens, the patient will have the option to be offered another organ donor and have the operation again in one week."[38] The site of the Oriental Organ Transplant Centre in early April, 2006, claimed that "the average waiting time (for a suitable liver) is 2 weeks".[39] The website of the Changzheng Hospital in Shanghai says: "... the average waiting time for a liver supply is one week among all the patients."[40]

In contrast, the median waiting time in Canada for a kidney was 32.5 months in 2003, and in British Columbia it was even longer at 52.5 months.[41] The survival period for a kidney is between 24 and 48 hours, and a liver about 12 hours.[42] The presence of a large bank of living kidney-liver 'donors' must be the only way China's transplant centres can assure such short waits to customers. The astonishingly short waiting times advertised for perfectly-matched organs would suggest the existence of a large bank of live prospective 'donors'.

A good deal of the material available on the websites of various transplant centres in China before March 9, 2006 (when allegations about large-scale organ seizures resurfaced in Canadian and other world media) is inculpatory. Understandably, much of it has since been removed. So these comments will refer only to sites that can still be found at archived locations, with the site locations being identified either in the comments or as endnotes. A surprising amount of self-accusatory material was still available to web browsers as of the final week of June, 2006. We list here only four examples:

(1) China International Transplantation Network Assistance Centre (Shenyang City)[43]

As of May 17, 2006 this website indicated in the English version (the Mandarin one evidently disappeared after March 9) that the centre was established in 2003 at the First Affiliated Hospital of China Medical University "… specifically for foreign friends. Most of the patients are from all over the world." The opening sentence of the site introduction declares, "Viscera (one dictionary definition: 'soft interior organs … including the brain, lungs, heart etc') providers can be found immediately!"[44] On another page[45] on the same site is this statement: "… the number of kidney transplant operations is at least 5,000 every year all over the country. So many transplantation operations are owing to the support of the Chinese government. The supreme demotic court, supreme demotic law – officer, police, judiciary, department of health and civil administration have enacted a law together to make sure that organ donations are supported by the government. This is unique in the world."

In the 'question and answer' section of the site are found the following:

> "Before the living kidney transplantation, we will ensure the donor's renal function … So it is more safe than in other countries, where the organ is not from a living donor."[46]

> "Q: Are the organs for the pancreas transplant(ed) from brain death (sic) (dead) patients?

> A: Our organs do not come from brain death victims because the state of the organ may not be good."[47]

(2) Orient Organ Transplant Centre Tianjin City[48]

On a page removed in mid-April 2006 (but it can still be located as an archive[49]) is the claim that from "January 2005 to now, we have done 647 liver transplants – 12 of them done this week; the average waiting time is 2 weeks." A chart also removed about the same time (but still available as an archive[50]) indicates that from virtually a standing start in 1998 (when it managed only nine liver transplants) by 2005 it had completed fully 2,248.[51]

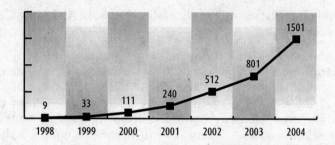

In contrast, according to the Canadian Organ Replacement Register 14, the total in Canada for all kinds of organ transplants in 2004 was 1,773.

(3) Jiaotong University Hospital Liver Transplant Centre Shanghai[52]

In a posting on April 26, 2006,[53] the website says in part:

> "The liver transplant cases (here) are 7 in 2001, 53 cases in 2002, 105 cases in 2003, 144 cases in 2004, 147 cases in 2005 and 17 cases in January, 2006."

(4) Changzheng Hospital Organ Transplant Centre, affiliated with No. 2 Military Medical University Shanghai[54]

A page was removed after March 9, 2006. (An archived page is available.[55]) It contains the following graph depicting the number of liver transplants each year by this Centre:

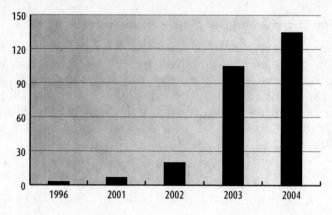

In the "Liver Transplant Application" form,[56] it states on the top: "… Currently, for the liver transplant, the operation fee and the hospitalization expense together is about 200,000 yuan ($66,667 CND), and the average waiting time for a liver supply is one week among all the patients in our hospital …"

In China, organ transplanting is a very profitable business. We can trace the money of the people who pay for organ transplants to specific hospitals which do organ transplants, but we cannot go further than that. We do not know who gets the money the hospitals receive. Are doctors and nurses engaged in criminal organ-harvesting paid exorbitant sums for their crimes? That was a question it was impossible for us to answer, since we had no way of knowing where the money went.

Before its removal from the Internet on April 25, 2006, the size of the profits for transplants was suggested in the following price list for the China International Transplantation Network Assistance Centre in Shenyang City:[57]

Kidney	U.S.$62,000
Liver	U.S.$98,000 – 130,000
Liver-kidney	U.S.$160,000 – 180,000
Kidney-pancreas	U.S.$150,000
Lung	U.S.$150,000 – 170,000
Heart	U.S.$130,000 – 160,000
Cornea	U.S.$30,000

A standard way of investigating any crime allegation where money changes hands is to follow the money trail. But for China, its closed doors mean that following the money trail is impossible. Not knowing where the money goes proves nothing. But it also disproves nothing, including these allegations.

A former prisoner from China interviewed by David Matas in July 2008 told a chilling story. It provides an insight into hospital operations from a prison perspective.

While in prison, the prisoner, whom we have given the pseudonym Lanny, was kept in various prison cells averaging 20 persons per cell.

In over ten instances, one of his cellmates was a prisoner sentenced to death. He became familiar with the pattern of execution of these prisoners.

A few days before execution, a man in a white coat would come and extract a blood sample from the prisoner. On the day of execution four or five men in white coats with white gloves would arrive. The prisoner would be escorted away by the men in white. Waiting outside, visible through the prison windows, was an ambulance hospital van in white with a red cross.

In one case, when Lanny was in interrogation, he saw one of these death penalty inmates in an adjoining room, with a needle with a syringe sticking out of his neck. The syringe was half full of liquid. An hour later the prisoner was still there, but the syringe was empty.

What Lanny learned from cell leaders was that prisoners sentenced to death were being organ-harvested for transplants. Their date of execution was set by arrangement with a nearby hospital, arranged for when organs were needed. The money paid for the transplant was split fifty-fifty between the hospital and the prison guards. As for the man with the needle in his neck, when Lanny returned from interrogation his cell leader told him that the prisoner was being injected with an anaesthetic to make him numb and preserve his organs until they were harvested.

In November 2006, Lanny was transferred to cell 311 in Wu Xi Number 1 prison, Wu Xi City, Jiangsu province (near Shanghai), from another cell in that same prison. Shortly after his arrival, the guards asked Lanny to sign a statement that prisoner Chen Qi Dong had died of illness. The guards wanted the statement to show the family.

Chen Qi Dong had been in cell 311 before Lanny arrived but died a few days before Lanny was transferred to that cell. Lanny never met him and refused to sign the statement about his cause of death. The others in the cell signed.

Cell 311 leader Wang Yao Hu – as well as seven or other eight cell members, including Wang Shi Cun from Wu Xi and Shai Hai – told Lanny what had happened to Chen Qi Dong. Chen was a Falun Gong practitioner who refused to recant and insisted on continuing the meditation and Falun Gong exercises while in prison. Guards beat and tortured him for doing so.

In reaction to his mistreatment, Chen Qi Dong went on a hunger strike. The guards in turn force-fed him by pouring congee down a tube jammed into his throat. But the congee was too hot and scalded his digestive system. Chen Qi Dong got a fever. At this point the man in white arrived and took a blood sample, a few days before Chen was taken from his cell. The day Chen left the cell for good, four men with white coats and white gloves came to fetch him. One of the prisoners in the cell, in interrogation that day, saw Chen in the next room, with a needle in his neck. Through a window, the prisoners in cell 311 could see waiting a white hospital ambulance van with a red cross. The cell leader told Lanny that Chen had been organ-harvested.

During his stay in prison, Lanny heard of two or three other such cases, but without the detail he heard in the case of Chen. There was a similar pattern in these cases. A Falun Gong practitioner refused to recant and continued his meditation and exercises in prison. The guards beat and tortured the practitioner in response. The beating and torture got out of hand to the point where the practitioner was permanently injured. The guards, in order to remove any trace of their own misdeeds, arranged for the telltale evidence to disappear through organ-harvesting of the practitioner.

Chapter Seven

Telephone calls

Two volunteer Mandarin-speaking investigators, "M" and "N", telephoned a number of hospitals and transplant doctors to ask about transplants. They began making calls for the World Organization to Investigate Persecution against the Falun Gong as soon as a media report surfaced on March 10, 2006 that Falun Gong practitioners were being killed for their organs. Once we began our work, we took advantage of some of the work that they had already done and asked them to continue to make calls for us. They carried on with these calls even after we finished the first version of our report, for the second version. The callers presented themselves as potential recipients or relatives of potential recipients. Phone numbers were obtained from the Internet. These calls resulted in a number of admissions that Falun Gong practitioners are the sources of organ transplants.

If the phone number was a general number of a hospital, the caller usually started by requesting to be connected to the transplant department of the hospital and then spoke with whoever picked up the phone in that department. The caller would ask that person for some general information about transplant operations. Usually hospital staff would talk to people wanting organ transplants or their family members, and actively located relevant doctors for them. If the doctor was not available, the caller would later call back for this specific doctor or chief-physician.

Although callers always began by speaking to a hospital or a doctor, sometimes they were referred to prisons or courts, because these were the distribution points for harvested organs. It may seem strange to call a court about organ availability, but systematic organ-harvesting in China began with executed criminals. It seems that after China moved on from harvesting organs of those prisoners to harvesting organs of other prisoners, the distribution point for organs remained the same.

One of the callers, "Ms. M", told one of the authors that in early March, 2006 she managed to get through to the Public Security Bureau in Shanxi. The respondent there told her that healthy and young prisoners are selected from the prison population to be organ donors. If the candidates cannot be tricked into providing the blood samples necessary for successful transplants, the official went on with guileless candour, employees of the office take the samples by force.

On March 18 or 19, 2006 M spoke to a representative of the Eye Department at the People's Liberation Army Hospital in Shenyang in northeastern China, although she was not able to make a full recorded transcript. Her notes indicate that the person identifying himself as the hospital director said the facility did "many cornea operations", adding, "We also have fresh corneas." Asked what that meant, the director replied, "… just taken from bodies."

At Army Hospital 301 in Beijing in April, 2006, a surgeon told M that she did liver transplants herself. The surgeon added that the source of the organs was a "state secret" and that anyone revealing the source "could be disqualified from doing such operations".

In early June, 2006 an official at the Mishan city detention centre told a telephone caller that the centre then had at least five or six male Falun Gong prisoners under 40 years of age available as organ suppliers. A doctor at Shanghai's Zhongshan hospital in mid-March of 2006 said that all of his organs come from Falun Gong practitioners. A doctor at Qianfoshan Hospital in Shandong in March, 2006 implied that he then had organs from Falun Gong persons and added that in April there would be "more of these kinds of bodies …" In May, Dr. Lu of the Minzu hospital in Nanning city said organs from Falun Gong practitioners were not available at his institution and suggested the caller call Guangzhou to get them. He also admitted that personnel from his hospital earlier went to prisons to select healthy Falun Gong persons in their 30s to provide organs.

In mid-March of 2006, Dr. Wang of Zhengzhou Medical University in Henan province agreed that "we pick all the young and healthy kidneys …" Dr. Zhu of the Guangzhou Military Region Hospital in April of 2006 said he then had some type B kidneys from Falun Gong, but would have "several batches" before May 1 and perhaps no more until May 20 or later. An official at the first detention centre in Qinhuangdao city in Liaoning province told a caller in mid-May 2006 that she should call the Intermediate People's Court to obtain Falun Gong kidneys. The same day, an official at that court said they had no live kidneys from Falun Gong, but had had them in the past, specifically in 2001. Finally, the First Criminal Bureau of the Jinzhou people's court in May of 2006 told the caller that access to Falun Gong kidneys currently depended on "qualifications".

Director Song at the Tianjin city central hospital in mid-March 2006 volunteered that his hospital had more than ten beating hearts. The caller asked if that meant "live bodies" and Song replied, "Yes, it is so." An official at the Wuhan city Tongji hospital two weeks later told the caller that "(i)t's not a problem" for his institution when the caller says, "… we hope the kidney suppliers are alive. (We're) looking for live organ transplants from prisoners, for example, using living bodies from prisoners who practise Falun Gong. Is it possible?"

The map of China which follows indicates the regions where admissions have been made to telephone investigators by detention or hospital personnel.

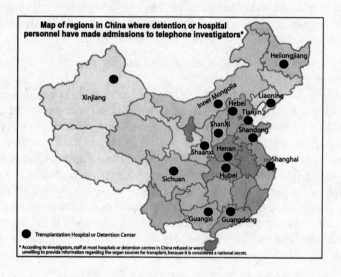

Map of regions in China where detention or hospital personnel have made admissions to telephone investigators*

● Transplantation Hospital or Detention Center

* According to investigators, staff at most hospitals or detention centres in China refused or were unwilling to provide information regarding the organ sources for transplant, because it is considered a national secret.

Caller M called about 80 hospitals. In some cases she asked for specific doctors in the called hospitals, and was able to speak to transplant doctors. Ten hospitals admitted they use Falun Gong practitioners as organ suppliers. Five hospitals said they could obtain Falun Gong practitioners as organ suppliers. Fourteen hospitals admitted they use live organs from prisoners. Ten hospitals said the source of organs is a secret and they could not reveal it over the phone.

Caller N made calls to close to 40 hospitals in China, out of which five admitted to using Falun Gong practitioner organs. N called back to talk to the doctors who made these admissions, and found they were still reachable at the hospitals. N also made calls to 36 detention centres and courts in China, out of which four admitted to using Falun Gong practitioner organs.

When calling hospitals, in some cases N would ask for specific doctors and was able to speak to transplant doctors. N's style was to ask directly the called parties if they use Falun Gong practitioners' organs. The typical response she got was that the caller did not expect this question at all, and would pause for a while to think how to respond. After the pause, about 80% did not admit that they used Falun Gong practitioners' organs. About 80% of those who did not admit to using Falun Gong practitioners' organs did admit that they use live bodies who are prisoners. Less than ten people simply hung up the phone once they heard the question about Falun Gong practitioners.

One of the authors has listened with a certified Mandarin-English interpreter to the recorded telephone conversations quoted below between officials and the callers. Certified copies of the relevant transcripts in Mandarin and English were provided to us.

The accuracy of the translations of the portions of them used in our report is attested to by the certified translator, Mr. C. Y., a certified interpreter with the Government of Ontario. He affirmed that he has listened to the recording of the conversations referred to in the report, and has read the transcripts in Chinese and the translated English versions of the conversations, and verifies that the transcripts are correct and the translations accurate. The original recordings of the calls remain available as well. One of us met with the two callers in Toronto on May 27, 2006 to discuss the routing, timing, recording, accuracy of the translations from Mandarin to English and other features of the calls.

We conclude that the verbal admissions in the transcripts of investigators' interviews can be trusted. There is no doubt in our minds that these interviews did take place with the persons claimed to be interviewed, at the time and place indicated, and that the transcripts accurately reflect what was said.

Moreover, the content of what was said can itself be believed. For one, the admissions made at the various institutions are contrary to the reputational interests of the government of China in attempting to convince the international community that the widespread killing of Falun Gong prisoners for their vital organs has not occurred.

Here are excerpts from transcripts of some of the calls:

(1) **Nanning City Minzu Hospital in Guangxi Autonomous Region (22 May 2006):**

"Q: Didn't you use Falun Gong practitioners' organs before?

A: Now it has changed from before ...

Q: Then they [the hospital in Guangzhou to which the caller was referred] use organs from Falun Gong practitioners?

A: Right, right, right ...

Q: It is said that the organs from Falun Gong practitioners are relatively healthy and better. Do they use this kind as well?

A: Right, right, right. Usually the healthy ones are chosen.

Q: What I mean is that the organs from Falun Gong practitioner are better. Do they use this kind as well?

A: Right, right, right ...

Q: ... what you used before, were they from detention centres or prisons?

A: From prisons.

Q: Oh, prisons. And it was from healthy Falun Gong practitioners, the healthy Falun Gong right?

A: Right, right, right. We would choose the good ones, because we will assure the quality of our operations.

Q: That means you choose the organs yourself?

A: Right, right, right ...

Q: ... Usually how old is the age of the organ supplier?

A: Usually in their 30s.

Q: In their 30s. Then you will go to the prison to select yourself?

A: Right, right, right. We must select it."

This particular call led to a remarkable response from the Government of China. Phoenix TV, a Hong Kong media outlet, produced a Government of China documentary response to our report. In this documentary, Lu Guoping acknowledges having received the call from our caller. He confirms that he referred our caller to a hospital in Guangzhou. He acknowledges that the caller asked whether that hospital used organs from Falun Gong practitioners.

What changes in the documentary is the answer he said he gave. In the TV interview, he says:

> "I told her I was not involved in the surgical operations and had no idea where the organs come from. I told her I could not answer her questions. She then asked me whether these organs come from prisons. I replied no to her in clear-cut terms."

On the video, Dr. Lu is presented with a partial transcript of the call made to him found in our report. He reacts by saying:

> "The record of the phone call does not conform to the truth. Many parts of it have been distorted or mutilated. The report says that when I was asked where the organs removed from Falun Gong people came from, prisons or detention, houses I said they came from the prisons. But this was not my answer ... The report also says that when the person who called me asked whether we have to go to the prison to select body organs I answered yes and added we have to go there to make the choice. This question was actually not raised at all then."

There is no indication in the Phoenix TV documentary that we have a recording where Dr. Lu says in his own voice the words attributed to him in our report. Nor does either the doctor or the interviewer make any attempt to explain how we could possibly have got the voice of the doctor on a recording saying what he denies saying, interspersed seamlessly with what he admits saying, if he did not say what he denies saying. The suggestion left by the documentary is that we have altered a transcript. Because there is no acknowledgement of a recording, there is no suggesting we have altered the recording.

So here we have on our recording an admission from a doctor that personnel from his hospital ("we") used to go to a prison to select Falun Gong practitioners for their organs. Moreover, we have a further admission that the voice we have on our recording is the voice of the very person our recording says he is. This is as close to a smoking gun as we are ever likely to get.

(2) **Mishan City Detention Centre, Heilongjiang province (8 June 2006):**

"M: Do you have Falun Gong [organ] suppliers? …

Mr. Li: We used to have, yes.

M: … what about now?

Mr. Li: … Yes …

M: Can we come to select, or you provide directly to us?

Mr. Li: We provide them to you.

M: What about the price?

Mr. Li: We discuss after you come …

M: How many [Falun Gong suppliers] under age 40 do you have?

Mr. Li: Quite a few …

M: Are they male or female?

Mr. Li: Male …

M: Now, for … the male Falun Gong [prisoners], how many of them do you have?

Mr. Li: Seven, eight, we have [at least] five, six now.

M: Are they from countryside or from the city?

Mr. Li: Countryside."

(3) **Oriental Organ Transplant Centre (also called Tianjin City No. 1 Central Hospital), Tianjin City (15 March 2006):**

"N: Is this Director Song?

Song: Yes, please speak …

N: Her doctor told her that the kidney is quite good because he [the supplier] practises ... Falun Gong.

Song: Of course. We have all those who breathe and with heartbeat ... Up until now, for this year, we have more than ten kidneys, more than ten such kidneys.

N: More than ten of this kind of kidneys? You mean live bodies?

Song: Yes it is so."

(4) Shanghai's Zhongshan Hospital Organ Transplant Clinic (16 March 2006):

"M: Hi. Are you a doctor?

Doctor: Yes, I am ...

M: ... So how long do I have to wait [for organ transplant surgery]?

Doctor: About a week after you come ...

M: Is there the kind of organs that come from Falun Gong? I heard that they are very good.

Doctor: All of ours are those types."

(5) Qianfoshan City Liver Transplant Hospital, Shandong province (16 March 2006):

"Receptionist: Hold a second. I'll get a doctor for you.

Doctor: Hello. How are you?

M: ... How long have you been doing [these operations]? ...

Doctor: ... Over four years ...

M: The supply of livers ... the ones from Falun Gong, I want to ask if you have those types?

Doctor: It is ok if you come here.

M: So that means you have them?

Doctor: ... In April, there will be more of these kinds of suppliers ... now, gradually, we have more and more.

M: Why will there be more in April?

Doctor: This I can't explain to you ..."

(6) Shanghai Jiaotong University Hospital's Liver Transplant Centre (16 March 2006):

"M: I want to know how long [the patients] have to wait [for a liver transplant].

Dr. Dai: The supply of organs we have, we have every day. We do them every day.

M: We want fresh, alive ones.

Dr. Dai: They are all alive, all alive ...

M: How many [liver transplants] have you done?

Dr. Dai: We have done 400 to 500 cases ... Your major job is to come, prepare the money, enough money, and come.

M: How much is it?

Dr. Dai: If everything goes smoothly, it's about RMB 150,000 ... RMB 200,000.

M: How long do I have to wait?

Dr. Dai: I need to check your blood type ... If you come today, I may do it for you within one week.

M: I heard some come from those who practise Falun Gong, those who are very healthy.

Dr. Dai: Yes, we have. I can't talk clearly to you over the phone.

M: If you can find me this type, I am coming very soon.

Dr. Dai: It's ok. Please come.

M: ... What is your last name? ...

Dr. Dai: I'm Doctor Dai."

(7) Zhengzhou Medical University Organ Transplant Centre in Henan Province (14 March 2006):

"Dr. Wang: ... For sure, [the organ] is healthy ... If it's not healthy, we won't take it.

M: I've heard that those kidneys from Falun Gong practitioners are better. Do you have them?

Wang: Yes, yes, we pick all young and healthy kidneys …

M: That is the kind that practises this type of [Falun] Gong.

Wang: For this, you could rest assured. Sorry I can't tell you much on the phone.

M: Do you get [them] out of town?

Wang: … We have local ones and out-of-town ones …

M: What is your last name?

Wang: Wang."

(8) Tongji Hospital in Wuhan City, Wuhan City, Hunan Province (30 March 2006):

"N: How many [kidney transplants] can you do in a year?

Official: … Our department is the one that does the most in the whole Hubei province. We do a lot if the organ suppliers are ample.

N: … We hope the kidney suppliers are alive. [We're] looking for live organ transplants from prisoners, for example, using living bodies from prisoners who practise Falun Gong. Is it possible?

Official: It's not a problem."

(9) General Hospital of Guangzhou Military Region, Guangdong Province (12 April 2006):

"N: Is this Dr. Zhu? …

Zhu: Yes, that's me.

N: I'm from hospital 304 … I have two relatives in hospital 304. We don't have enough kidney supply right now. We did a lot of [kidney transplants] in 2001, 2002, and 2003 …

Zhu: Right …

N: We found that kidneys from young people and Falun Gong [practitioners] are better. How about your hospital, such as kidneys from Falun Gong?

Zhu: We have very few kidneys from Falun Gong.

N: But you still have some?

Zhu: It is not hard for [blood] type B. If you come here, we can arrange it quickly, definitely before May 1.

N: There will be a batch before May 1?

Zhu: Several batches.

N: Will you have some after May 1?

Zhu: After May 1, you may need to wait until May 20 or later."

(10) The First Criminal Bureau of the Jinzhou Intermediate People's Court (23 May 2006):

"N: Starting from 2001, we always [got] kidneys from young and healthy people who practise Falun Gong from detention centres and courts ... I wonder if you still have such organs in your court right now?

Official: That depends on your qualifications ... If you have good qualifications, we may still provide some ...

N: Are we supposed to get them, or will you prepare for them?

Official: According to past experience, it is you that will come here to get them."

(11) Kunming Higher People's Court (31 May 2006):

"N: ... We contacted your court several times in 2001. Your court can provide us with those live kidney organs from those young and healthy Falun Gong practitioners ... ?

Official: I am not sure about that. Such things are related to national secrets. I don't think this is something that we can talk about on the phone. If you want to know more information about these things, you'd better contact us in a formal way, okay?"

(12) Air Force Hospital of Chendu City (29 April 2006):

"Investigator: The patient he emphasizes that he wants the organ of the young and healthy. The best is from those who practice Falun Gong. Will he have this kind of chance?

Chief Physician Xu: Yes.

Investigator: Yes?

Chief Physician Xu: He will have this opportunity …

Investigator: It should be from the young and healthy, who practice Falun Gong!

Chief Physician Xu: No Problem."

(13) No. 1 Hospital Affiliated with Jiaotong University of Xi'an (11 April 2006)

"Investigator: How long I have to wait for the organ supply?

Dr. Wang: … It probably will be before the month of May.

Investigator: Is the kidney from live body?

Dr. Wang: Also have liver from the live body.

Investigator: Also have liver from the live body?

Dr. Wang: We have, we have …

Investigator: The source of the organs is from live human body?

Dr. Wang: Correct.

Investigator: There are some labour camps that jail Falun Gong practitioners, and then the organs are removed from their live bodies …

Dr. Wang: Yes, yes. What we care is the quality. We don't care about the source. What would you say? Now in China, there are thousands of cases of the liver transplant. Everyone is the same. It is impossible that because some information was leaked out and then everyone stops doing the organ transplant."

(14) Shanghai Ruijin Hospital (25 October 2006):

"Investigator: Do you use live kidneys [for transplant]?

Doctor: Yes.

Investigator: Well, we have a relative in Shenyang, he said that it seemed that there were fairly larger numbers of kidneys used over there, and they were better in quality. He refers to that kind from Falun Gong, right? Do you use this kind as well? …

Doctor: Yes.

Investigator: Wow, you use that kind as well.

Doctor: Every hospital is the same …

Investigator: I understand, it is because the Falun Gong kind is much healthier, right?

Doctor: Correct."

(15) No. 1 Hospital affiliated to Inner Mongolia Medical College (14 November 2006)

"Doctor: Recently we might have [liver sources] …

M: That type, the Falun Gong type is good …

…

M: How much does it cost to do a liver transplant?

Doctor: We are relatively inexpensive – 150,000-200,000 yuan.

M: How long do we have to wait?

Doctor: About a month …

M: That type, the Falun Gong type [organ supplier] is better …

Doctor: I know, I know. After you are over here, I'll talk to you. I'm afraid that I couldn't explain to you very well right now.

M: Right, that kind who practices Falun Gong, they are very healthy.

Doctor: I know, I know.

M: Can you find them? If it is …

Doctor: Sure, I can."

Chapter Eight

The numbers

The number of organ transplants in China is huge – up to 20,000 in 2005, according to the *China Daily* newspaper. China has the second largest number of such operations done in the world, just after the U.S.A. The large volumes coupled with the short waiting times means that there has to be a large number of potential donors on hand at any one time. Where is and who is this large donor population?

There are many more transplants than identifiable sources. We know that some organs come from prisoners sentenced to death and then executed. Very few come from willing donor family members and the brain-dead. But these sources leave huge gaps in the totals. The number of prisoners sentenced to death and then executed, plus willing sources, comes nowhere close to the number of transplants.

The number of prisoners sentenced to death and then executed is itself not public. We are operating only from numbers provided by Amnesty International, sourced from Chinese public records. Those numbers, when one considers global execution totals, are large, but nowhere near the estimated totals of transplants.

China has had no organized system of organ donations.[58] In this, it is unlike every other country engaged in organ transplant surgery. Donations from living donors have been allowed for family members. The Government announced in August 2009 that it was launching a national organ donation system.

We are told that there is a Chinese cultural aversion to organ donation. Yet Hong Kong and Taiwan, with essentially the same culture, have active organ donation programs.

The absence until now of an organ donation system in China tells us two things. One is that organ donations are not a plausible source for organ transplants in China.

Because of the cultural aversion to organ donation in China, even an active organ donation system would have difficulty supplying the volume of transplants now occurring. But the problem is compounded when there is not an active effort to encourage donations.

Donations matter in other countries because donations are the primary source of organs for transplants. We can conclude from the absence of a serious effort to encourage donations in China that, for China, donations do not even matter. China has, without donations, such a plethora of organs available for transplants that encouraging organ donations becomes superfluous.

The absence of a serious effort to encourage organ donations, in combination with short waiting times for transplant surgery in China and the large volume of transplants performed, tells us that China is awash in living organs for transplant – from people the authorities have ready on hand to be killed for their organs. That reality does nothing to dispel the allegation of organ-harvesting of unwilling Falun Gong practitioners.

At least 98% of the organs for transplants in China come from someone other than family donors.[59] In the case of kidneys, for example, only 227 of 40,393 transplants – about 0.6% – done between 1971 and 2001 came from family donors.[60]

It was only in 2005[61] that the government of China admitted to using the organs of prisoners sentenced to death and then executed, although the practice had been going on for many years. The regime has had no barriers to prevent marketing the organs of "enemies of the state".

According to tabulations constructed from the Amnesty International reports[62] of publicly-available information in China, the average number of prisoners sentenced to death and then executed between 1995 and 1999 was 1,680 per year. The average between 2000 and 2005 was 1,616 per year. The numbers have bounced around from year to year, but the overall average number for the periods before and after Falun Gong persecution began is the same. Execution of prisoners sentenced to death cannot explain the increase of organ transplants in China since the persecution of Falun Gong began.

According to the Chinese Code of Criminal Procedure, the death penalty can be imposed in two different fashions – by immediate execution or with two-year suspension. A death sentence with a two-year suspension will never be carried out if during the two years the prisoner avoids committing another intentional crime.

Death sentence with immediate execution truly means, according to law, immediate. The time period of seven days is specified. The law says that the death sentence shall be carried out within seven days of the death sentence order.[63]

There is no system of clemency or pardon in China for those sentenced to death. The combination of the requirement of immediate execution and the absence of a clemency system means that, in principle, there is no death row. The jails should not have, if the law is being followed, prisoners sentenced to death and waiting to be executed.

The absence of a death row means that, in principle, there is no organ bank of prisoners sentenced to death. The reality of the law in China, as elsewhere, is not always the same as the law as it reads on paper. However, compliance with the law, which, in spite of everything, does in China at least occasionally occur, works against the existence of an organ donor bank of prisoners sentenced to death. Prisoners sentenced to death are not a reliable a source of organs.

According to public reports[64] there were approximately 30,000 transplants in total done in China before 1999 and 18,500[65] in the six-year period 1994 to 1999. Shi Bingyi, vice-chair of the China Medical Organ Transplant Association, says there were about 90,000[66] transplants in total up until 2005. That meant that transplants went up from 18,500 in the six-year period prior to the persecution of the Falun Gong to 60,000 in the six-year period after the persecution of the Falun Gong began. Since the death penalty volume was constant, that left 41,500 transplants in the six-year period 2000 to 2005 where the only explanation for the sourcing was Falun Gong practitioners.

The other identified sources of organ transplants, willing family donors and the brain-dead, have always been tiny. In 2005, living-related kidney transplants consisted of 0.5% of total transplants.[67] The total of brain-dead donors for all years and all of China is nine up to March 2006.[68] There is no indication of a significant increase in either of these categories in recent years.

Again, this sort of gap in the figures does not establish that the allegation of harvesting of organs from Falun Gong practitioners is true. But the converse, a full explanation of the source of all organ transplants, would disprove the allegation. If the source of all organ transplants could be traced either to willing donors or executed prisoners, then the allegation concerning the Falun Gong would be disproved. But such tracing is impossible.

Estimates of executions in China of prisoners sentenced to death are often much higher than the figures based on publicly-available records of executions. There is no official Chinese reporting on overall statistics of executions, leaving totals open to estimation.

One technique some of those involved in estimating executions have used is the number of transplant operations. Because it is known that at least some transplants come from executed prisoners and that family donors are few and far between, some analysts have deduced from the number of transplants that executions of prisoners sentenced to death have increased.

This reasoning is unpersuasive. One cannot estimate execution of prisoners sentenced to death from transplants unless executions of prisoners sentenced to death are the only alleged source of transplants. Falun Gong practitioners are another alleged source. It is impossible to conclude that those practitioners are not a source of organs for transplants because of the number of executions of prisoners sentenced to death, given that the number of executions of prisoners sentenced to death has been deduced from the number of transplants.

Can the increase in transplants be explained by increased efficiency in harvesting from prisoners sentenced to death and then executed? The increase in transplants in China paralleled both the persecution of the Falun Gong and the development of some transplant technology. But the increase in transplants did not parallel the increase of all transplant technology. Kidney transplant technology was fully developed in China long before the persecution of Falun Gong began. Yet kidney transplants shot up, more than doubling once the persecution of Falun Gong started. There were 3,596 kidney transplants in 1998 and nearly 10,000 in 2005.[69]

A second reason that multiple organ-harvesting from executed prisoners sentenced to death does not explain the increase in organ transplants is overall disorganization of organ-matching in China. There is no national network for the matching and sharing of organs. Doctors decry the wastage of organs from donors, bemoaning the fact that "only kidneys were used from donors, wasting of other organs".[70] Each hospital manages its own organ supply and waiting list. Patients go from one hospital where there are no ready organs for transplants to other hospitals where transplant surgery takes place at once.[71] Hospitals refer patients from their own facility – where they say they have no readily available organs for transplant – to another hospital which they say does have organs for transplant.[72] This disorganization diminishes the efficient use of organs.

A third reason that multiple organ-harvesting from executed prisoners sentenced to death does not explain the increase in organ transplants is the experience elsewhere. Nowhere have transplants jumped so significantly with the same number of donors, simply because of a change in technology.

The number of organ transplants in Canada[73] each year has not changed substantially in the past decade. During the same period in the U.S.,[74] there has been a slight increase each year except 2008, when the number decreased by a small amount from the 2007 total. In Japan,[75] the number has fluctuated from year to year with an overall increasing trend. This information is drawn from the statistics of the national organ transplant network for each country.

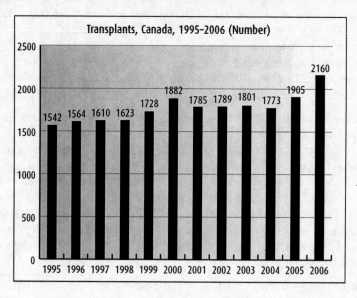

Transplants by Donor Type U.S. Transplants Performed January 1, 1988 – June 30, 2009 Based on OPTN data as of September 11, 2009			
	All Donor Types	Deceased Donor	Living Donor
To Date	464,060	364,033	100,027
2009	14,191	10,970	3,221
2008	27,963	21,746	6,217
2007	28,364	22,052	6,312
2006	28,939	22,207	6,732
2005	28,116	21,213	6,903
2004	27,039	20,048	6,991
2003	25,472	18,658	6,814
2002	24,909	18,291	6,618
2001	24,233	17,641	6,592
2000	23,257	17,334	5,923
1999	22,017	17,008	5,009
1998	21,518	16,973	4,545
1997	20,309	16,263	4,046
1996	19,755	15,980	3,775
1995	19,396	15,921	3,475
1994	18,298	15,210	3,088
1993	17,631	14,733	2,898
1992	16,134	13,563	2,571
1991	15,756	13,329	2,427
1990	15,001	12,878	2,123
1989	13,139	11,221	1,918
1988	12,623	10,794	1,829
Organ Procurement Transplant Network			www.optn.org

The increase in organ transplants in China parallels the increase in persecution of the Falun Gong. These parallel increases of Falun Gong persecution and transplants, in themselves, do not prove the allegations. But they are consistent with them. If the parallel did not exist, that hypothetical non-existence would undercut the allegations.

Organ transplant surgery in China is a booming business. There were only 22 liver transplant centres[76] operating across China before 1999 and 500 in mid-April of 2006.[77] The number of kidney transplantation institutions increased from 106[78] in 2001 to 368[79] in 2005.

The money to be made has led to the creation of dedicated facilities, specializing in organ transplants. The Peking University Third Hospital Liver Transplantation Centre[80] was founded in October 2002, the Beijing Organ Transplantation Centre[81] in November 2002, the Organ Transplant Centre of the People's Liberation Army Number 309 Hospital[82] in April 2002, the People's Liberation Army Organ Transplant Research Institute[83] (Organ Transplant Centre of the Shanghai Changzheng Hospital) in May 2004, and the Shanghai Clinical Medical Centre[84] for Organ Transplants in 2001. The Oriental Organ Transplant Centre[85] in Tianjin began construction in 2002. It has fourteen floors above ground and two floors underground with 300 beds. It is a public facility, built by Tianjin City. It is the largest transplant centre in Asia.

The establishment of these facilities is both an indicator of the volume of organ transplants and a commitment to their continuation. The creation of whole facilities dedicated to organ transplants bespeaks long-term planning.

The organ source for virtually all Chinese transplants is prisoners. There is a debate whether these prisoners have all previously been sentenced to death or whether some of them are detained Falun Gong practitioners who have been sentenced to jail terms only (or not sentenced at all). But there is no debate over whether the sources of organs are prisoners; that much is incontestable. The establishment of dedicated organ transplant facilities in China is an overt assertion of the intent to continue organ-harvesting from prisoners.

The Government of China has said, both in law and through official statements, that it would cease organ-harvesting from prisoners sentenced to death who do not consent to organ-harvesting. And there is no such thing as meaningful consent to organ-harvesting from a prisoner sentenced to death.

Human Rights Watch has reported that consent is obtained from executed prisoners in only a minority of cases. The organization writes that even in this minority of cases:

> "… the abusive circumstances of detention and incarceration in China, from the time a person is first accused of a capital offense until the moment of his or her execution, are such as to render absurd any notion of 'free and voluntary consent.'"[86]

The creation of these dedicated facilities raises questions about the source of so many organs transplanted in the past. It also makes us ask what will be the source for the many organs which China apparently intends to transplant in the future. From whom will these organs come? The source of prisoners sentenced to death will presumably disappear or diminish substantially if China is genuine in applying to those prisoners its law and stated policy about requiring consent of donors.

The Chinese authorities, to build these dedicated organ transplant institutions, must have the confidence that there exists now and into the foreseeable future a ready source of organs from people who are alive now and will be dead tomorrow. Who are these people? A large prison population of Falun Gong practitioners provides an answer.

Since our report came out, there has been a change in Chinese law discussed in Chapter Twelve. The effect of this law is to decrease transplant tourism. The decrease in transplant tourism has gone hand in hand with an increase in transplants to patients within China. There is no substantial fall-off in total organ transplants.

Before January 1, 2007, the death penalty could be imposed by regional courts, the Higher People's Courts. As of January 1, 2007, any death penalty imposed by a regional court has to be approved by the central Supreme People's Court.

This shift in procedures reduced the pool of prisoners sentenced to death, in the estimate of Amnesty International, by about half. Fewer people sentenced to death means that fewer people with such sentences are available for organ transplants.

Amnesty International figures of prisoners sentenced to death and then executed are: 2004 – 3,400; 2005 – 1,770; 2006 – 1,010; 2007 – 470; 2008 – 1,718. Statistics from the Government of China show that organ transplant volumes have not declined as much as this declining supply. The China Liver Transplant Registry reports these figures: 2004 – 2,219; 2005 – 2,970; 2006 – 2,781; 2007 – 1,822; 2008 – 2,209.

The year 2007 shows a decrease in liver transplants, consistent with the fall-off in the execution of prisoners sentenced to death and the change in the organ transplant law. Yet, the fall-off in liver transplants in 2007 was nowhere near the reduction in execution of prisoners sentenced to death.

From 2006 to 2007 the decrease in execution of prisoners sentenced to death was 53%. The decrease in liver transplants was 34%.

Moreover, in 2007 there were two downward pulls on liver transplant volumes. There was a Health Ministry requirement imposed in 2007 that transplants take place only in registered hospitals. This requirement completely shut down transplants in non-military, non-registered hospitals and temporarily shut down transplants in later-registered hospitals until they were registered.

This dual downward pull should have created a decrease in transplants substantially more acute than the decrease in the execution of prisoners sentenced to death. Yet the opposite has occurred.

Persons executed after being sentenced to death were, according to Amnesty International, in 2004 close to the all-time high recorded in 1996. The figures in 2008 for prisoners executed after being sentenced to death were nowhere near as high, about half. Yet liver transplant volumes in 2008 bounced back to 2004 levels.

How was China able in 2007 to hold its reduction of liver transplant volumes to only 34% in the face of the imposition of a licensing requirement for non-military hospitals doing transplants and a 53% reduction in what Chinese officials claim to be their almost exclusive source for organs? How has China been able to return to historically high liver transplant volumes in 2008 in the absence of a commensurate increase in execution of prisoners sentenced to death? The only plausible answer is an increase in sourcing of organs from the only other significant available source – Falun Gong practitioners.

The United Nations

The United Nations Rapporteur on Torture, Manfred Nowak, and the U.N. Rapporteur on Religious Intolerance, Asma Jahangir, addressed our concerns in their 2007 and 2008 reports. They wrote in 2007:

> "Allegation transmitted: Organ harvesting has been inflicted on a large number of unwilling Falun Gong practitioners at a wide variety of locations, for the purpose making available organs for transplant operations ... It is reported that there are many more organ transplants than identifiable sources of organs, even taking into account figures for identifiable sources, namely: estimates of executed prisoners annually, of which a high percentage of organs are donated, according to the statement in 2005 of the Vice Minister of Health Mr Huang Jiefu; willing donor family

members, who for cultural reasons, are often reluctant to donate their organs after death; and brain-dead donors. Moreover, the reportedly short waiting times that have been advertised for perfectly-matched organs would suggest the existence of a computerized matching system for transplants and a large bank of live prospective donors. It is alleged that the discrepancy between available organs and numbers from identifiable sources is explained by organs harvested from Falun Gong practitioners, and that the rise in transplants from 2000 coincides and correlates with the beginning of the persecution of these persons ..."[87]

The Government of China responded but without addressing the concerns raised. As a result, the Rapporteurs reiterated their concerns in 2008 with these words:

"A critical issue was not addressed in the Government's previous responses, in particular: It is reported that there are many more organ transplants than identifiable sources of organs, even taking into account figures for identifiable sources, namely: annual estimates of executed prisoners by whom a high percentage of organs are donated, according to the statement in 2005 of the Vice Minister of HLTH, Mr. Huang Jiefu; willing donor family members, who for cultural reasons, are often reluctant to donate their organs after death; and brain-dead donors. Moreover, the short waiting times that have been advertised for perfectly-matched organs would suggest the existence of a computerized matching system for transplants and a large bank of live prospective donors. It is alleged that the discrepancy between available organs and numbers from identifiable sources is explained by organs harvested from Falun Gong practitioners, and that the rise in transplants from 2000 coincides and correlates with the beginning of the persecution of these persons. The Special Rapporteurs note reports that on 15 November 2006, Vice-Minister Huang reiterated at a conference of surgeons in Guangzhou that most organs harvested come from executed prisoners. And notwithstanding the reported stringent criteria in place for donors, including for those sentenced to death, the Government informed in its response of 28 November, that voluntary donations, and donations between relatives are the two other legitimate sources of transplant organs. According to the allegations, based on data from the China Medical Organ Transplant Association, between the years 2000 and 2005 there were 60,000 transplantations performed, or approximately 10,000 per year for six years. This period coincides with the alleged rise in the persecution of Falun Gong practitioners. In 2005, it is reported that only 0.5% of total transplants were accounted for by donations by relatives; non-relative brain-dead donors were around nine in 2006; and estimates – given that the Government does not make public statistics on executions – for 2005 indicate 1,770 executions were carried out, and 3,900 persons sentenced to death. It is alleged that the discrepancy between the number of transplants carried out and the number of available sources is made up from the harvesting of organs from Falun Gong practitioners. However, it is also reported that the true number of executions is estimated to be around 8,000 to 10,000 per year, rather than the figure of 1,770 executions referred above. As the Special Rapporteur on torture recommended in his report on his visit to China, he reiterates that the Government (E/CN.4/2006/6/para. 82, recommendation q) should use the opportunity of the restoration of the power of review of all death sentences by the Supreme People's Court to publish national statistics on the death penalty. A full explanation of the source of organ transplants would disprove the allegation of organ harvesting of Falun Gong practitioners, particularly if they could be traced to willing donors or executed prisoners. The request for an explanation for the discrepancy in the number of transplants between the years 2000 to 2005 and the numbers from identifiable sources of organs is reiterated."[88]

The Chinese government, in a response sent to the Rapporteurs by letter dated March 19, 2007 and published in the report of Professor Nowak to the U.N. Human Rights Council dated February 19, 2008, stated that:

"Professor Shi Bingyi expressly clarified that on no occasion had he made such a statement or given figures of this kind, and these allegations and the related figures are pure fabrication."

Moreover, the Government of China, lest there be any doubt, asserted that:

"China's annual health statistics are compiled on the basis of categories of health disorder and not in accordance with the various types of treatment provided."[89]

Shi Bingyi was interviewed in a video documentary produced by Phoenix TV, a Hong Kong media outlet. That video shows Shi Bingyi on screen saying what the Government of China, in its response to Nowak, indicates he said, that the figures we quote from him he simply never gave. He says on the video:

"I did not make such a statement because I have no knowledge of these figures I have not made detailed investigation on this subject how many were carried out and in which year. Therefore I have no figures to show. So I could not have said that."

Yet, the actual source of the quotation is footnoted in our report. It is a Chinese source, the Health News Network. The article from the Network was posted on the website for transplantation professionals in China.[90] The text, dated 2006-03-02, stated, in part, in translation:

"Professor Shi said that in the past 10 years, organ transplantation in China had grown rapidly; the types of transplant operations that can be performed were very wide, ranging from kidney, liver, heart, pancreas, lung, bone marrow, cornea; so far, there had been over 90,000 transplants completed country-wide; last year alone, there was close to 10,000 kidney transplants and nearly 4,000 liver transplants completed."

This article, in June 2008, remained on its original Chinese website, though it has been taken down since. The original source of the information remained available within China through the Internet at the time Shi Bingyi denied the information.

Moreover, the information in this article continues to be recycled in Chinese publications. The official website of the Minister of Science and Technology of the People's Republic of China posts a newsletter of June 20, 2008 which states:

> "Up to date, China has performed some 85,000 organ transplants, only next to the United States in number. In recent years, China performed organ transplants on more than 10,000 patients a year ... Liver transplants have exceeded 10,000 in number ... Heart transplants went over 100 in number ..."[91]

The number of 90,000 total transplants in 2006 is not consistent with only 85,000 total transplants as of 2008. This calls for an explanation only those who provide the statistics can give. What is striking about the later article, aside from the statistical mismatch, is that it flies in the face of the official Chinese statement to the Rapporteurs that China's health statistics are compiled on the basis of categories of health disorder and not in accordance with the various types of treatment provided.

So what we have is a statement from Shi Bingyi on a Chinese-based website which was extant at the time of the denial, a statement which Shi Bingyi publicly denied ever having made. Moreover, despite the continued presence on this website of a statement showing that Shi Bingyi said what we wrote he said, the Chinese government accused us of fabricating the words we attributed to Shi Bingyi.

Neither the Government of China nor Shi Bingyi claimed that Health News Network has misquoted or misunderstood what Shi Bingyi said. At the time of the denial, there was no effort to hide or mask or take down from the Internet the publicly-posted article of the Health News Network where Shi Bingyi is quoted. The continuation of this article on a Chinese website – at the same time as China was removing from the Internet so much other information about organ transplants which we used in coming to our conclusions – amounted to a continuation to assert what is to be found in that article.

The United Nations Committee against Torture picked up the baton from the Special Rapporteurs. In its November 2008 concluding observations, it wrote:

> "While noting the State party's information about the 2006 Temporary Regulation on Human Organ Transplants and the 2007 Human Organ Transplant Ordinance, the Committee takes cognizance of the allegations presented to the Special Rapporteur on Torture who has noted that an increase in organ transplant operations coincides with 'the beginning of the persecution of [Falun Gong practitioners]' and who asked for 'a full explanation of the source of organ transplants' which could clarify the discrepancy and disprove the allegation of organ harvesting (A/HRC/7/3/Add.1). The Committee is further concerned with information received that Falun Gong practitioners have been extensively subjected to torture and ill-treatment in prisons and that some of them have been used for organ transplants (arts. 12 and 16).

> "The State party should immediately conduct or commission an independent investigation of the claims that some Falun Gong practitioners have been subjected to torture and used for organ transplants and take measures, as appropriate, to ensure that those responsible for such abuses are prosecuted and punished."[92]

We are independent from the Government of China and the Falun Gong community. The Committee against Torture did not mean to suggest anything different. What they were proposing was an investigation independent from the Government of China with which the Government of China would nonetheless co-operate by giving access to Chinese territory, documents, places of detention and witnesses in China without fear of intimidation or reprisals.

This issue then was further amplified by the United Nations Universal Periodic Review Working Group in February 2009. The Universal Periodic Review is a new element of the United Nations Human Rights Council which was created in 2006 to replace the failed U.N. Human Rights Commission. Under the Universal Periodic Review, every state gets reviewed once during a four-year cycle. China's turn came up February 2009 in Geneva.

Only states can intervene in the Universal Periodic Review Working Group debate. But it can be any state; it does not have to be a state which is a member of the Human Rights Council. The debate is an interactive dialogue, meaning China has a right to respond.

At the Universal Periodic Review Working Group, Canada recommended that China implement the recommendations of the Committee against Torture. The Government of China explicitly, in writing, rejected this recommendation.

Canada, Switzerland, United Kingdom, France, Austria and Italy recommended that China publish death penalty statistics. The Government of China said no to this recommendation too.

Chapter Nine

Sujiatun

The Epoch Times published a story in its March 9, 2006 issue with the headline "Over 6,000 Falun Gong practitioners detained in secret concentration camp in China" and a subheading "Over 6,000 Falun Gong practitioners are secretly detained at Sujiatun concentration camp". The source was a person whose identity was concealed, and who was described as a long-time reporter who worked for a Japanese television news agency and specialized in news in China.

The Epoch Times then published a story in its March 17 issue under the headline "New witness confirms existence of Chinese concentration camp, says organs removed from live victims". The lead sentence of this article, written under the byline of Ji Da, states:

> "A former employee of Liaoning Provincial Thrombosis
> Hospital of Integrated Chinese and Western Medicine told
> *The Epoch Times* during a recent interview that the
> Sujiatun Concentration Camp in China was actually part
> of a hospital."

The sources for these two stories have been identified only by pseudonyms – Annie and Peter.

Harry Wu came out with a statement on June 8 casting doubt on the testimony of Annie. But that doubt had developed much earlier. Wu wrote a letter "To whom it may concern" on March 21, 2006, that the testimony of Annie and Peter amounted to "possible fraud", "distorted facts", "fabricated news". Wu is executive director of the Laogai Research Foundation and the China Information Centre located in Washington D.C. He spent nineteen years in Chinese labour camps.

A spokesman for the U.S. Department of State in a daily press briefing on April 14 was asked about the reports of organ-harvesting of Falun Gong practitioners in Sujiatun. The spokesman replied that officers and staff from the Embassy in Beijing and the Consulate in Shenyang visited the area and the site mentioned in the reports and "found no evidence that the site is being used for any function other than as a normal public hospital".

Peter and Annie spoke to a public rally in Washington D.C., on April 20, 2006. Annie said that she felt the need to speak out because the U.S. and Chinese governments "have denied the existence of this incident".[93] So a controversy had developed about the reports of Peter and Annie.

As noted, Wu questioned the credibility of Annie and Peter on March 21. Yet his investigators in China did not complete their investigations and report to him till well after this letter was written. Wu writes:

> "Meanwhile, I asked the CIC reporters in China to make an investigation on the Sujiatun allegation. Since March 12, the investigators searched around the whole District of Sujiatun. On March 17, they even managed to visit the two military camps located in Sujiatun. On March 27, they secretly visited the Liaoning Provincial Thrombosis Hospital of Integrated Chinese and Western Medicine in Sujiatun. On March 29, they visited the Kangjiashan Prison at the neighbourhood of Sujiatun. However, with all these first-hand investigations, they had not found anything that could be an evidence of the Falun Gong allegation of Sujiatun Concentration Camp. During and after their investigation, they sent back photos and written reports to me about their findings respectively on March 15, March 17, March 27, March 29, March 30 and April 4."[94]

Though some investigations were conducted prior to the writing of the March 21 letter, the bulk were conducted subsequently. In particular, the visit to the relevant hospital occurred on March 27, six days after the letter was written. So Wu formed his views about Sujiatun before his investigators had completed their work. His views were not based on the full reports of his investigation. His investigation, for the most part, was used to confirm views already formed and publicly communicated.

Wu never met with or interviewed any of the three persons he has accused of lying – Annie (the ex-wife of the surgeon), the surgeon and Peter, the Japanese television news agency reporter. We could have understood his deciding to come to no conclusion whether these three were lying or telling the truth. However, to conclude that they were lying without interviewing them and without completing his investigation is unfair both to them and to the truth-seeking process.

An interview allows for judgments on demeanour, spontaneity, directness or evasiveness, relevance and attention to detail. It gives an opportunity to clarify misunderstandings. It allows the interviewer to find out not only what the person knows, but how the person knows it, to find out what information is first-hand and what information is second-hand.

We have interviewed both Annie and Peter. David Kilgour, before he went into politics, was a trial lawyer and Crown prosecutor for many years. He has had the benefit of engaging in numerous cross-examinations during his professional career and is well able to sort out those who lie from those who tell the truth.

Wu characterizes as "technically impossible" the volume of organ-harvesting which Annie says her husband did.[95] Yet, what is technically possible for organ harvesting is a matter of expert knowledge. To our knowledge, Wu has no specialized credentials which would allow him to assert what is technically possible for organ-harvesting. He neither quotes nor cites nor refers to any expertise to substantiate his claim of what is technically possible.

Annie reports that her husband engaged in cornea-harvesting of about 2,000 Falun Gong practitioners. Dr. Mohan Rajan writes: "The process of removing the eye takes only 20 minutes".[96] PS Prakasa Rao writes: "Eye removal takes only 10-15 minutes ..."[97] Contrary to Wu's assertions, it is technically possible for the volume of cornea-harvesting Annie describes, given the short time the operation takes.

Annie refers to secret underground chambers in which Falun Gong prisoners were kept. She does not claim that she has seen these chambers, but only heard of them from someone who had seen them.

Wu describes Annie's reference to secret underground chambers as "speculations". However, the existence of large underground structures in Shenyang City proper and in the Sujiatun district of the greater metropolitan Shenyang area are a matter of public knowledge. These structures have been reported in a local Shenyang newspaper.

They are described on the website of the Sujiatun District Chinese Party Committee.[98]

Peter told us that in 2003, in Sujiatun, he saw the exterior of a brick walled enclosure. This enclosure was within walking distance of the hospital, but ten minutes by taxi, because of the road system. It was not part of the hospital, nor part of the hospital compound. Since he last saw the enclosure, there has been a lot of construction in the area. He does not know if this enclosure is still there.

Peter described this enclosure to *The Epoch Times* in an interview published in the March 10, 2006 issue. He said that Falun Gong practitioners were detained at this centre. The report quotes Peter as saying:

> "The concentration camp has a crematorium to dispose of bodies. There are also many doctors on site. No detainees have managed to leave the concentration camp alive. Before cremation, the internal organs are all removed from the body and sold."

Peter explained to us that he did not enter inside the enclosure, nor did he personally talk to anyone who was working there. What he was telling *The Epoch Times* about what went on there was what he had heard from people who lived or worked in the neighbourhood. He understood that these people in turn knew this information because people who worked at the detention centre lived in the neighbourhood and communicated to others what was going on inside.

The Epoch Times then interviewed Annie, for its issue of March 17, 2006. Annie, in response to questions about the detention centre/concentration camp, talked about her hospital. The result was an *Epoch Times* story stating that Annie had confirmed what Peter had told them. Although the headline to the article is "New Witness confirms existence of Chinese Concentration Camp, says Organs Removed from Live Victims", one can see from reading the article that Annie does not talk about the detention centre Peter described. She does not confirm the existence of that detention centre. She states: "For the majority of the Falun Gong practitioners, nobody knew where they were being secretly kept."

In the body of the article where Annie is interviewed, a subheading inserted by the paper has the words "Concentration camp details". But what follows has nothing to do with the detention centre Peter described and refers only to the hospital where Annie worked.

The interviewer, when asking Annie about the hospital, puts one question this way: "Did the hospital's medical staff inside the concentration camp know about this?" Annie answers the question by talking about the hospital where she worked, without reference to any concentration camp.

Wu was able to pick that up just from reading *The Epoch Times*. In his June 6, 2006 commentary, he writes: "The secret prison Peter described is different from what Annie says."

What Peter actually saw, as opposed to what he heard – a brick walled enclosure – is in itself not all that probative. What he heard, since it comes from unidentified sources and is second- or third-hand, is a trigger for investigation, but nothing more.

What Annie heard is different. She heard directly from an identified source, her husband, who confessed to personal involvement in organ-harvesting. Was the husband truthful in telling his wife what he was doing?

We have no reason to believe that the husband would lie to Annie. There is no credible explanation we have heard why Annie's husband would say to his own wife that he had participated in atrocities if he had not done so.

On May 20, 2006, David Kilgour interviewed Annie. The following transcript was edited (to protect those who would otherwise be in danger due to publication of the interview) and abridged.

Kilgour: In 2001, when did the procurement of food supplies for [Sujiatun Hospital] go up?

Annie: About July, in the summer.

Kilgour: July 2001. You were in the accounting department?

Annie: Statistics and Logistics Department.

Kilgour: Statistics and Logistics Department. What happened? The procurement of food went up first and then the surgical equipment?

Annie: In July 2001, there were many people working in the Statistics and Logistics Department. Some of them from procurement brought the receipts to me for signature after they made the purchase. On the receipts I noted sharp increases in the food supplies. Also, the people in charge of the logistics were delivering meals to the facilities where Falun Gong practitioners were detained. Other medical staff came to our department to report the purchase of the medical equipment. From the receipts, the medical equipment supplies also sharply increased.

Kilgour: By the way, the facilities to detain Falun Gong practitioners, was it the underground facilities?

Annie: In the backyard of the hospital, there were some one-storey houses typically built for construction workers. After several months, the consumption of food and other supplies gradually decreased. At that time people guessed that maybe the detainees were sent to an underground facility.

Kilgour: When did the supply decrease? September? October?

Annie: After about four or five months.

Kilgour: End of 2001?

Annie: Yes.

Kilgour: How much of an increase did you estimate it was from the food [receipts you saw]? How many people you estimated were there?

Annie: The person in charge of getting the food and in charge of sending food to Falun Gong practitioners detained told me that there were about 5,000 to 6,000 practitioners. At the time, a lot of public security bureaus and hospitals in many areas were detaining many Falun Gong practitioners. A lot of people working at the hospital, including me, were not Falun Gong practitioners. So we didn't pay attention. If it were not for what happened in 2003, when I found my ex-husband was directly involved in it, I probably wouldn't be interested in this at all. A lot of the staffers working in our department are family members of the officials in the government health care system. For some matters, we knew it in our hearts but none of us would discuss these things.

Kilgour: When they decreased the procurement, where did you think the practitioners went?

Annie: We thought they were released.

Kilgour: At the end of 2001, you thought they were released?

Annie: Yes.

Kilgour: All 5,000 had been released?

Annie: No, there were still Falun Gong practitioners detained in the hospital, but the number was gradually decreasing. Later, in 2003, I learned that Falun Gong practitioners had been transferred to the underground complex and other hospitals, because our hospital couldn't hold so many people.

Kilgour: They left the houses or cabins in the backyard to go to underground?

Annie: Yes, I later got to know this in 2002.

Kilgour: Did you say that you were not the person to send food to them when practitioners were detained in the houses or cabins in the backyard?

Annie: No, I was not.

Kilgour: Did you know who supplied their meals after they left your jurisdiction?

Annie: I didn't know.

Kilgour: I heard a lot of these people were killed for their organs. 2001 and 2002. Was it the correct understanding?

Annie: During the years of 2001-2002, I didn't know anything about organ-harvesting. I only knew the detention of these people.

Kilgour: So you didn't discover this until you husband told you in 2003.

Annie: Right.

Kilgour: Did he tell you that in 2001-2002 he had already started doing these operations?

Annie: Yes, he started in 2002.

Kilgour: Your former husband began in 2002?

Annie: Yes.

Kilgour: Did you roughly know if there were [organ removal] operations since 2001?

Annie: The operations started in 2001. Some were done in our hospital, and some were done at other hospitals in the region. I found out in 2003. At the beginning, he also did the operations, but he did not know they were Falun Gong practitioners. He was a neurosurgeon. He removed corneas. Starting from 2002 he got to know those he operated on were Falun Gong practitioners. Because our hospital was not an organ transplant hospital – it was only in charge of removal – how these organs were transplanted, he didn't know.

Kilgour: Your ex-husband started to take organs from Falun Gong practitioners starting from when?

Annie: At the end of 2001, he started to operate, but he didn't know these live bodies were Falun Gong practitioners. He got to know that in 2002.

Kilgour: What kind of organs did he take out?

Annie: Corneas.

Kilgour: Just corneas?

Annie: Yes.

Kilgour: Were these people alive or dead?

Annie: Usually these Falun Gong practitioners were injected with a shot to cause heart failure. During the process these people would be pushed into operation rooms to have their organs removed. On the surface the heart stopped beating, but the brain was still functioning, because of that shot.

Kilgour: What was the injection called?

Annie: I don't know the name of it but it caused heart failure. I was not a nurse or a doctor. I don't know the names of the injections.

Kilgour: Causing heart failure, most, or all, or some cases?

Annie: For most people.

Kilgour: So he would take corneas of these people, then what happened to these people?

Annie: These people were pushed to other operation rooms for removals of heart, liver, kidneys, etc. During one operation when he collaborated with other doctors, he learned they were Falun Gong practitioners, that their organs were removed while alive, and that it was not just cornea removal. They were removing many organs.

Kilgour: They did it in different rooms, didn't they?

Annie: In the later period of time, when these doctors co-operated together, they started doing the operations together. At the beginning, fearing information could leak out, different organs were removed by different doctors in different rooms. Later on, when they got money, they were no longer afraid any more. They started to remove the organs together. For other practitioners who were operated on in other hospitals, my ex-husband didn't know what happened to them afterwards. For the practitioners in our hospital, after their kidneys, liver, etc. and skin were removed, there were only bones and flesh, etc. left. The bodies were thrown into the boiler room at the hospital.

In the beginning, I did not fully believe this had happened. For some doctors who had operation accidents, they may form some illusions. So I checked with other doctors and other officials from the government health care system.

Kilgour: In 2003 or 2002?

Annie: 2003.

Kilgour: Your husband only did corneas?

Annie: Yes.

Kilgour: How many cornea operations did your ex-husband perform?

Annie: He said about 2,000.

Kilgour: Corneas of 2,000 people, or 2,000 corneas?

Annie: Corneas of around 2,000 people.

Kilgour: This is from 2001 to 2003?

Annie: From the end of 2001 to October 2003.

Kilgour: That was when he left?

Annie: It was the time that I got to know this and he stopped doing it.

Kilgour: Where did these corneas go?

Annie: They were usually collected by other hospitals. There was an existing system handling such business of the removal and sales of the organs to other hospitals or other areas.

Kilgour: Nearby or far away?

Annie: I don't know.

Kilgour: All the heart, liver, kidneys, and corneas go off to other hospitals?

Annie: Yes.

Kilgour: Did you know what prices they sold them for?

Annie: I don't know at the time. However, in the year 2002, a neighbour had a liver transplant. It cost 200,000 yuan. The hospital charged a little bit less for Chinese than foreigners.

Kilgour: Which year, 2001 or 2002?

Annie: 2002.

Kilgour: What was your husband told? How did they justify? These were perfectly healthy people?

Annie: In the beginning, he wasn't told anything. He was asked to help out in other hospitals. However, every time when he did such a favour, or provided this kind of help, he got lots of money, and cash awards – several dozen times his normal salary.

Kilgour: What was the total amount of money he got out of the 2,000 cornea removals?

Annie: Hundreds of thousands of U.S. dollars.

Kilgour: Were they paid in U.S. dollars?

Annie: Paid in Chinese yuan. Equivalent to hundreds of thousands of U.S. dollars.

Kilgour: How many doctors were working on these organ removals in the hospital, and in which area? Are we talking about 100 doctors, or dozens, or 10?

Annie: I don't know how many people were doing it specifically. But I know that about four or five doctors who were acquaintances of us at our hospital were doing it. And in other hospitals, doctors of general practice were also doing this.

Kilgour: Are there any records in the statistics department regarding how many people were operated upon?

Annie: There was no proper procedure or paperwork for this kind of operation. So there was no way to count the number of operations in the normal way.

Kilgour: After practitioners transferred underground at the end of 2001, did you know where their food supplies were from?

Annie: Food still came from our department; just the amount gradually decreased. At the end of 2001 we thought they were released. In 2003, I learned that they were not released but were transferred underground or to other hospitals.

Kilgour: Was the underground facility run by the military army or by the hospital? You said food was still from the hospital.

Annie: We weren't responsible for the procurement of the food for the people detained and kept underground. That is why there was so much difference in the procurement of food when people were transferred to the underground complex. But the food of some of the detainees was provided by the hospital, and for others it was not. The decrease in food was not proportional to the decrease in the number of detainees.

Kilgour: What did your husband tell you about the underground facility? Five thousand people killed, or more than 5,000?

Annie: He didn't know how many people were detained underground. He only heard from some others that people were detained underground. If three operations were done every day, after several years of operation, for the

5,000-6,000 people, not many people would be left. This whole scheme and the trading of organs were organized by the government health care system. The doctors' responsibility was simply to do what they were told to do.

Kilgour: He didn't go down to the underground facility himself?

Annie: He didn't.

Kilgour: Rudimentary operations in the underground facility?

Annie: He had never been there.

Kilgour: All of those people, were they dead when they were operated on? Or their hearts stopped? Did he know that they were killed afterwards? They weren't yet dead.

Annie: At the beginning, he didn't know these were Falun Gong practitioners. As time went by, he knew they were Falun Gong practitioners. When they did more of these removals of organs and became bold, these doctors started to do the removals together; this doctor extracted the cornea, another doctor removed the kidney, the third doctor took out the liver. At that time, this patient, or this Falun Gong practitioner, he knew what was the next step to treat the body. The heart stopped beating, but they were still living. If the victim's skin was not peeled off and only internal organs were removed, the openings of the bodies would be sealed and an agent would sign the paperwork. The bodies would be sent to the crematorium near the Sujiatun area.

Kilgour: Only if the skin was removed, they would be sent to the boiler room?

Annie: Yes.

Kilgour: Usually what was the "supposed" cause of death given?

Annie: Usually no specific reason when the bodies were sent to the crematorium. Usually the reasons were "The heart stopped beating", "heart failure". When these people were rounded up and detained, nobody knew their names or where they were from. So when they were sent to the crematorium, nobody could claim their bodies.

Kilgour: Who administered the drug to cause the heart to stop beating?

Annie: Nurse.

Kilgour: Nurse working for the hospital?

Annie: Nurses brought over by these doctors. Doctors, including my ex-husband, came to this hospital in 1999 or 2000. He brought his nurse over. When organ-harvesting first started, nurses were assigned to the doctors. Wherever the doctors go, their nurses go with them as far as the organ removal operations were concerned.

Kilgour: How many did you think were still alive?

Annie: Initially I estimated there were about 2,000 people left at the time I left China in 2004. But I cannot give a figure any more, because China is still arresting Falun Gong practitioners and there have been people coming in and going out. So I cannot give a figure now any more.

Kilgour: How did you come to this number 2,000 in 2004?

Annie: According to how many my ex-husband did and how many other doctors did. And how many sent to other hospitals. Good doctors are well connected within the health care system. Many of them used to be classmates in medical schools. The number was estimated by the few doctors involved. When we were together in private, they discussed how many people in total. At that time, these doctors did not want to continue. They wanted to go to other countries or transfer to other fields. So the total number of deaths was calculated and derived by these doctors involved.

Kilgour: What is their estimate of how many people were killed?

Annie: They estimated 3,000-4,000 people.

Kilgour: This is the estimate by all of the doctors?

Annie: No. By three doctors we were familiar with.

Kilgour: Do you have anything else you want to say?

Annie: Chinese or non-Chinese, they think it is impossible Sujiatun detained so many Falun Gong practitioners. They focused on just this Sujiatun hospital. Because most people do not know there are underground facilities. I want to say, even if things were over for Sujiatun, in other hospitals this issue continues. Because I worked in Sujiatun, I know about Sujiatun. Other hospitals and detention centres' inspecting and putting control on these facilities will help reduce the deaths. For Chinese people, one person comes out, there are still family members in China. They still dare not come out to speak the truth. They are afraid it could put their family members in danger. It doesn't mean that they don't know about it.

Chapter Ten

Corroboration

Researchers looking at the issue independently of the authors have come to the same conclusion to which we have come – Kirk Allison of the University of Minnesota, British transplant surgeon Tom Treasure, and Yale student researcher Hao Wang. Many academic publications insist on peer review by two qualified researchers in the field before publication. Because of the independent verification through Kirk Allison, Tom Treasure and Hao Wong our own work has passed this peer review threshold. This chapter presents the work of these researchers in their own words.

Tom Treasure

The Falun Gong, organ transplantation, the holocaust and ourselves published in the *Journal of the Royal Society of Medicine*[99]

The numbers of organ transplants performed in China and the speed with which organs become available has raised international concern about the source of organs. It is publicly declared that organs come from executed criminals and that consent is given. However, there are allegations of an even more macabre scenario – that prisoners are systematically subjected to surgery specifically to remove their organs for transplantation. In this essay I explore the plausibility of this claim against our knowledge of doctors' complicity with the events leading to the Holocaust and the practicalities of contemporary organ transplantation.

Organ transplantation has increased in China at a remarkable rate. One institution reported 647 liver transplant operations in about a year. The waiting times are between 1-2 weeks according to Chinese hospital web pages. Price lists are available with U.S. dollar charges well below others in a global health market and under a tenth of those in the U.S.A.[100] To become organ donors people have to die young, and under particular circumstances, which means that organs are generally scarce and waiting times can be long. In China there is a numerical gap between the likely number of donors and the number of organs evidently available, in spite of that fact that organ donation has met with resistance in Chinese culture. From May 2006 organ transplantation came under regulation for the first time;[101] but the question still arises about how these transplant teams have achieved such rapid expansion and such short waiting times. An allegation has been made that in China the bodies of healthy living people have been systematically eviscerated and their organs taken for transplantation.[102]

It is now accepted as fact that the organs of executed criminals in China are used for transplantation. It is claimed that they consent, but can this be freely given? That apart, an argument of the greater good and lesser evil can be invoked: if an individual has lost the right to life under judicial process, perhaps he has also lost the right to have his kidneys buried with him. Why should they be wasted when two innocent victims of renal failure could have an improved and extended life?

However, there is a still greater concern. As part of an expansion in religious activity into the ideological vacuum left by the collapse of communism, a spiritual movement called the Falun Gong has emerged. Practitioners meet to perform their exercises and to meditate. They are pacifist by inclination and seek to meld modern science with Chinese traditions. It is hard to determine why they have attracted such disfavour, but they are cast as seditious and undesirable.[103] It seems that they are incarcerated in their tens of thousands in order to correct their way of thinking. Apparently when arrested, they are routinely blood tested. There is no reason to believe that it is for the benefit of the Falun Gong – blood group matching, however, is critical to organ donation. The suspicion that Falun Gong practitioners are a source of organs is central to the investigative work of David Matas and David Kilgour who have formulated the allegation.

The recipients are predominantly those travelling internationally for health care. If Matas and Kilgour are correct, the organs come from incarcerated members of an innocent sect – and the perpetrators are of necessity medical practitioners. As the allegation unfolds, the story seems horrific to the point of being almost beyond belief. So alarmed was I on learning of this allegation that I struggled to make sense of it. The element of the story that horrifies me most, if it is true, is that it is my medical colleagues, the doctors, who perpetrate these acts. This is the only element that I have the capacity to address. While I cannot get more evidence than has already been offered, I can at least test this allegation for credibility.

Transplantation of kidney, liver, cornea, heart and lung offer benefit in survival and/or life quality for the recipients, in an approximate descending order of quality adjusted life years (QALYs) gained. The sum total of QALYs donated by the dead person to others is considerable; very great indeed if multiple organs are donated and successfully transplanted into several individuals. To achieve that goal the operation on the donor and the allocation of organs must be expertly coordinated. I have been party to both removing and transplanting various organs.

My personal involvement peaked in the weekend when I successfully transplanted hearts into three patients within 72 h. A necessary preliminary was the process of removing those organs and is incompatible with organ removal after execution. What happens is that an anaesthetic team continues to monitor and carefully adjust the vital physiology of the person declared brain-dead, solely in order to maintain viable organs for transplantation. The heart and lungs are kept functioning while meticulous dissection and mobilization of the liver are completed. Then, in a rapid sequence, the organs – heart, lungs, liver, kidneys and then corneas – are removed, preserved and taken away. These are the necessary practicalities of the donor's operation – it should be noted that it is not compatible with retrieving organs after any process of judicial execution. The unprepared normal person might well find this both macabre and repulsive, but transplant teams necessarily become inured to these emotional and visceral responses.

How have we arrived at this point? Medical ethics are neither absolute nor static. In the West we have repeatedly challenged prior beliefs and stretched the norms of behaviour in the last few decades. For example, termination of pregnancy and manipulation of fertility (in both directions) have attracted extensive negotiation and there is still no unanimity on many points. The distinction between life and death has been redefined, specifically for the benefit of transplantation. A kidney from a cadaver can recover while the recipient is supported on dialysis, but once the myocardium necroses, the heart is irretrievably dead. It was the absence of a heartbeat that defined death until the advent of heart transplantation very publicly forced the issues in the late 1960s. Once the process of dying is completed to the point that the heart stops or fibrillates, it is likely to be damaged beyond recovery. For heart transplantation to succeed, death had to be redefined as brain death. Transplantation unquestionably pushed the boundaries of what doctors would and would not do and, in turn, society accepted the new definitions. For multiple organ donation to be achieved something that would have been horrific in another time became not only tolerable but laudable under the new rules. The blunting of our visceral responses and the redefining of ethical boundaries are steps that could lead us, if we are not careful, to the ethicists' slippery slope and must be recognized as such. But can there be any possible precedent which would make even remotely credible the allegation that doctors engage in the systematic harvesting of organs from non-consenting healthy victims?

In the 1930s the first steps on the road to the Holocaust were taken – and they were taken with the complicity of doctors.[104] How this came about merits attention for, if we do not recognize the facts and understand how it happened, how can we guard against it happening again? In Germany, as everywhere, there were people in long-term institutional care. Such patients vary in their capacity for interaction with their carers: at one end of the spectrum there is no evidence of awareness or any capacity for sensate being. The view arose, as it inevitably does, that if their lives were to slip quietly away it would be no loss. Perhaps it would be a blessing. It would surely be a relief for their families. And then there were the saved resources of time, money and love and devotion from parents and nurses that could be released for a better purpose. Their state was captured in the German phrase *lebensunwertes Leben* meaning 'life unworthy of life'.

The ethical question was whether it was permissible to take any active steps to bring about their end; in parallel, the medical question that arose was how it might be done. This in itself is important because, if the stark truth of what we are doing can be masked by the argument of secondary intent, it may be found permissible to bring about the end of life. Various methods were considered. Putting in place a policy of increasing sedation to reduce any possible distress was one. Another was starvation by systematic underfeeding or feeding a diet designed to be deficient in some essential component. But how to implement the policy?

A team of doctors was asked to devise a questionnaire, a form, on which could be collected information about the individual's functional level. The job was done and criteria were established. These questionnaires were completed on all potential *lebensunwertes Leben* patients by another set of doctors. It seems likely that the carers who completed these forms were inclined to overstate the degree of disability, evidently in the belief that this would bring more care to their charges rather than less. The forms then went to three independent assessors who, in turn, were asked to take a view, against proffered criteria, as to whether this was a life worth living. The second and third assessor could see the previous opinions on the form, which had the effect of encouraging unanimity. The forms were returned to a bureau and medical transport teams were dispatched to bring those individuals identified as *lebensunwertes Leben* to another facility where the treatment was administered. Finally, a doctor would phrase a plausible death certificate. And so it was done. The cogs turned but none knew the purpose of the whole machine. There was a paper trail, which is why we can be sure that what I have written actually happened. There were let-outs for those who got an inkling of what was going on and demonstrated themselves to be 'not up to the task'. They could be relieved of these duties and transferred to other work. With the onset of war, incomprehensible horror ensued but it was the policies and methods developed for the *lebensunwertes Leben* which provided a blueprint for what followed, and doctors were implicated throughout.

So how does this relate to transplantation? Of its nature there are also cogs turning to drive this machine. The carers of the potential donor see no future for their ventilator-dependent charges. They inform transplant coordinators who have a laudable mission to maximize the opportunities for the many potential recipients and work towards obtaining consent from the families. An international network, established on the basis of fairness, is informed of the availability of donor organs. The designated retrieval team, usually trainee surgeons or so-called 'research' or transplant fellows, go where they are sent. It is nearly always at the dead of night, when the operating theatres are free and road and air routes are clear, and it is always under extreme time pressure to maximize the quality of the organs. Meanwhile the transplant teams call recipients on waiting lists and set up urgent transplant operations, in several different hospitals – all against the clock. The time pressure, the geographical dispersion, the complexity of the matching of multiple organs, the need to respect confidentiality and the anonymity of donor and recipient, and the sheer logistics of it all, means that no member of the medical staff has an overview of the whole process. Nor would they be expected to in China. This is what makes it plausible that it could happen and that doctors themselves could be largely unaware of it, or at least sufficiently distant to turn a blind eye and a deaf ear.

Revealing the exact source of all donor organs, with a complete and transparent paper trail, would be sufficient to refute the allegations; but, interestingly, it may well be difficult to do so even in countries more open than China is at present. In the circumstances in which I was involved, there was an explicit understanding that the process only starts when it is what the donor would have wished. However, the fact is that I have never been in a position to inspect the documentation of the consent process. The hearts arrived in our operating room without a name attached and, by then, the recipient was anaesthetized and we were well on the way to removing the sick heart.

Factors that make the allegations plausible are the partitioning of the logistic elements and technical steps just as described for transplantation anywhere, and the necessity for haste. What makes it credible is the numerical gap between the reported number of transplants compared with what is possible in other countries, the short waiting times and the confidence with which operations are offered in the global health market, and the routine blood testing of the Falun Gong.

Kirk Allison

Prepared Statement of Kirk C. Allison, Ph.D., Director, Program in Human Rights and Health, School of Public Health, and Associate Director, Program in Human Rights and Medicine, Medical School, University of Minnesota to the "ongoing war on human rights" hearing before the Subcommittee on Oversight and Investigations of the Committee on International Relations, U.S. House of Representatives One Hundred Ninth Congress Second Session September 29, 2006.[105]

Chairman Rohrabacher, Ranking Member Delahunt, Congresswoman McCollum and esteemed Committee Members, thank you for your attention to this issue and for the privilege of presenting testimony. In my remarks I am speaking for myself rather than for my institution, and, secondly, my concern is general as I am not a Falun Gong practitioner.

Since July 1999 the systematic persecution of non-violent Falun Gong practitioners constitutes the single greatest concentration of human rights violations in China against a specific group since the Cultural Revolution. A program of ideological eradication has been systematically pursued under a double strategy: Publicly with high visibility in terms of state propaganda, but hermetically in actions of detainment and sanction outside conventional judicial processes.[106]

Nonetheless events and practices have been recounted in affidavits, structurally inferred from publicly available information, forensically, and through telephone inquiries. While the People's Republic of China repudiated the International Covenant of Civil and Political Rights signed by Taiwan, it ratified the International Covenant of Economic, Social and Cultural Rights.

This includes "the right of everyone to the enjoyment of the highest attainable standard of physical and mental health" and the right to take part in cultural life[107] "without discrimination of any kind as to race, colour, sex, language, religion, political or other opinion, national or social origin, property, birth or other status."[108] Notably on 4 October 1988 China also ratified the Convention against Torture and Other Cruel, Inhuman or Degrading Treatment or Punishment, but rejected the Committee Against Torture's power of inquiry (Article 20).

Manfred Nowak, the China mission Special Rapporteur regarding civil and political rights, including the issue of torture and detention, concluded in 2005: The combination of deprivation of liberty as a sanction for the peaceful exercise of freedom of expression, assembly and religion, with measures of re-education through coercion, humiliation and punishment aimed at admission of guilt and altering the personality of detainees up to the point of breaking their will, constitutes a form of inhuman or degrading treatment or punishment, which is incompatible with the core values of any democratic society based upon a culture of human rights.[109] Mr. Nowak notes that Falun Gong practitioners comprise 66% of victims of alleged torture in China.[110]

Those who defend practitioners are sanctioned as is the case of Attorney Gao Zhisheng whose third open letter in 2005 protesting the treatment of Falun Gong practitioners (among others) resulted in closure of his law firm and loss of his law license. He has recently been in detention since 15 August 2006.

The systematic program of ideological eradication of Falun Gong coincided with an inexplicable increase in whole organ transplantation, and international organ transplant tourism to China. This raises the question of the organ source.

In July of 2005 Huang Jiefu, Vice Minister of Health, indicated as high as 95% of organs derive from execution.[111] Under the 1997 Criminal Law capital crime offenses were expanded from 27 in 1979 to 68, with over half for non-violent crime.[112] While the number of executions is a state secret, Liu Renwen of the Chinese Academy of Social Sciences Law Institute estimated 8,000 executions in 2005.[113] Regional claims of low rates are contradicted by strong circumstantial evidence: Amnesty International reports that Yunnan Province admitted to 17 executions in 2002 but purchased 18 mobile execution vans in 2003 at about $60,000 each.[114] Such mobile vehicles have been cited as providing a smooth transition from execution to organ extraction[115] with physician involved in both phases.

Coordination of execution by gunshot followed by organ extraction without consent has also been cited in Congressional testimony by Dr. Wang Guoqi, far beyond the latitude of Article 3 of China's Provisional Regulations on the Use of Executed Prisoners' Corpses or Organs (1984).[116] While the World Medical Association's Resolution on Physician's Conduct Concerning Human Organ Transplantation of 1994 enjoins "severe discipline" for physicians involved in the non-consensual extraction of organs from executed prisoners,[117] on 22 May 2006 the Council of the World Medical Association called on China to cease using executed prisoners as sources for organ transplantation carte blanche.[118] Coordination across the state bureaucracy between execution and transplantation is clear.

The website of the China International Transplant Centre states openly: So many transplantation operations are owing to the support of the Chinese government. The Supreme Demotic Court, Supreme Demotic Law officer, Police, Judiciary, Department of Health and Civil Administration have enacted a law together to make sure that organ donations are supported by the government. This is unique in the world.[119] In this sense, the confluence of the Falun Gong persecution and organ sourcing is a variation on a larger theme noted in popular press[120] and before Congress.[121] While a new 'temporary' regulation to curb the blatant selling of organs came into force on 1 July 2006,[122] transplant tourism at high prices continues.

A BBC story on Wednesday of this week reported "organ sales thriving in China"[123] while officials state non-consensual organ removal a fabrication.[124] Yet consent "free of undue pressure"[125] is difficult to conceive in a context of impending execution with little recourse to substantive appeal, aside from the reported extrajudicial tissue typing and selection of Falun Gong detainees. Concerning Falun Gong practitioners as non-voluntary victims, the most compelling evidence has been compiled by David Kilgour and David Matas in the Report into Allegations of Organ Harvesting of Falun Gong Practitioners in China of 6 July 2006.

Using Chinese information, the source of some 41,500 organs between 2000 and 2005 remains ambiguous and unaccounted for. Systematic blood testing of arrested Falun Gong practitioners is known.[126] The report assesses overlapping evidence pointing with high likelihood to organ sourcing from Falun Gong practitioners. In my meeting with practitioners in June 2006[127] evidence included transcripts of queries to identified hospitals on organ availability.

Falun Gong sources were characterized as being of high quality and often available in as short a time as a week, in some cases with a guarantee of a backup organ. My statement on 24 July 2006 titled "Mounting Evidence of Falun Gong Practitioners used as Organ Sources in China and Related Ethical Responsibilities"[128] made several points: The short time frame of an on-demand system requires a large pool of donors pre-typed for blood group and HLA matching. It is consistent with execution timing.

Given a 12- to 24-hour window for kidney tissue, and a 12-hour window for liver, matching for transplant tourists cannot be assured on a random-death basis. Queried physicians indicated selecting live prisoners to ensure quality and compatibility.[129]

The coordination of transplantation can take place only through communication, in particular in an on-demand context. Given the seriousness of the matter, it is fitting for this Committee to initiate an independent investigation from which, on the basis of evidence, whether confirmatory or exculpatory, clear policy can be articulated, and appropriate pressure exercised. The current level of evidence calls for this step.

Thank you for the opportunity to present this testimony to the subcommittee.

Hao Wang

China's Organ Transplant Industry and Falun Gong Organ Harvesting: An Economic Analysis by Hao Wang
Advisor: T.N. Srinivasan, Yale University
April 2007

Abstract

This thesis evaluated the allegation that systematic, large-scale organ seizures from unwilling Falun Gong practitioners have been supplying the majority of organs for the organ transplant industry in China since 1999. Despite the tremendous growth in the organ transplant industry after 1999, the known sources of organ supply – namely the living donors, brain-dead, non-heart-beating donors and executed prisoners – have not shown significant growth over time and fail to explain the huge quantity of annual transplants.

The detained population of Falun Gong practitioners is found to have the requisite population size and characteristics of a large 'organ bank'. They are the only prison group that provides an adequate explanation for the explosive growth in the volume of China's organ transplants between 2000 and 2005. It is the conclusion of this paper that the organs of detained Falun Gong practitioners are being systematically harvested for use in China's organ transplant industry and that such practice is an industrialized form of the Communist Party's systematic persecution against Falun Gong.

The full text of this thesis is available on our website.[130]

Part II: Acting on the Evidence

Chapter Eleven

Responses

The Chinese government has a pattern of response to evidence of human rights violations inflicted on Falun Gong practitioners. Its response to our work was part of this pattern.

The Government of China conducts a global campaign against the Falun Gong consisting of harassment, bullying, spying, disinformation, and pervasive and persistent anti-Falun Gong propaganda. The incitement to hatred which generates the persecution against the Falun Gong within China has become a primary message that embassies of China bring to the rest of the world. This global disinformation campaign against the Falun Gong has three basic prongs. One is getting out the Chinese government's own propaganda. The second is blocking in every way possible the flow of any contrary information. The third is initiatives from those trying to please China.

When it comes to propaganda against the Falun Gong, China's party-state does not make an effort to be accurate. The lies are shameless, blatant, patent, unabashed.

The Chinese are disciples of the big lie technique of former German Nazi leader Adolf Hitler. Hitler in his 1925 autobiography *Mein Kampf* defined the big lie propaganda technique as a lie so colossal that no one would believe that someone "could have the impudence to distort the truth so infamously".

The most obvious Chinese use of this technique is the constant labelling of the Falun Gong as an evil cult, though it has none of the characteristics of a cult. But the big lie is not just a single lie. It has many different facets.

The global Chinese campaign we have seen is unlike anything we see from Zimbabwe or North Korea or any of the other major human rights violators. As courtroom lawyers, we are used to having people disagree with us. But we have never seen anything like the disagreement with our report from the Government of China. The Chinese government's disagreement studiously avoids the plausible and gravitates towards the outrageous.

The Government of China Embassy in Canada issued its first response to our report the same day as our report, July 6, 2006 – and a second one dated July 26, 2006. The first statement dismissed our report out of hand. That meant that the Government of China engaged in no investigations to determine whether or not what the report contained was true. The second statement was almost three weeks after the release of our report, so Chinese officials had had time to delve into our report and produce contradictory information. But there was none.

The sole factual quarrel the Government of China had with the report had nothing to do with the substance of the report. It correctly noted that we placed two cities in the wrong provinces. We had indicated in an appendix that Wu Han is in Hunan, when it is in Hubei, and that Qin Huangdao is in Shandong, when it is in Hebei. These two errors – and they are the only ones anyone has been able to identify – do not justify questioning the analysis or conclusions of the report. Indeed, in two respects they strengthen it.

If this is all that anyone – including the Chinese government, with all its resources and inside knowledge – can produce to question the facts in our report, one can legitimately say that our report sits on a rock-solid foundation. Secondly, the practice of organ-harvesting from Falun Gong practitioners is even more widespread than we had originally reported, since, through our error, we had omitted reference to the existence of the practice in Hebei province. We had identified another site, Qianfoshan, in Shandong province, where the practice was occurring.

Both Government of China statements attribute initial reports of harvesting of organs in Sujiatun Hospital to Falun Gong practitioners. However, those initial reports about Sujiatun Hospital originated not from Falun Gong practitioners but from the ex-wife of a surgeon at Sujiatun Hospital. Neither the ex-wife nor her former husband is a Falun Gong practitioner.

Both Chinese government statements refer to a shifting Falun Gong narrative in consequence of a disproof of the original story about Sujiatun Hospital. Yet the ex-wife of the surgeon did not change or shift her story at any time.

The second Chinese Government response refers to the statement of the ex-wife of the surgeon, which she made to us and which we reproduced in our report, that her husband removed the corneas of 2,000 Falun Gong prisoners in two years. The Government of China questions this figure on the basis that "he would have to finish three cornea transplantations within one day and every day without rest", and then argues, "This is an absurd lie which no one with common sense would believe."

The Government of China response mixes up transplanting and harvesting. The testimony of the ex-wife was organs harvested from two thousand persons, not two thousand transplants. She did not claim that her husband was engaged in transplant surgery. The husband was, according to her testimony, removing the corneas from the eyes of Falun Gong practitioners, not placing those corneas into the eyes of recipient patients.

Harvesting surgery is, obviously, quicker than the combination of harvesting and transplanting. Moreover, corneas, unlike other organs, are dead tissue. They do not need to be transplanted immediately once harvested. They can survive on the shelf for a considerable period. As explained in Chapter Nine, a cornea harvest can be completed in twenty minutes. For an operation that length of time, what the ex-wife said about the volume of corneas harvested in two years does not put her testimony in doubt.

The second Chinese government statement refers to the fact that journalists and diplomats visited Sujiatun Hospital after the initial reports had surfaced and found no evidence that the site was being used for organ-harvesting of Falun Gong practitioners. We would not have expected these visitors to find anything even if the initial reports of organ-harvesting from the ex-wife of the surgeon were true. An operation leaves no trace in an operating room after it is completed. Operating rooms are cleaned up, sanitized, made antiseptic after each and every operation.

The first Chinese government statement then says: "It is obvious that their purpose is to smear China's image." We have no wish to smear China's image. Our sole concerns are respect for the truth and human dignity.

Both Chinese statements say:

> "China has consistently abided by the relevant guiding
> principles of the World Health Organization endorsed in

1991, prohibiting the sale of human organs and stipulating that donors' written consent must be obtained beforehand and donors are entitled to refuse the donation at last minute."

This was belied by the facts. The China International Transplantation Network Assistance Centre Website, until April of 2006, set out a price list for transplants.[131] As well, many individuals can attest to paying for organ transplants in China. The statement in both responses that China has consistently abided by the principle stipulating that donors' written consent must be obtained beforehand is also belied by the facts.

Both Chinese government statements say:

"China has issued a regulation on human organ transplants, explicitly banning the sale of organs and introducing a set of medical standards for organ transplants in an effort to guarantee medical safety and the health of patients. The regulation requires medical institution which is qualified for practising human organ transplant to register at provincial level health department. Unregistered medical institutions are forbidden to practice human organ transplant. If the government finds any registered institution violating the regulation, it will cancel the registration and punish the people responsible."

This legislation came into force only a few days before our report was first released on July 1, 2006. It is not an answer to our findings about what happened before that date. Moreover, in China, there is a huge gap between enacting legislation and enforcing it.

Our first reply, issued long before the second Chinese government response, made this point. Yet the second Chinese government response just repeats word for word what was in their first response on this point.

The Government of China wrote in its first response: "It is very clear that Falun Gong's rumour has ulterior political motives." None of our findings are based on rumour. Every finding we make is sourced and independently verifiable.

This claim of rumour is a constant Chinese government refrain. David Matas went to Israel to speak on May 30, 2007 at a symposium on organ transplants at Beilinson Hospital near Tel Aviv. The Chinese embassy in Israel circulated a statement at the symposium that the report we wrote on organ-harvesting of Falun Gong practitioners contains:

> "... verbal evidence without sources, unverifiable witnesses and huge amount of unconvincingly conclusive remarks based on words like 'probably', 'possibly', 'maybe' and 'it is said', etc. All these only call into question the truth of the report."

Nevertheless, all one has to do to is to look at our work to see that every statement we make in it is independently verifiable. There is no verbal evidence without sources. Where we rely on witnesses we identify them and quote what they say.

We have searched our manuscript for these words. At no place do we do link the words "probably", "possibly", "maybe" or the phrase "it is said" to our conclusions. Nor had we done so in the two versions of our report, which are word-searchable on the Internet.

As well, what could the politics of the Falun Gong possibly be? They are not a political party or movement with a political agenda. The Chinese Government describes their political agenda, in its second response, as being "against everything from China" – a bizarre charge, but all too typical of the hyperbole into which the Government launches when discussing this group.

The Falun Gong, to be sure, oppose human rights violations in China. But China is different from the Communist Party of China. And China is more than just human rights violations.

Human rights are not political. They are universal. The notion of politics suggests a legitimate debate between opposing points of view. But there is no legitimate debate between respect for human rights and violations of human rights. Violations of human rights are always wrong. Respect for human rights is always right.

The two Government of China responses attack us as not independent, and Falun Gong as an evil cult. Yet our work has to be judged on its merits. Attacking us is not an appropriate response.

The second Government of China response is primarily an elaboration on the "evil cult" attack on Falun Gong. The second response has eight paragraphs. Only three deal with organ-harvesting. One talks about Canada-Chinese relations. Four paragraphs, the bulk of the response, are a venomous attack on Falun Gong, replete with false, slanderous allegations. It is this sort of slander which, in China, depersonalizes and dehumanizes the Falun Gong and makes possible the violation of their basic human rights. Indeed, the fact that the Government of China would make a hate-filled attack on Falun Gong the focus of its response to our report reinforces the analysis of the report.

Some people, for reasons of political or diplomatic or economic convenience, will swallow anything said by the Communist Party of China, true or not. For them, what is relevant is only that it is said by the Communist Party of China. Its truth is a matter of indifference. However, we have met others for whom the truth matters, who are not associated in any way with the Communist Party of China, but still assert, without having read our work, that it is based on rumour. The only explanation is that these dupes have heard or read Chinese Communist propaganda about our work and have been misled by the big lie.

When the Chinese government puts words in quotation marks and asserts that they come from our work, there is a tendency to assume that these quotes are real. Many people cannot believe that someone could have the nerve to distort the truth so grossly.

The most simple and obvious vehicle for Chinese propaganda is Chinese embassy websites. Go to any Chinese embassy website anywhere in the world and you will find posted there an attack on the Falun Gong.

The Embassy of China in Canada website home page has three links connecting the reader to anti-Falun Gong propaganda.[132] One is entitled "Cult Falun Gong". The second is "Memorandum on Falun Gong". The title of the third is "Response to the so-called Revised Report on China's Organ Harvesting". No other topic merits more than one link. Tibet has only one link. So does Taiwan.

Politicians or civil servants who meet with Falun Gong, as well as media who interview them, are often the recipients of spammed anti-Falun Gong propaganda. A lead spammer is Charles Liu, who also uses the name Bobby Fletcher. He is a down-the-line Chinese government apologist, generally parroting positions of the Government of China, including denial of the existence of the Tiananmen Square massacre of

1989. But his main efforts have been directed to discrediting the Falun Gong, through directed e-mails, discussion groups, letters to the editor and Internet blogs. The *Western Standard* magazine reported:

> "Liu's actions mirror disinformation campaigns waged by the Chinese government in the past. Typically, these include the deliberate spreading of false or misleading facts to sow confusion or doubt among the conflicting accounts."[133]

The Government of China publishes, prints and distributes Chinese and local language newspapers in foreign countries which are nothing more than anti-Falun Gong propaganda tracts. In Canada, an example is *La Presse Chinoise*. It is a small Montreal newspaper with a usual print run of 6,000 copies. In August 2006 it published an issue thirty-two pages long, printed 100,000 copies and distributed them across Canada. This issue had no advertisements. It was distributed for free. And it contained no news whatsoever, only an attack on the Falun Gong. The issue did not say it was financed by the Government of China. But according to an investigative report by Mark Morgan of *La Grande Époque*, that was the reality.[134]

The Embassy of China in whatever national capital it is located will write letters to editors of local newspapers, setting out Chinese propaganda and disinformation. As well, embassies will send letters or e-mails to friendly reporters, filled with the usual Communist bumph. Letters are often published in the papers to which they are addressed, which gives free, widespread, local language distribution to this propaganda. Stories are written that the Government of China objects to this or that, as if there were justification or grounding to the objection. For instance, the Chinese embassy in Canada sent off in January 2007 an e-mail to the *Ottawa Citizen* protesting the NTD TV Chinese New Year dance spectacular then just performed in Ottawa. The *Ottawa Citizen*, in all seriousness, published a story setting out the Chinese embassy objections.[135]

Chinese government goes from hi-tech to lo-tech in its abuse of Falun Gong, from digital media to simple flyers handed out at meetings. Embassy and consular officials wander around to public gatherings handing out anti-Falun Gong literature.

One such set of flyers, handed out by officials of the Calgary consulate led to a hate crimes investigation. The Chinese officials placed anti-Falun Gong hate literature outside a conference room of the American Family Foundation Conference at the University of Alberta in Edmonton in June 2004. The Edmonton Police recommended hate crimes prosecution of Chinese consular officials Cao, Jianye and Yeh, Chi Yao for this distribution.[136]

There is a similar story with the electronic media. CCTV-4, a Chinese government TV satellite broadcaster, sought permission to broadcast into Canada on a digital basis. On December 22, 2006 the Canadian Radio-television and Telecommunications Commission concluded that this broadcaster had a history of abusive comment, incitement to hatred and contempt, incitement to violence and threats to physical security against the Falun Gong.[137] The CRTC approved the application, but with a warning that unless CCTV-4 is free of abusive comment it would be removed from the list of eligible satellite services authorized for digital distribution in Canada.[138]

One form of harassment of Falun Gong practitioners is incessant phone calls with taped messages. The messages harangue the listeners in Chinese and English in three-minute recorded statements demonizing the Falun Gong. The tapes include Chinese patriotic songs.

Some practitioners have received as many as twenty-five calls a day. Calls have been made to homes, cellphones and workplaces. The calls fill up message machines. Calls made to cellphones pile up charges which are based on use. The high frequency of the phone calls prompts phone owners to turn off their cellphones.

Complaints to phone companies or the police lead nowhere. The calls have been traced to mainland China. Foreign police and phone companies can do nothing about such calls.

Write to the Chinese embassy to ask them to stop the persecution of the Falun Gong and it will send you by return mail a barrage of anti-Falun Gong propaganda. The embassy sends out booklets and video compact disks filled with disinformation about the Falun Gong. The embassy sends out this same disinformation unsolicited to government officials, members of legislatures and parliaments, and even civic officials who raise concerns or who might possibly raise concerns about the treatment of the Falun Gong.

If anyone wants a guided tour and a heavy dose of anti-Falun Gong propaganda, China is more than happy to oblige, all expenses paid. Academics are usually self-respecting enough to avoid these tours. They are prepared to go so far as to keep silent about the Falun Gong in order to get access to China.

Some journalists are different. They take the trips and figure that they are maintaining journalistic ethics as long as they report the reality of Falun Gong persecution in the same articles as the disinformation the Chinese propaganda machine has fed them.

Though the Government of China prefers working through intermediaries it can bully or pay, when all else fails it will send a representative to repeat in person anti-Falun Gong slander. That is what happened at the organ transplant forum at which David Matas spoke in May 2007 at Beilinson Hospital in Israel.

Once the Chinese embassy found out that the event was going ahead with Matas on the speakers' list, they sent down a spokesman to reply to his intervention. They distributed on every chair before the symposium a paper titled "Position Paper of Chinese Government on Allegations of So Called organ harvest". It contained the usual nonsense.

The Chinese remarks were mostly not about our report; they were, rather, a slanderous attack on the Falun Gong, and had nothing at all to do with organ-harvesting. These remarks were incitement to hatred, akin to Holocaust denial, manifesting the very bigotry which led to the violation that they were denying.

The Government of China uses its embassies and consulates to mount public displays against the Falun Gong. For instance, the Chinese consulate in Toronto, Canada has displayed an array of anti-Falun Gong posters along the wall where people wait in line to apply for visas. The title of the exhibition is "Combat Cults and Protect Human Rights". The posters state "Falun Gong is a Scourge".

For blocking to be effective, China needs to know not only what is being said, but also what is being planned. Accordingly China engages in spying – or what is euphemistically called intelligence-gathering – on the Falun Gong. Defectors tell us that this intelligence-gathering is the primary task of Chinese embassies around the world. Falun Gong practitioners everywhere are constantly being monitored and spied on by the Government of China. This is an invasion of privacy of Falun Gong practitioners. But the consequences are a good deal worse than that.

Defectors Chen Yonglin and Hao Fenguin made public statements about the Chinese Falun Gong intelligence-gathering and spy network. Chen defected from the Chinese consulate in Sydney, Australia in May 2005. Hao worked for the 610 Office in Tianjin City, China. (As indicated in Chapter Two, the 610 Office is the bureaucracy in China designated with responsibility for repression of the Falun Gong.) Hao visited Australia in February 2005 and sought asylum once there.

Chen said that there were as many as 1,000 Chinese government spies in Australia. Hao confirmed Chen's statement.[139]

The Falun Gong has on occasion been spied on by persons who practise Falun Gong in order to accumulate information about other Falun Gong practitioners, information which is then communicated to the Government of China. A few of these people have been unequivocally identified. For a number of others, there is suspicion but no certainty.

Falun Gong practitioners find that their e-mail accounts are hacked. It is possible for customers to find out from their Internet service providers the locations from which the e-mail accounts have been accessed. Falun Gong practitioners who have made inquiries discover that their e-mail accounts are being accessed from places they have never been.

In order for an e-mail account to be accessed, the person accessing the account would need the password for that account. The passwords of those Falun Gong practitioners are presumably identified by prior hacking efforts or by double agency. If one Falun Gong practitioner uses the computer of a second practitioner to access the e-mail account of the first practitioner and the second practitioner (the one whose computer is used) is an agent of the Government of China, then Chinese officials have access to the password of the first practitioner.

One use to which the Chinese government puts information gathered through its spying is to send computer viruses to Falun Gong practitioners and those in contact with them electronically. The virus sender assumes the identity of one person on a listserv so that the message with the virus appears to be coming from someone known to the listserv.

In the course of arranging a visit David Matas made in 2007 to Australia to speak at NGO events paralleling the APEC summit, he, along with the rest of a listserv he was on, received such a virus. A technical expert traced back the virus to mainland China.

Fortunately, the virus did not infect his computer because of the systems he uses. Others were not so lucky. The receipt of viruses by Falun Gong practitioners traced to mainland China is commonplace.

Websites hosting information about the Falun Gong are subject to cyber-attacks from China. For instance, the website Bestnet, which hosted a mirror site of a Falun Gong site, reported on July 30, 1999 a denial-of-service attack which "appears to be coming from sources inside China".[140] Webmaster John Walker wrote: "The Government of China may use intimidation to rule inside its own borders but I'll be damned if I will let them get away with it here."

A denial-of-service attack is a flooding of requests with incomplete information which eventually causes the target machine to crash. Internet sleuths were able to trace the Internet protocol address. From that they were able to find the name and street address of the owner of that IP address. Though the name of the owner was innocuous, the street address was the headquarters of the Government of China Ministry of Public Security.[141]

The Government of China does not just attempt to disrupt live events. It wades into the media as well, attempting to use its diplomatic weight to shut up or distort local media information about the persecution of the Falun Gong. Again, here is an example from Canada. The CBC announced that it was broadcasting in November 2007 a TV documentary by Peter Rowe on the persecution of the Falun Gong in China which featured our report. The Government of China phoned up the CBC (something the CBC admitted) and the CBC pulled the show. It was replaced with an old documentary on Pakistan because, so the CBC spokesman said, recent turmoil in Pakistan made the rebroadcast timely.

But, as it turned out, timeliness was not the concern. The CBC went back to the producer Peter Rowe and asked for changes. He initially balked and then made some. But the changes he made were not enough. After the producer refused to co-operate any further, the CBC made more changes on its own and then broadcast its concocted product.

The CBC version of the documentary was broadcast, on November 20. Since the original version had already been aired, without notice, in the middle of the night in Montreal a few days earlier, and became available on YouTube, it was possible to compare the two.

The parts deleted from the original version were items which constituted hard evidence to substantiate the findings we had made of the mass killings of Falun Gong. One item deleted was the playing of tapes of telephone admissions from hospitals in China acknowledging that they were selling Falun Gong organs. Chinese government denials remained.

The additions were typical Chinese propaganda. The CBC on its own, for instance, added this screen to the documentary: "Amnesty

International does not have conclusive evidence to back up the allegation the Falun Gong are killed for their organs."

Yet, silence is not evidence of anything. Amnesty International silence on a human rights violation is not proof and not even evidence that a violation is not occurring. The organization does not claim to be a verifier or source or encyclopaedia of all human rights violations.

The CBC, before the commercial which led into the documentary, flashed onscreen, with footage of Falun Gong practitioners, a bit of Chinese propaganda straight up: "China regards Falun Gong as a cult." For people who know nothing about the Falun Gong that sort of introduction was bound to mislead.

Not to be outdone by the CBC, Radio-Canada went one further in a show which aired in October 2008. Crescent Chau had published, through *La Presse Chinoise*, standard Communist Party propaganda against Li Hongzhi and the Falun Gong – material which was, according to the Quebec Court of Appeal, defamatory. The libels led Falun Gong practitioners to protest in front of the offices of *La Presse Chinoise.*

Radio-Canada reported these protests in a way that would have warmed the heart of the most hardened Chinese government bureaucrat. Falun Gong was depicted as an organization which is "highly structured" with "no shortage of money", composed of different organs working in lockstep. This mythical organization was then blamed for tension in Montreal's Chinatown – because some practitioners had the nerve to protest their being libelled by Crescent Chau and *La Presse Chinoise.* Radio-Canada preyed on the ignorance of the Canadian public to propagate the Communist Party line, blaming the victims for protesting their victimization, adding to the propaganda by describing the Falun Gong as "little known and bothersome", and "whose presence creates malaise".

Yet Falun Gong is not an organization. Nor does it have any money. Indeed, the very notion of a set of exercises having money is a form of Orwellian newspeak only a communist party and its fellow travellers could concoct. If other innocents with no connection to China who engaged in a common harmless practice were to protest outside a metro daily because the daily reported that, when they were not practising, they were engaged in bestiality or vampirism – some of the milder charges Crescent Chau and *La Presse Chinoise* levied against Falun Gong practitioners – it is unlikely Radio-Canada would report the protests as some sort of conspiracy.

The Epoch Times is a globally-distributed newspaper which is general in nature but which has a focus on Chinese human rights violations. Many Falun Gong practitioners are involved in the paper. Businesses which advertise in *The Epoch Times* report anonymous threatening telephone calls, as well as calls from the local Chinese consulate urging them not to advertise in the paper. So do businesses which serve as distribution depots for the newspaper, places where the newspaper can be picked up by customers.

The telephone calls slander the Falun Gong and warn the advertisers and distributors of a loss of business if they persist. For instance, a travel agent in England was warned that, if his agency continued to advertise in *The Epoch Times,* his agency would no longer be able to book flights on Chinese airlines. Though these callers did not identify themselves as Government of China representatives, only representatives of the Government of China would be in a position to utter such threats.

These threats have had an impact. *The Epoch Times* reported a drop-off in advertising and number of distribution points after the calls began. In England these calls were the subject of a complaint to the U.K. Foreign Office. However, the Foreign Office refused to take any action, claiming that there was insufficient proof that the calls were made.

Because of limited bandwidth, radio and TV broadcasters have needed regulatory permission to broadcast. The Government of China has lobbied foreign broadcast regulators, asking them to use their powers to keep off the air any broadcaster who would provide information about the persecution of the Falun Gong.

New Tang Dynasty TV applied in February 2005 to the Canadian Radio-television and Telecommunications Commission (CRTC) for approval to broadcast in Canada. NTD TV is a global satellite TV network which began in 2002. It broadcasts in Chinese, as well as other languages. Its programming is more than 90% Mandarin. It is independent of the Government of China and reports on Chinese human rights abuses. Because of that, it has aroused the enmity of the Government of China.

Zhang Jiyan, the defecting wife of a Chinese diplomat, smuggled out of the Chinese embassy in Canada a document showing an embassy plan "to knock down NTD TV's attempt to enter the cable television network". Huikang Huang, deputy head of the Chinese embassy, suggested rallying Chinese Canadians and Chinese visa students to write to the CRTC to oppose the NTD TV application.[142] Subsequently the public record shows that the CRTC did in fact receive nearly identical letters opposing the application from the National Congress of Chinese Canadians, the Federation of Ottawa Carleton Chinese Organizations and the Chinese Student Association of the University of Ottawa.[143] The NTD TV application to the CRTC, nonetheless, succeeded.[144]

The Chinese government establishes organizations abroad which are nominally independent from the government but in fact act as its agents. Many universities have Chinese student organizations which are tightly connected to the local Chinese embassy or consulate. The Chinese government uses threats of exit visa denials and intimidation of the family back home to get students abroad to spy on their classmates and intimidate the Falun Gong.

David Matas was witness to the activities of these groups at Columbia and Princeton universities when he spoke there in April 2007. A group came to the venue at Columbia with banners and red flags, which security personnel required them to leave outside. They nonetheless held up placards which said in Chinese and English that Falun Gong is an evil cult. David Matas had obtained the e-mail which they had used to bring their colleagues out, and for his talk proceeded to read through it and react to it. Not liking what they were hearing, the group left his talk and the room en masse in midstream. In Princeton, there was a similar gang protest, though this time the Chinese government agents were allowed to bring in posters which they held up at the back of the room.

The Chinese government gives grants for universities to establish Confucius Institutes. These institutes are supposedly for Chinese studies. But once established, they become spy outlets for the Chinese government and leverage on the university to attempt to ban Falun Gong activity.

The use to which a Confucius Institute is put depends on the local embassy or consulate which grants the funds. We have been to some universities which report that the ethnic Chinese staff of these institutes, once established, become targets of Chinese government officials seeking out information about Falun Gong activity on campus.

Tel Aviv University removed in 2008 an exhibit on Falun Gong meditation. Professor Yoav Ariel, a lecturer in the East Asian Studies Department, confirmed that he had ordered the exhibit removed because of a request by the Chinese embassy. Ariel said that the university must take into consideration its ties with Chinese universities, with which it conducts student exchanges. The university has had a

Confucius Institute, endowed by the Government of China, since 2007.[145]

Another use the Government of China makes of intelligence-gathered information is to attempt to thwart every public event which would disclose the persecution of the Falun Gong. The Government of China leans on hosts, asking them to cancel such events. One particularly sorry example of this is the global Chinese government effort to undermine the touring dance spectacular sponsored by NTD TV. For instance, the Chinese embassy in Sweden called on city officials in Stockholm and Linkoping to cancel the venues for the Chinese dance spectaculars scheduled there for January 2008 because the performers had links to the Falun Gong.[146]

A similar effort was successful in Seoul and Pusan, South Korea. In 2007, two venues in Seoul, the National Theatre of Korea and the Convention and Exhibition Centre, terminated their contracts with the dance company as the result of pressure from the Chinese embassy.[147] (A successful lawsuit against the Convention and Exhibition Centre meant that the event was eventually performed at a later date.) In 2008, the Korean Broadcasting Corporation theatre in Pusan behaved in a similar fashion, backing out of a contract for a dance performance after the Government of China protested.[148]

Where an event is going ahead despite Chinese efforts to cancel it, the Government of China as a second recourse tries to shape the event. It asks for changes to, or deletions of, elements of the program which its officials claim are offensive to China.

Here is an example. We have already mentioned the organ transplant forum in May 2007 at Beilinson Hospital, at which David Matas was asked to speak. When Matas arrived in Israel on the Sunday before that event, he was told that the Chinese embassy had asked Israeli Foreign Affairs to cancel the event. The Foreign Affairs Assistant Deputy Minister Avi Nir and the Health Assistant Deputy Minister Boz Lev put the request to the Beilinson Hospital, which refused. Foreign Affairs and Health then asked the hospital to withdraw the invitation to him to speak even if the program continued. The hospital refused that too. Foreign Affairs and Health then asked the hospital to withdraw the invitation to Roy Bar Ilan, a Falun Gong practitioner, to be part of the closing panel. This the hospital did, even though the program, as advertised even on the day of the event, included his name.

The event was a marathon, going from 5:00 p.m. to 9:00 p.m. with a dozen speakers. For the very last portion of the symposium, there was a panel of all the previous speakers plus a few new ones. The new ones made short statements and then all speakers took questions from the floor.

David Matas took advantage of this question period to raise his own question. He prefaced the question by saying that it was not about China but about Israel, since there were many Falun Gong practitioners in Israel, including several in the room. He asked Roy Bar Ilan, who was in the audience and who, he noted, was supposed to be on the panel, to answer the charges the Chinese embassy official had made against the Falun Gong.

The chair, in response to that question, without giving Roy a change to answer it, said, abruptly and unceremoniously, that the symposium was over. And it was. No thanks were given. There was no applause for the speakers. Everyone simply dispersed.

One phenomenon we have both experienced is diplomatic Chinese efforts to prevent parliamentarians and government officials from meeting with us. On a trip to Australia, in August 2006, David Kilgour spoke on our report at a forum in Melbourne hosted by Liberal Party member Victor Perton. The Melbourne Chinese consulate had sent a letter to all members of the Legislative Assembly asking them not to attend the forum.

Similarly, when David Matas was in Finland in September 2006 meeting with the Finnish parliamentary human rights committee, its chair informed him that the Chinese embassy had called, urging them not to meet with him. The chair replied that embassy officials were welcome to meet separately with the committee, but that the committee would nonetheless meet with him.

Where events go ahead despite the best Chinese efforts to stop them, the Government of China tries to discourage people from attending them. Letters are sent from embassies and consulates to notables and dignitaries, slandering the events and the Falun Gong and urging non-attendance. For instance, a letter from the Consulate General of the People's Republic of China to New York Assemblyman Michael Benjamin dated December 11, 2007 urged him not to support in any form the dance spectacular hosted by NTD TV in New York in 2008, suggesting that to do so would impair U.S.-China relations. Assemblyman Benjamin indicated he would attend the event regardless, and made the letter public.

The general approach of Chinese officials to foreign officials and political leaders on the subject of the Falun Gong is a mix of incitement to hatred and bullying. For instance, in a letter in March 2003 to

Canadian Member of Parliament Jim Peterson, the Chinese chargé d'affaires in Canada "advised the Canadian government of the sensitivity of the issue [of the Falun Gong] in the overall bilateral relations [between Canada and China]".[149] In other words, sympathy to the plight of the Falun Gong would impact adversely on Canadian-Chinese bilateral relations.

The Chinese consulate in Toronto wrote city councillors in 2004 urging them to oppose a motion for the proclamation of a Falun Gong week. The letters said: "If passed, the motion will have a very negative effect on our future beneficial exchanges and co-operation." Among the "beneficial exchanges and co-operation" Toronto City Councillor Michael Walker heard mentioned as threatened were the sale to China of a Canadian-made nuclear reactor (the CANDU), the construction by the Canadian company Bombardier of a rail link to Tibet, and a two-panda loan to the Metro Toronto Zoo.[150]

At Columbia University, an organization titled the Columbia University Chinese Students and Scholars Association had posted a threat on its website in April 2007 when David Matas was speaking there on our report. The threat was this: "Anyone who offends China will be executed no matter how far away they are."

When David Matas spoke at the forum in Broadbeach, Gold Coast, Australia August 4, 2008, the forum was connected through the Internet to participants in China, over 150 in total. The local as well as the Internet participants asked questions after the formal presentation was over. One of the Internet participants was a Chinese government police official. This is the question, in translation, he asked David Matas:

"Are you afraid of death? You are brutally interfering in our Party's internal policies. Are you afraid of our revenge? Our revenge against you, we'll take revenge against you, are you not afraid of that?"

Incitement to discrimination leads to discrimination. While hate propaganda is most effective in a closed society like China, it has its insidious effect even in open societies.

Active discrimination becomes a way of getting the message out. If Falun Gong practitioners are denied access to service and benefits, even abroad, simply because they are practitioners, it becomes a way of discouraging the practice.

For example, the Ottawa Chinese Seniors Association terminated the membership of Daiming Huang because she practises Falun Gong. As well, the Association confronted her about her beliefs, organized petitions against her practices, and subjected her to demeaning comments about her beliefs. The Human Rights Tribunal of Ontario in January 2006 ruled that this was discrimination, exposing the woman to contempt and loss of standing, and isolation within her community, and was an affront to her dignity. The Tribunal ordered the Association to pay Mrs. Huang $18,000.00 as well as to allow Falun Gong practitioners to become members of the Association.[151]

The opportunities for the Government of China on its own to inflict discrimination abroad on Falun Gong practitioners are few. Mostly the Government of China has to act through local agents. However, there are some matters which, by the very nature of sovereignty, remain within their control abroad.

Chinese nationals abroad whom the Chinese government has identified as Falun Gong practitioners will be denied passport renewal unless they renounce in writing their belief in Falun Gong. We have visited dozens of countries in order to promote the recommendations of our report. In the course of those visits, we met many Falun Gong practitioners in different countries who have been denied passport renewal. They have been told by their embassies that the reason is that they are Falun Gong.

For Chinese nationals abroad, the absence of a passport causes difficulties with the host countries. The Universal Declaration of Human Rights states: "No one shall be arbitrarily deprived of his nationality."[152] Passport renewal denial based on the beliefs of the passport holder violates this right.

China uses its visa entry and exit system for anti-Falun Gong propaganda purposes. Known Falun Gong practitioners are not allowed to leave China. And no one is allowed entry who is known to be Falun Gong or sympathetic to Falun Gong, especially where the purpose is as benign as even simply meeting other Falun Gong practitioners in private. This is true even of Hong Kong. More than 70 Falun Gong practitioners from Taiwan were denied entry to Hong Kong in February 2003 to attend an experience-sharing conference. This denial is currently the subject of court proceedings.

It would be going too far to say that the only China scholar who is reliable is a person who has never been to China. But there is a grain of truth in that assertion. Scholars who criticize the human rights record of the Government of China, particularly its treatment of the Falun Gong, are unlikely to get visas to enter China.

Another example is the Olympics. According to an Associated Press report of November 8, 2007, Li Zhanjun, director of the Beijing Olympics media centre, in reacting to news stories of a Bible ban during the Olympics, said texts and other items from major religious groups that are brought into China for personal use by athletes and visitors are permitted. Li also said religious services – Christian, Muslim, Jewish, Hindu and Buddhist – would be available to athletes in the Olympic Village. However, he said, the policies do not apply to Falun Gong. Li added:

> "We do not acknowledge Falun Gong because it is a cult. Falun Gong texts, Falun Gong activities in China are forbidden. Foreigners who come to China must respect and abide by the laws of China."

Local laws are never a justification for violation of international standards. Though the Government of China says foreigners must respect local laws, that statement, like almost everything else China says about the Falun Gong, is misleading. It is China which must respect the international prohibition against discrimination on the basis of belief.

While journalists the Government of China has identified as sympathetic are given a royal tour, all expenses paid, journalists identified as likely to report on Chinese human rights violations are denied visas. An example is the visas granted reporters accompanying Canadian Prime Minister Paul Martin on his visit to China in January 2005. Originally, Danielle Zhu and David Ren of NTD TV were granted visas for the trip. But then the visas were revoked. PEN Canada protested the revocations, but to no avail.[153]

China insists that the people with whom it does business not have Falun Gong practitioners in their employ. It insists that anyone who deals with China in any way practise the discrimination China does. Just as Nazi Germany in the pre-war days refused to deal with anyone who was Jewish, no matter what their status abroad, today the Government of China refuses to deal with anyone, no matter what the connection of the person to the business or project or government with which they are dealing, who is a Falun Gong practitioner.

For instance, the Government of Canada funds projects in China through the Canadian International Development Agency. Canadian recipients of CIDA funding provided through contribution agreements which mandate the beneficiaries to do work in China are required by the Government of China not to allow any Canadian citizens who are Falun Gong practitioners to participate in the work funded by the contribution agreement.

Theft of copies of *The Epoch Times* is endemic. It is distributed free in bulk at boxes and commercial establishments for passersby to pick up. In many places, the newspapers disappear from their distribution points soon after they are dropped off. Distributors have caught culprits stealing the papers who acknowledge being paid to do it without saying who is paying them. Though complaints are laid with the police, the police will not prosecute, saying it is not a crime to steal what is free.

The problem reached such proportions in California that the legislature actually enacted a law to deal with it.[154] The legislation, passed in September 2006, creates an offence of taking more than 25 copies of a free newspaper if done to deprive others of the opportunity to read the newspaper. The person who introduced the bill, Assembly Minority Leader George Plescia, Republican, La Jolla, acknowledged that the bill was a response to, amongst other incidents, the disappearance of thousands of copies of *The Epoch Times* in the San Gabriel Valley.[155]

The most grotesque form of blocking of protest against Chinese human rights violations is the beating of protesters. These beatings are not as systematic as the other forms of blockage. But they occur with regularity.

An example is Argentina, where a group of protesters were beaten in December 2005. At the time Luo Gan, head of the 610 Office, was visiting Buenos Aires. During his visit, the Falun Dafa Association filed a criminal lawsuit against him, relying on his presence as the basis for court jurisdiction. The next day Falun Gong practitioners protesting at Congress Square in Buenos Aires were assaulted by a group which, according to Amnesty International, were "connected to officials of the Chinese government". The practitioners were beaten. Their banners and photo displays were stolen.

The police were present at the beatings but did nothing to stop the attackers. A policeman told one Falun Gong practitioner that the police had orders not to interfere with the attack. The Amnesty International director for Argentina, Pablo Marsal, said: "Officials of another country are violating our Argentine sovereignty in our country."[156]

Chapter Twelve

Laws and policies

Chinese laws and policies

In China there is a huge gap between enacting legislation and enforcing it. To take one example, the preamble of the Constitution of China promises for China a "high level" of democracy. But, as the Tiananmen Square massacre vividly demonstrated, China is not democratic.

The first Chinese law on transplants, enacted in 1984, contemplated harvesting organs from prisoners "who volunteer to give their dead bodies or organs to the medical institutions".[157] It even contemplated involuntary donations from "uncollected dead bodies or the ones that the family members refuse to collect".[158]

The law insisted that organ transplantation occur only at hospitals granted special permits by the Department of Public Health in the province where the hospital is found.[159] But that did not happen. Transplant surgery in China spread like wildfire. Transplantation units sprang up everywhere. The list of approved institutions was far more limited than the list of actual institutions engaged in transplantation surgery.

Until July 1, 2006, the practice of selling organs in China was legal. A law banning their sale came into effect on that date. But the 2006 law on organ transplants was not enforced. In late November 2006 Belgian senator Patrik Vankrunkelsven called two different hospitals in Beijing, pretending to be a customer for a kidney transplant. Both hospitals offered him a kidney on the spot for 50,000 euros.

As noted in Chapter Two, Deputy Health Minister Huang Jiefu in November 2006 decried the selling of organs from executed prisoners sentenced to death and said, "Under-the-table business must be banned." It had already been banned, on July 1. His speech can be taken as an official acknowledgment that the ban is not working.

A Chinese law on transplants in May 2007 required that transplants be performed only in registered hospitals, and prohibited the sale of organs. This law, unlike previous laws, appears to have had an effect. Foreign transplant tourism has been curtailed. We say this not because of what the Government of China says but because of the evidence we have been getting from those outside China seeking transplants and from their doctors.

What is one to make of these changes? Can we now say that the problem has been solved? Liars suffer the punishment of not being believed when they act out of character and tell the truth. The Government of China has said once again, "We will stop doing this." The Chinese party-state has passed legislation once again forbidding the practice. Is this time different? There are a number of reasons to be wary.

The official announcement of the 2007 law made no reference to the 2006 measure. The enactment of law which is not enforced and then an announcement of the enactment of a similar law a year later gives the impression that China is playing a game of smoke and mirrors, trying to make it appear that something is being done rather than actually doing something.

An announcement of a change is not the same as a change. Enactment of a law is not the same as implementation of a law. The 2006 law superseded an old law, on the books for decades, which was not enforced. The 2007 law could be different; but history has to leave observers sceptical.

It would seem that a precondition for resolving any problem is acknowledging that the problem exists. Those who enacted the new law are not prepared to do this. The official announcement of the 2007 law states: "Most organs are donated by ordinary Chinese at death after the voluntary signing of a donation agreement." This statement is patently untrue and is contradicted by information from other official Chinese sources.

If the Chinese officials are prepared to lie about the present when they talk about this new law, what hope is there that they are telling the truth about the future? How can a law resolve the problem of sourcing organs from prisoners when those who enact the law are not prepared to acknowledge that this sourcing even exists?

In a state where the political arm controls the police, the army, the prosecution and the courts, there is no need for legislation to give the state power to do anything. Legislation serves a propaganda, or, if you will, educational purpose. Especially in a country of over one billion people, it is this propaganda or educational purpose which is paramount. Legislation is a vehicle for communicating a state message.

What is the message of a law which pretends the problem which generated it does not exist? What does this pretence say to those responsible for creating the problem? The message, we suggest, is: "Go ahead, carry on. We have not noticed and we will not notice. We are enacting this law for outsiders so that they can think something is being done, not for you."

It is hard to take seriously any suggestion that the authorities are cracking down on misbehaviour when they refuse to acknowledge that this misbehaviour is taking place. While anti-corruption campaigns in China do not amount to much, at least there is an acknowledgement that there is corruption. Would anyone in China take seriously an anti-corruption campaign which refused to acknowledge that there was corruption? Can anyone even in China take seriously legislation to ban the use of improperly sourced organs when the Government of China refuses to acknowledge that organs are improperly sourced?

Moreover, there is in China no organ donation system. There is a cultural aversion to donating organs which makes organ donations difficult even in those Chinese societies with active donation systems – in Taiwan and Hong Kong.

The only realistic way of weaning the Chinese from organ-harvesting of prisoners is shifting to organ-harvesting of the brain-dead. But organ-harvesting of those whose hearts still beat is illegal in China even when their brains are dead. The new law does not change that illegality.

We cannot put much hope in a law which makes illegal a practice which if implemented would end transplant surgery in China altogether. It is unrealistic to expect such a law to be enforced.

Organ-harvesting of non-consenting prisoners is also illegal, but it happens anyway. So it is perfectly possible for organ-harvesting of brain-dead people to take place in China without a law and even in violation of a law. The advantage of such a law is that it would help to shift Chinese transplant culture and practice.

The authorities, officially, cannot encourage a shift from one illegal activity to another illegal activity. Indeed, any effort to do so would undermine the credibility of their efforts to ban the first activity. China will have to enact a law allowing for organ-harvesting of the brain-dead if the rest of the world is to take seriously Chinese claimed efforts to move transplant surgery organ sourcing away from prisoners.

The original proposal for the law change which took effect on July 1, 2006 was to legalize organ-harvesting from the brain-dead. But the new law in the end did not contain this provision. The official explanation was cultural aversion, that the traditional Chinese attitude towards death is considered to be the moment when a person's heartbeat and breathing cease.[160]

It is certainly not for us to say what Chinese cultural attitudes should be. Even if we were to venture an opinion, we are confident it would have no impact. But this much seems clear: The Government of China is going to have to choose. Either it is going to have to shift to a national system of organ donation and organ-harvesting from the brain-dead or it is going to have to shut down organ transplantation in China altogether. The present situation, where organs are almost completely sourced from prisoners, has to stop.

Progress is not the same as achievement. There has, to be sure, been a fall-off in transplant surgery in China. There are news reports that some foreign customers have gone away disappointed. Hospitals are, under the new law, going through a process of accreditation. Is this fall-off attributable to the new law? It seems not entirely. For one, the reports of disappointed customers started before the new law came into effect. The rejection of customers is new, but not as new as the law.

What is also significant for the drop-off is a change in another law, the law about the death penalty. As noted in Chapter Eight, as of January 1, 2007 the death penalty had to be approved by the central Supreme People's Court and could not be imposed solely by regional courts; this change reduced the pool of prisoners sentenced to death, in the estimate of Amnesty International, by about half.

If there are fewer organs available from prisoners sentenced to death, why not just increase the harvest of organs from jailed Falun Gong practitioners? The answer to this question lies in the non-fungibility of the Chinese organ supply. Some hospitals and some doctors can access organs from Falun Gong practitioners. Others cannot. Some hospitals and doctors can access organs only from prisoners sentenced to death. It is these doctors and hospitals which have to start turning away customers when the supply of organs from prisoners sentenced to death falters.

There is a difference between a fall-off and a complete stop. Until China organizes a functional national organ donation scheme and both legalizes and operationalizes harvesting of organs from the brain-dead, only a complete end to transplant surgery in China, except for the odd case of family donors, can convince observers that the 2007 law is being respected.

The Department of Health of the Government of China, which is applying the new law, does not control the military. Yet it is the military which is the primary organ harvester of prisoners. It is the military who have privileged access to prisons and prisoners.

Patients have told us that, by and large, either they went to military hospitals for operations or, when they received transplants in civilian hospitals, they were operated on by military personnel. Regulating civilian hospitals, which are only secondarily the source of the problem, and doing nothing about military hospitals, which are the primary source of the problem, will not solve the problem.

If the Chinese government is doing anything at all to prevent organ-harvesting from prisoners, the reason is international pressure and concern. It seems foolhardy to relax that pressure and concern before the problem is completely resolved. It is predictable that as soon as the international focus disappears, so will Chinese efforts at reform.

The decrease in transplant tourism has gone hand in hand with an increase in transplants to patients within China. We found, before the new law came into force, when the Chinese focus was on the foreign market, that waiting times for foreign customers were much shorter than waiting times for Chinese nationals. Chinese nationals waiting for transplants were understandably miffed by this preferential treatment to foreigners.

According to Chinese official sources, there are 1.5 million people in China who suffer from organ failures and need transplants every year.[161] The Ministry of Health of the Government of China announced that from June 26, 2007 Chinese patients would be given priority access to organ transplants over foreigners.[162]

Transplants are still happening with lightning speed. For instance, an article entitled "Life-Saving Kidney Lands in Island-City" on December 27, 2006, published in *Peninsula Metropolitan News* in Qingdao City, Shandong Province, reported that only 16 days elapsed between a patient having been diagnosed with uremia and completion of a kidney transplant.

Even if the sourcing of organs for transplants from Falun Gong practitioners were to cease immediately, or ceased yesterday, that is not the end of the problem. The harvesting that did take place was a crime against humanity. Crimes against humanity call out for redress. Perpetrators of crimes against humanity must be brought to justice.

As noted in Chapter Eight, the United Nations Committee against Torture recommended that China "ensure that those responsible for such abuses [torture and use for organ transplants of some Falun Gong practitioners] are prosecuted and punished".[163]

Foreign laws and policies

The sort of transplants in which the Chinese medical system engages are illegal everywhere else in the world. But it is not illegal for a foreigner in any country to go to China, benefit from a transplant which would be illegal back home, and then return home. Foreign transplant legislation everywhere is territorial. It does not have extraterritorial reach.

Many other laws are global in their sweep. For instance, in many countries child sex tourists can be prosecuted back at home as well as in the country where they have had sex with children. This sort of legislation does not exist for transplant tourists who pay for organ transplants without bothering to determine whether the organ donor has consented.

There have been some legislative initiatives. For instance, Belgian senator Patrik Vankrunkelsven is proposing an extraterritorial criminal law which would penalize transplant tourists who purchase organs abroad where the donors are prisoners or missing persons. But these legislative proposals are still in an early stage.

Many states have travel advisories, warning their citizens of the perils in travel to one country or another. The advisories often warn of political violence, or even weather-related problems. But no government has posted a travel advisory about organ transplants in China, to warn its citizens that, in the words of The Transplantation Society, "almost all" organs in China come from prisoners. The Canadian travel advisory for China, posted on the Department of Foreign Affairs website, gives extensive information – almost 2,600 words – and has a section about health, but organ transplants are not mentioned.

Some – and, we would hope, most – would-be recipients of organ transplants would hesitate to go to China for transplants if they knew that their organs were coming from people who were non-consenting prisoners. But right now there is no systematic communication to would-be recipients concerning the source of organs in China, either through governments or the medical profession.

Transplant surgery used to require both tissue and blood type matching for the transplant to succeed. The development of transplant anti-rejection drugs has allowed for transplant surgery to circumvent tissue matching. It is possible, with heavy use of anti-rejection drugs, to transplant from a donor to a recipient whose tissues do not match. Only blood type matching is essential. Tissue matching is preferable, to avoid heavy reliance on anti-rejection drugs, but is no longer essential. The Chinese medical system relies heavily on anti-rejection drugs. China imports these drugs from the major pharmaceutical companies.

International pharmaceutical companies behave towards the Chinese transplantation system the same way everyone else does. They ask no questions. They have no knowledge whether or not their drugs are being used in recipients who received organs from involuntary donor prisoners.

Many countries have export control acts, forbidding the export of some products altogether and requiring state permission for the export of other products. But no state, to our knowledge, prohibits export to China of anti-rejection drugs used for organ transplant patients.

For instance, the Canadian Export and Import Permits Act provides:

> "No person shall export or attempt to export any goods included in an Export Control List or any goods to any country included in an Area Control List except under the authority of and in accordance with an export permit issued under this Act."[164]

But anti-rejection drugs for transplants are not included in the Area Control List for China.

Some state-administered health plans pay for health care abroad in the amount that would be paid if the care were administered in the home country. Where that happens there is not, to our knowledge, in any country a prohibition of payment where the patient obtains an organ transplant in China.

Transplant tourists need aftercare in their home country. They continue to need prescription and administration of anti-rejection drugs. States which provide government funding for health services typically provide funding for this sort of aftercare. How the organ recipient got the organ is a matter of indifference to the funders. The fact that the organ may have came from an unconsenting prisoner in China who was murdered for the organ is simply not relevant to foreign state funding of aftercare for the recipient.

Chapter Thirteen

Doctors

Many countries have self-governing transplant professions with their own disciplinary systems. Transplant professionals who violate ethical guidelines can be ejected from their profession by their colleagues without any state intervention.

For transplant professionals in China, we found nothing of the sort. When it comes to transplant surgery, as long as the state does not intervene, anything goes. There is no independent supervisory body exercising disciplinary control over transplant professionals independent of the state.

The Wild West system of transplant surgery in China makes it easier for abusive practices to occur. State involvement and criminal prosecution are inevitably less systematic than professional discipline. Because the penalties for criminal prosecution are greater than the penalties for professional discipline – potential jail time rather than just barring someone from the profession – prosecution cases are more rare than discipline cases.

The absence of a functioning transplant professional discipline system does not mean that abuses are occurring. But it certainly makes it more likely that they will occur.

There are huge gaps in foreign transplant ethics. In many of the countries from which transplant tourism to China originates, transplant professionals have organized ethical and disciplinary systems. But it is rare for these systems to deal specifically with transplant tourism or contact with Chinese transplant professionals or transplants from prisoners sentenced to death. The watch words here seem to be "out of sight, out of mind".

The Transplantation Society, an international non-governmental organization, opposed the transplantation of organs from prisoners sentenced to death, but only in July 2006. Their statement said:

> "Because of the restrictions in liberty in a prison environment it is impossible to ascertain whether prisoners are truly free to make independent decisions, and thus an autonomous informed consent for donation cannot be obtained. Therefore, The Transplantation Society is opposed to any use of organs from executed prisoners."

The Society recognized that in China prisoners sentenced to death are a major source of organs. Indeed, their statement called executed prisoners "the major source". In November 2006 the Society issued a letter to all its members about interaction with China on transplants, which failed to draw the logical conclusion from this reality.

The Society says about the presentation of transplant studies from China at Transplantation Society meetings:

> "... presentations of studies involving patient data or samples from recipients of organs or tissues from executed prisoners should not be accepted."

But then the Society also says:

> "Experimental studies that do not involve the use of material from executed prisoners or material from recipients of organs or tissues of executed prisoners should be considered for acceptance on scientific merits."

The November letter treats collaboration on studies the same way. It states:

> "Collaboration with experimental studies should only be considered if no material derived from executed prisoners

or recipients of organs or tissues from executed prisoners is used in the studies."

But it also states collaboration with clinical studies can be considered if the study:

"... does not violate the Helsinki Declaration of the World Medical Association: Ethical Principles For Medical Research Involving Human Subjects and does not violate the Policy and Ethics Statement of The Transplantation Society for example through the involvement of recipients of organs or tissues from executed prisoners."

This November letter is even more categorical on the source of organs in China. The letter is "almost all" organs are "likely" to have been obtained from executed prisoners.

There is a mismatch between the factual conclusions of the letter and the policy. It would seem that, if almost all organs are from prisoners sentenced to death, then almost all patient data or samples on which studies are based involve recipients of organs from prisoners sentenced to death. It would further seem that, in consequence, no experimental studies from China should be considered for acceptance or collaboration. But the policy does not say that.

Studies from China do not source the organs to prisoners sentenced to death or Falun Gong practitioners. How are outsiders to know the source of those organs when there is no Chinese disclosure? Are outsiders expected to assume that organs are properly sourced unless Chinese professionals admit otherwise? That seems to be what the November letter is suggesting. But surely that suggestion is foolish.

This blind eye to the Society's own factual conclusions is evident from the policy of contact. The Society will permit doctors from China to become members of the Society if they "sign the Statement of The Transplantation Society for Membership agreeing to conduct clinical practice according to The Transplantation Society policy". Does not the Society care whether or not its members actually conduct clinical practice according to The Transplantation Society policy? It seems that for the Society mere agreement is enough. If actual conduct, rather than mere agreement mattered, the Society would ban Chinese doctors from membership as long as "almost all" transplants in China come from prisoners.

Contact between transplant professionals outside of China and in China, in a context where "almost all" Chinese transplants come from prisoners, can only facilitate continuing transplantation from prisoners. Yet the Society actively encourages this contact. The Society policy states:

> "Giving lectures or sharing expertise through visiting colleagues and transplant programs in China should provide an excellent opportunity for dialogue and for sharing our positions on standards of care, acceptable sources for organs and transplantation ethics."

Put another way, this policy encourages professionals to go to China and say, in one breath, "Do not harvest organs from prisoners," and in the next breath, "Here is how to be better at the work of harvesting you are now doing." The Society invites its members to join in its ambiguity.

The policy towards trainees is even more blatant. The Society answers with a plain and simple "Yes" to the question "Should members of The Transplantation Society accept clinical or pre-clinical trainees from transplant programs that use organs or tissues from executed prisoners?" The fact that such trainees will go back to China to harvest organs from prisoners is treated all too lightly. The policy states:

> "Care should be taken to ensure, as far as possible, that it is their intention that their clinical career will comply with the standards of practice outlined in The Transplantation Society Policy & Ethics Statement."

But, as long as "almost all" organs in China come from prisoners, that compliance is impossible. The only intention which would be relevant in this context would be an intention not to engage in transplant surgery.

On referrals, the Professional Code of Conduct of the Medical Council of Hong Kong has two principles worth emphasizing. One is that "if there is doubt" as to whether the consent is given freely or voluntarily by the donor, the profession should have nothing to do with the donation. And the very least one can say about China, in light of the fact that "almost all" transplants come from prisoners, is that there is doubt in almost every case whether the consent is given freely or voluntarily by the donor.

The second is that the onus is on the foreign professionals to ascertain the status of the Chinese donor. The foreign professional is not acting ethically as long as he or she makes no inquiries or only cursory ones. Before referring a patient to China the foreign professional, after investigation, has to be satisfied beyond any doubt that consent was given freely or voluntarily by the donor.

Specifically, the Professional Code of Conduct of the Medical Council of Hong Kong states:

> "27.1 Doctors should observe the following principles and familiarise themselves with the provisions of the Human Organ Transplant Ordinance (Cap. 465) particularly section 4 of the Ordinance which is reprinted at Appendix D. Commercial dealings in human organs are prohibited, both inside and outside the HKSAR (Hong Kong Special Administrative Region).
>
> 27.2 The benefit and welfare of every individual donor, irrespective of whether he is genetically related to the recipient, should be respected and protected in organ transplantation.
>
> 27.3 Consent must be given freely and voluntarily by any donor. If there is doubt as to whether the consent is given freely or voluntarily by the donor, the doctor should reject the proposed donation.
>
> 27.4 In the case of a referral for an organ transplant outside the HKSAR from any donor, a doctor would be acting unethically if he made the referral without ascertaining the status of the donor or following these principles."

The Hong Kong principles are the exception rather than the rule. Global professional ethics do little or nothing to staunch the foreign demand for organs from China

If one applies the Hong Kong principles to The Transplantation Society Chinese contact policy, one would have to conclude that it fails to meet the ethics test. The Transplantation Society policy does not put the onus on foreign professionals to determine the source of donor organs in China. The policy, furthermore, does not reject any contact with Chinese transplant professionals as long as there is some doubt about the source of organs. Quite the contrary, for, despite the fact that "almost all" organs are sourced from prisoners, the policy nonetheless contemplates contact in a wide variety of ways.

On transplant tourism, the Transplantation Society Policy and Ethics statement provides:

> "Transplant tourism is a recently described phenomenon that may entail exploitive practices of organ transplantation for recipients who travel outside their country of residence to purchase an organ from a vendor. A practice of transplant tourism that has no transparency or professional oversight violates ethical principles of care. The Transplantation Society is opposed to practices of transplant tourism that exploit donors and recipients."

In other words, a practice of transplant tourism that has transparency and professional oversight would not violate ethical principles of care. What form does the transparency and professional oversight have to take? The policy does not say.

The World Medical Association has also failed to confront adequately abuse of organ transplantation in China. From the moment the Chinese Medical Association joined the World Medical Association in 1997 Chinese doctors have been violating the latter's ethical standards. The World Medical Association has been looking into these violations and slowly moving towards eviction. But the process has inched forward at a glacial pace.

The World Psychiatric Association evicted the Soviet Union for abuse of psychiatry. Psychiatrists worldwide condemned the Soviet Union by resolution in 1977. The Soviets withdrew from the Association in 1983 when faced with almost certain expulsion. The precedent is exemplary. Why is the World Medical Association not following that precedent?

Ever since China began organ transplants, it sourced the organs from prisoners without their consent, in violation of the most basic ethical standards. The first victims of this practice were prisoners sentenced to death. But as the demand for organs and the money to be made from transplants increased, the supply of prisoners sentenced to death

169

was quickly exhausted. China moved on from prisoners sentenced to death to other prisoners – Falun Gong practitioners, prisoners sentenced to nothing.

We should not need to convince anyone that killing innocents for their organs is a violation of medical ethics. So is killing prisoners sentenced to death. The Government of China denies that it is killing Falun Gong practitioners for their organs. But it no longer denies that it is killing prisoners for their organs.

The debate we have with the Government of China is not whether organs are coming from prisoners. It is only a debate about what sorts of prisoners are the sources of organs. But, for the ethical standards of the World Medical Association, resolving that debate should not matter.

As bad as it is to put people in psychiatric hospitals for their beliefs, killing people for their organs is far worse. The inaction of the World Medical Association in the face of Chinese medical practices is deeply disturbing.

The complicity of Chinese doctors in organ-harvesting from prisoners has been a problem for a decade, since China joined the World Medical Association. (China had first joined in 1989, but left in 1991 for failure to pay its dues; it successfully applied to rejoin in 1997.)

The World Medical Association realized that there was a problem in China in 1997, long before the persecution of the Falun Gong began. If the Association had acted decisively then, we might not face the problem we do now. From the very start, organ-harvesting from prisoners was an issue.

The German Medical Association moved to defer the application of China to join until it was clear whether Chinese doctors took part in the transplantation of organs from prisoners. The motion was overwhelmingly defeated. Dr. Anders Milton, Chair of the World Medical Association Council said:

> "It is important that the Chinese Medical Association is once again a member of the World Medical Association so that we can discuss with them the allegations that doctors in China take part in the transplantation of organs from executed prisoners which we deplore."

The Association announced in April 1998 a conference to be held later in the year, in China, on medical ethics and human rights. It was spurred by reports of organs being taken from "executed and living prisoners" in China. The conference, as far as we can tell, never took place.

The Association and its Chinese members issued a joint statement also in April 1998 condemning as "illegal and completely unacceptable" the involuntary or forced removal and sale of organs. This statement by the Chinese became one of a long series of such statements made while the practice flourished, without any visible impact on the practice. Dr. Anders Milton, in another of his naive statements, said: "If further allegations are made about organ trafficking we can rely on the Chinese Medical Association to try to rectify the situation."

The Association adopted a policy statement on organ donation and transplantation in October 2000, revised in October 2006, which stated that:

> "Because prisoners and other individuals in custody are not in a position to give consent freely and can be subject to coercion, their organs must not be used for transplantation except for members of their immediate family." (paragraph 16)

But about China, nothing was done. There was a revival of interest in 2006. A World Medical Association Council meeting of May 2006 in South Africa called on China "immediately" to cease the practice of using prisoners as organ donors. They demanded that their Chinese members condemn the practice and ensure that Chinese doctors are not involved in it. The resolution reiterated the old 2000 policy.

A year later, this call for immediate cessation, like the calls nine years earlier, had produced more or less nothing. Chinese legislation had changed on July 1, 2006 to ban the sale of organs but the practice continued. The statement from Deputy Health Minister Huang Jiefu that "Apart from a small portion of traffic victims, most of the organs from cadavers are from executed prisoners" was made more than four months after the new legislation came into force.

To be fair to the World Medical Association, they were far from being the only organization which fell into the trap of thinking the human rights situation in China was improving or might improve through their own efforts. Many governments have fallen into the same trap, including our own government, the Government of Canada.

The Government of China offered a human rights dialogue to Canada as a *quid pro quo* for not co-sponsoring at the old United Nations Human Rights Commission a resolution expressing concern about human rights violations in China. It was an offer which Canada foolishly accepted.

Canadian academic Charles Burton evaluated in April 2006 the Canada-China bilateral dialogue, at the request of Canada's Ministry of Foreign Affairs. He reported that Chinese participants in the dialogue were low-level officials who spent much of the time of the meetings just reading scripts – and they were the same scripts year after year. There was no obvious connection between these meetings and what actually happened in China. Senior Chinese Communist officials resisted taking the dialogue seriously; they saw it as an affront to China's national dignity for China to be made to answer to foreigners for domestic policy decisions.

The inspiration we draw from the activity of the World Psychiatric Association against Soviet abuse of psychiatry is far from new. Psychiatric professor emeritus Abraham Halpern of New York Medical College wrote to the World Medical Association in September 2006, made reference to the report we wrote about organ-harvesting, and called on the Association to take a number of steps. Proposed steps included appointment of an investigative committee of the World Medical Association to visit China, and expulsion of the Chinese Medical Association from the World Medical Association if the Government of China did not stop illegal organ-harvesting. In that letter, he reminded the Association of the action of the World Psychiatric Association against the Soviet Union for the wrongful involuntary incarceration of non-mentally-ill dissidents in maximum security forensic psychiatric hospitals.

He wrote a follow-up letter in April 2007 asking for an emergency meeting of the Council of the World Medical Association on the issue. He wrote that action by the Medical Association is the type of step which

"... has proven effective in the past in the Soviet Union and even in China itself in connection with stopping the wrongful incarceration in maximum security forensic institutions of non-mentally-ill dissidents in the Soviet Union and Falun Gong adherents in China."

The Association sent a mission to China, led by the then head of the Council of the Association, Dr. Yoram Blachar from Israel. The mission reported to the Association Council meeting held in May 2007. Blachar, continuing to strike the naive tone set by his predecessor Dr. Milton, said that he was encouraged by new legislation in China prohibiting trade in organs.

The World Medical Association should not grasp at straws. There may be a temptation, in order to avoid a confrontation with China, to accept the new law as movement in the right direction and leave it at that. It would be a mistake to succumb to that temptation.

The Chinese party-state has lied so often before, the abuse of transplant surgery has gone on now for so long, that China is no longer entitled to the benefit of the doubt. Only when the World Medical Association can be certain beyond any reasonable doubt that the abuse has stopped should China be allowed continued membership in the Association.

What appears to move the Government of China far more than dialogue is embarrassment, the loss of face or fear of loss of face. The World Medical Association is far more likely to have an impact on Chinese behaviour through expulsion than it ever will through dialogue.

The World Psychiatric Association eventually agreed in 1989 to readmit the Soviet Union, provided four conditions were met. They were that the Soviet Psychiatric Association:

1) acknowledge that systematic abuse of psychiatry for political purposes had taken place,
2) promise to discontinue the abuses,
3) rehabilitate the victims, and
4) democratize the psychiatric profession.[165]

Whether it be the price of continued membership or the price of readmission after expulsion, the Chinese Medical Association, to continue membership in the World Medical Association should do no less. Rehabilitation of the dead has no significance in this context. But redress does. Redress can take a variety of forms. But at the very least it involves acknowledgement of the reality of what happened.

For membership to continue, the Chinese Medical Association should:

1) acknowledge that systematic abuse of transplant surgery has taken place,
2) promise to discontinue the abuses,
3) provide redress for the victims, and
4) democratize the transplant surgery profession.

But there is more. The issue for the World Medical Association is not just sourcing organs from prisoners. While it is possible to gloss over the question whether organs come only from prisoners sentenced to death or also from Falun Gong practitioners, it is not desirable to do so.

The World Psychiatric Association provides yet another example, this time about the Falun Gong. Chinese psychiatrists, like the Soviet psychiatrists before them, abused psychiatry to mistreat perceived opponents of their government, its fantasized enemies – in the case of China, the Falun Gong. The World Psychiatric Association, after their reaction to the Soviet psychiatric abuse, could not just ignore Chinese psychiatric violations. But they succumbed to the temptation of an agreement with the Chinese psychiatrists.

The Association and the Chinese psychiatrists agreed in May 2004 that there were:

> "... instances in which some Chinese psychiatrists failed to distinguish between spiritual-cultural beliefs and delusions, as a result of which persons were misdiagnosed and mistreated."

The parties further agreed that these instances were attributable to a "lack of training and professional skills of some psychiatrists rather than [to] systematic abuse of psychiatry". The Chinese Society of Psychiatrists agreed to take steps to "educate [its] members" about the issues that led to misdiagnosis and mistreatment and said it welcomed the World Psychiatric Association's "assistance in correcting this situation" and improving psychiatric diagnosis and treatment throughout the People's Republic of China.

Abraham Halpern, a voice of reason in all this, reacted this way:

> "The allegations of psychiatric abuse in China involve mistreatment, torture, and fraudulent diagnoses in the case of

large numbers of political dissidents and Falun Gong practitioners and should not be dismissed as mere 'failures in
accurate diagnosis'."

The organ-harvesting of Falun Gong practitioners is systematic and
not just the failure, in a few instances, to follow appropriate transplant
procedures. The numbers of organs harvested from Falun Gong practitioners, according to our calculations in the tens of thousands, allow
for no other description.

Yet, if the Chinese government were to admit to the World Medical
Association that there were instances of involuntary organ-harvesting
of Falun Gong practitioners for transplants – as they admitted to the
World Psychiatric Association that there are instances of involuntary
incarceration of non-mentally-ill Falun Gong practitioners in psychiatric hospitals and clinics – that would be something. The World
Psychiatric Association precedent tells us that the World Medical
Association should insist, as the price of continued Chinese membership in the Association, that the Chinese Medical Association be prepared to admit at least that much.

In a news release dated 5 October 2007 the World Medical Association
announced at the annual General Assembly in Copenhagen an agreement with the Chinese Medical Association. The Chinese Medical
Association agreed that organs of prisoners and other individuals in
custody must not be used for transplantation except for members of
their immediate family.

In a letter to the World Medical Association, the Vice President and
Secretary General of the Chinese Medical Association, Dr Wu
Mingjiang, said:

> "We would like to inform you that after discussions in the
> Chinese Medical Association, a consensus has been
> reached, that is, the Chinese Medical Association agrees to
> the World Medical Association Statement on Human
> Organ Donation and Transplantation, in which it states
> that organs of prisoners and other individuals in custody
> must not be used for transplantation, except for members
> of their immediate family.
>
> "The Chinese Medical Association will, through its influ-
> ence, further promote the strengthening of management

of human organ transplantation and prevent possible violations of the regulations made by the Chinese Government. We also hope to work more closely with the WMA and exchange information and views on the management of human organ transplantation."

Dr Edward Hill, chair of the World Medical Association, said the announcement by the Chinese Medical Association was a very positive step forward and added:

> "We shall now continue our dialogue with the Chinese Medical Association and include other national medical associations in a project to find best practice models for ethically acceptable organ procurement programmes. This would help not only China and its high demand for organs, but also other regions in the world that have the same problems of coping with a severe shortage of organs."

The agreement between the World Medical Association and the Chinese Medical Association to end organ sourcing from prisoners in China except for prisoners donating organs to their immediate family members is welcome. We were pleased to see that the agreement covered all prisoners and not just prisoners sentenced to death. This broader terminology means that in principle the agreement encompasses also Falun Gong practitioners who are held in detention but sentenced to nothing. Yet it does not remove all our concerns.

1.   The Chinese Medical Association is not a governmental entity. Its promise to avoid organ sourcing from prisoners indicates the good will of some Chinese medical doctors. However, it is not binding on the government, and is not binding on doctors in China who are not members of the Chinese Medical Association. The Chinese Medical Association cannot make decisions for the government. The government sets the rules for associations and not vice versa. The practice of sourcing organs from prisoners, whether prisoners sentenced to death or Falun Gong practitioners, was and is tolerated by the Chinese government. Only the Chinese government can stop this practice.

2. Even if it had been the Government of China which had entered into the agreement instead of the Chinese Medical Association, it is questionable whether the agreement would be effective. As noted in Chapter Twelve, the Chinese government has over time issued several laws and regulations prohibiting the selling of organs without the consent of the source. The very repetition of such laws is evidence that these laws are not effective.

3. The Chinese government has had a history of duplicity in this field. One example is the case of Dr. Wang Guoqi. On June 27, 2001 he testified before the Subcommittee on International Operations and Human Rights of the U.S. Congress, that organs for transplants are sourced from prisoners. The Chinese government called him a liar. This position was held until 2005, when for the first time Chinese officials admitted publicly that they indeed harvested organs from prisoners.

4. Liu Zhi of the Chinese Medical Association's international department said that the agreement with the World Medical Association has no legal effect. He expressed the hope that the agreement would influence China's 500,000 doctors and government decisions. This statement, in our view, minimizes the effect the agreement might have. At the very least, the Chinese Medical Association can insist that its own members comply with the terms of the agreement as a precondition for continued membership in their association. The fact that the Chinese Medical Association has not done this indicates a less-than-wholehearted support for the agreement.

5. The agreement does not address the issues of onus and standard of proof. In many cases in China, doctors are supplied an organ and told a source, but make no independent determination whether what they are told about the source is accurate or not.

   The agreement with the Chinese Medical Association would not mean very much if Chinese Medical Association doctors could claim respect for the agreement simply by turning a blind eye to practices around them. The agreement needs to ensure that Chinese transplant professionals are respecting the substance of the agreement as well as its form.

6. There is no verification system in place to determine whether or not the agreement with the Chinese Medical Association is being kept. Such a verification system needs to be independent from the Government of China and the Chinese Medical Association itself. There has to be transparent documentation of

the sources of organs used by Chinese Medical Association doctors in transplant operations. The Chinese Medical Association should make accessible to the World Medical Association, to human rights organizations such as Amnesty International and Human Rights Watch, and to human rights lawyers' organizations, transplantation numbers which involve its members, donor names and the names of the immediate family members who may receive transplants from prisoners.

Regrettably, today in China, there is no publicly available information on numbers of convicts sentenced to death and executed. This information should be publicly available. That would, one would think, be a simple task, now that the Supreme People's Court in Beijing must approve all death sentences. The Chinese Medical Association should ask the Government of China to make this information available.

7. In China, transplant surgery has become essential for financing the medical profession and hospitals. A dramatic decrease of transplant surgeries would impose financial burden on the health care system. Without an increase in government funds to the health care system, it is unlikely that hospitals will cease relying on transplants for money. While sourcing of organs and payment for organs are conceptually distinct, they are linked in reality. The need for funds pushes doctors and hospitals toward increasing transplant numbers and using historically available sources, prisoners.

8. The Chinese Medical Association agreement does not bind military doctors who are not among its members, nor does it bind military hospitals. Organ recipients indicate that military doctors and hospitals are heavily involved in organ transplant surgery.

9. The agreement with the Chinese Medical Association does not change the Chinese infrastructure for organ transplants. China still does not have a public organ donation program. There is still no law allowing for organ sourcing from those who are brain-dead but cardiac-alive. According to Deputy Health Minister Huang Jiefu, 95% of all organs for transplants come from prisoners. The implementation of the agreement with the Chinese Medical Association, in the absence of an organ donation system and a brain-dead law, would mean that organ transplantation in China would be almost non-existent, a most unlikely result.

10. The mere fact that the recipient is an immediate family member of the prisoner does not automatically mean that the prisoner has freely consented to the donation. Our concern about this exception is heightened by the fact that people in China can be sentenced to death for a wide variety of economic and political crimes (for example tax fraud). We are aware that this exception is found in the World Medical Association's Policy on Human Organ Donation and Transplantation. However, it is not to be found in the ethical principles of The Transplantation Society. In our view, the prohibition without exception which The Transplantation Society has adopted is preferable to the prohibition with the immediate family member exception, which the World Medical Association has adopted. The case of China highlights why this exception is problematic.

We note the statement of the former chair of the World Medical Association, Dr Yoram Blachar, who led the World Medical Association delegation to China, that differences between the two sides remained. The World Medical Association needs to continue to press the Chinese Medical Association on this issue until this appalling practice in China of killing prisoners for their organs ends entirely.

Chapter Fourteen

Strategy

The pursuit of human rights in China, as in any country, has to be approached strategically. What is the most effective way of combating human rights violations in China?

The best strategy is the most direct, combating human rights violations front and centre, rather than peripherally. The Communist Party of China rules China through repression. Since its inception the Party has killed tens of millions of persons to achieve and maintain power, more than Nazi Germany and the Stalinist Soviet Union combined. Repression of human rights in China takes many forms with many victims.

Because they have beliefs different from the Communists and tell the world about Chinese party-state violations, the Communist Party of China persecutes Falun Gong, democracy activists, ethnic minorities and global religions – Tibetan Buddhists, Muslim Uighurs and Christians, human rights defenders, journalists, and Internet bloggers. It persecutes the Falun Gong more than any other group.

Though Chinese Communists are annoyed with the efforts of other victim groups, it is only the Falun Gong they feel poses a true threat. It is only the Falun Gong the Communists fear provide a viable alternative to the ideological pre-eminence of the Communist Party in China. Communism in China today has evolved into an ideological vanity project for those in power. At a time when no one could figure out what to make of Jiang Zemin's "Three Represents" socio-political musings, the Chinese people were subscribing to Falun Gong beliefs in the millions. Before their repression the Falun Gong were more numerous than any other group, more numerous than the Communist Party itself.

It would be incongruous for oppressors to back off from what they see as their worst threat and remain unwavering in their hostility to other perceived enemies. Unravel the repression against the Falun Gong and all other victim groups will benefit.

Embracing the Falun Gong is practical. Who else, after all, has the newspapers, the TV, the radio, the numbers, the persistence day after day, year after year, city after city, country after country, to pursue human rights in China? Activism for promotion of respect for human rights in China around the world is, more than any other form, Falun Gong activism. For activists to cut themselves off from Falun Gong is to cut themselves off from their best and strongest allies in the struggle for promotion of human rights in China.

As a matter of strategy as well as principle, the expression of concerns about human rights violations should lead with condemnation of the worst violations first. Falun Gong has the ignominious honour of leading by far the long parade of human rights victims in China. As noted in Chapter Two, they represent two-thirds of the torture victims and half the people in detention in re-education-through-labour camps. Falun Gong practitioners and prisoners sentenced to death are the sole victims of organ-harvesting, the killing of innocents for their organs for transplant surgery.

It is dismaying, in light of the disproportionate victimization of this one group, how little their suffering receives attention from governments, intergovernmental organizations and non-governmental organizations concerned about human rights in China. The mobilization of concern about repression of the Falun Gong has not been nearly commensurate with the gravity of the situation. This behaviour is reminiscent of those who in the 1930s and 40s opposed Nazism without saying anything against anti-Semitism. Opposing human rights violations in China while remaining silent about Falun Gong victimization ignores the kernel at the centre of human rights violations in China.

The unprecedented and grotesque nature of organ-harvesting in particular allows for greater mobilization in protesting human rights violations in China generally. For some who hear of, say, torture or arbitrary detention in China, the reaction may be that they have heard this all before – too many times. People can quickly become jaded about almost anything, including the traditional forms of human rights violations. In contrast, when people hear about killing innocents for their organs, they sit up and take notice.

There is a common inclination to focus on the better documented over the worse violations. Yet that inclination suffers from an overly narrow audience selection. Protests of human rights violations have three basic audiences – the perpetrators, the victims and the public at large. For the perpetrator audience, in this case the Government of China, it is indeed easier to discuss the better documented over the worse. It is harder for the perpetrator to deny the better documented. Lesser documentation and greater harm both drive the perpetrator to denials, a seeming dead end.

To this concern there are two answers. One is that for the other two audiences, the victims and the public at large, it is far better to focus on the worse over the better documented. Surviving victims of human rights violations suffer both physically and mentally. A large part of their mental suffering is their sense of betrayal, their feeling of abandonment, the despair of being left alone to their fate. Expressions of concern about human rights violations, though they may not move the perpetrators to change their behaviour, surely move the victims to help them cope with their suffering. Crimes against humanity are crimes against us all. By showing solidarity with the victims, we acknowledge that we too are victims of these crimes.

Though there are no surviving Falun Gong victims of organ-harvesting, there are many surviving family members who believe, with good reason, that this is how and why their loved ones died. Organ-harvesting of Falun Gong practitioners is a violation which all Falun Gong practitioners everywhere feel keenly. It would mock that feeling to ignore that violation.

For the public at large, focusing on the better documented over the worse violations looks Machiavellian. For all matters, but for human rights above all, the public expects human rights activists to act on principle. That means protesting the worst violations first.

Unless respect for human rights is promoted by humanity at large, human rights principles will wither. By putting aside the worse violations in favour of those with more traction with perpetrator governments, we ignore our most crucial support, the public, in the struggle for respect for dignity for all.

Even when it comes to dealing directly with the Government of China, there is something to be said for raising worse violations which China denies than lesser violations which China admits. Many of the lesser violations in China are either embedded in law or so widespread that the Government of China just says, "We are trying," and leaves it at that. For a violation China denies, it should be uncontroversial to work with China to set in places safeguards to prevent the violation from happening.

For instance, it is Chinese policy, though regrettably not practice, for organ-harvesting to be done only with the consent of the donor. How can China say no to co-operation in setting up a functioning, documented, verifiable, supervised, standardized, comprehensive consent system for organ donation?

Once we decide on the victims and violations we wish to focus, what next? Who should be our target audience?

Those inside China are heavily propagandized and brutally terrorized. For the Communist Party of China, it is all too easy to ignore internal opposition. The Government of China rules by force, not by consent. It is imposed, not elected. If individuals in China do not agree with the Party, the attitude of the Government is: "So much the worse for them!" If the dissenters keep their opinions to themselves, they may be lucky and be ignored. If they express their opinions too openly, too persistently, they are arrested, beaten, tortured, made to disappear.

That was the experience of human rights lawyer Gao Zhisheng, who has had the courage to stand up within China to the Government of China. He wrote that you cannot be a human rights lawyer in China without being a human rights case yourself.

Gao had become a successful private lawyer starting from the most disadvantageous beginning imaginable. He was born in a cave. His parents could not afford to send him to school, so he listened outside classroom windows. Yet by 2001 China's Ministry of Justice had rated Gao as one of China's top ten lawyers. He had advocated on behalf of a long list of clients in difficult situations – including coal miners suing their employers and a client demanding compensation for his home confiscated in preparation for the 2008 Olympics.

Three of his clients were Yang Maodong, Zheng Yichun and Pastor Cai Zhuohua. Yang was detained for providing legal advice to villagers in Taishi, Guandong province, who were attempting to unseat a village leader for corruption. Zheng, a journalist and former professor, was sentenced to seven years imprisonment for his online writings. Pastor Cai Zhuohua was imprisoned for three years for such practices as printing and selling copies of the Bible.

Gao wrote three open letters protesting the persecution of the Falun Gong. The letters were written in December 2004, October 2005, and December 2005. Following the second letter, the Beijing Bureau of

Municipal Justice suspended the operation of his office for one year. In December, his licence to practice was revoked.

The response of Gao to this behaviour was to resign publicly from the Communist Party and to write his third letter. Following the third letter, he received calls from the police. They told him that he had crossed the line. The police said that he, his wife and children were all under investigation. Starting in December, he and his family were put under constant police surveillance.

In January 2006 Gao was arrested by the police for filming them. This time, the police threatened to kill him. He was released after a short detention, but a few days after his release (still in January) a car with covered licence plates followed by a military vehicle also with covered licence plates attempted to run him over.

Gao responded by organizing a relay hunger strike. Lawyers and rights activists fasted in turn for one or two days to protest state persecution. In response, the state arrested his office staff. Gao had kept his office open despite his disbarment, but from mid-February he had to continue his work without staff.

After the first reports surfaced of organ-harvesting of Falun Gong practitioners in March 2006 (the reports which precipitated our own investigation), the voice of Gao would not be stilled. He wrote about and condemned the practice. He expressed his willingness to join the Coalition to Investigate Persecution against the Falun Gong, the group that had mandated our work.

To do our investigation, we wanted to go to China. An application for a visa is more likely to succeed when the application is accompanied by an invitation from someone in the country from which the visa is sought. We cast about in several directions for an invitation from China to do this work. The person who responded was Gao Zhisheng.

In his invitation letter, Gao wrote, "As all my [land] telephones and networks have been cut off, I can only communicate [by cellphone] through reporters and the media." And that is indeed how we got our invitation letter, through the media. Gao phoned in our invitation to a reporter. The reporter in turn phoned one of our interpreters to pass on the invitation. The reporter then filed the invitation with her newspaper, *The Epoch Times,* which printed it in their issue of June 11, 2006.

We felt uneasy about what Gao had done, because he was putting himself at risk by inviting us in this manner. He anticipated and answered this concern in his letter, writing:

"You may be worried that my support and invitation to you may endanger me. But the danger I am facing is not because of my support and invite to you, it is because we face an evil dictatorship system. Therefore, the danger already exists. The source of danger lies in this evil inhuman system, not what we choose to do."

No visa was subsequently issued to us by the Chinese embassy in Ottawa. On August 15, 2006 Gao was arrested, tortured, prosecuted for inciting subversion, convicted on December 12, and sentenced on December 22 to three years in jail. Though the jail sentence of three years was suspended for five years provided Gao complied with the conditions of the suspension, he went into house arrest. After he made public a letter he wrote protesting Chinese Communist human rights abuse, he was abducted in September 2007 by officials, and disappeared. He was returned home briefly in February 2009 and, after he released a statement about his torture, was again abducted.

Today he remains among the disappeared. One has to applaud his raw courage. We have nominated him for the Nobel Peace Prize.

However, it would be unrealistic to expect many others to be as courageous as he has been. It would be too much to ask others to risk suffering what Gao Zhisheng has suffered.

A dictatorship, in any case, is more likely to pay attention to external opposition than internal opposition. External opposition is hard to suppress or ignore.

Democratic governments cater to their electorates sometimes to the detriment of international opinion. With tyrannies, it is the opposite. They do not really care much about what locals think of them because, almost no matter now unpopular the regime is, it can maintain power through terrorizing the local population.

On the other hand, tyrannies care about international opinion. International opinion impacts on their legitimacy, their respectability, their status, their hold on power. Since it cannot be suppressed in the same way that local criticism can, international criticism has to be answered.

While this observation is generally true, it is more true for China than any other country. China's government is unique among the tyrannies of the world. It is a global power with economic and political outreach around the planet. Other tyrannies are hermit kingdoms, cut off from the rest of the world, and may ignore criticism abroad while stifling it at home. Burma and North Korea are almost as indifferent to external as to internal criticism. For Zimbabwe, Sudan, Cuba and Iran the story is much the same. China, though, cares because its global ambitions depend on its global image.

If we are going to mobilize concern about China's government outside of China, who should be our targets? Should it be people who are ethnic Chinese, Chinese nationals outside of China, people in government or business or the arts or sports or academia who have some dealings with China? Or should it be people with no connection to China whatsoever?

Just as any opposition from inside China is welcome to the cause, so too is any opposition which comes from people outside who have a connection to China. But we would suggest that the best strategy would be to attempt to mobilize those with no connection to China.

One reason is that the crimes of the Government of China are not just crimes against the Falun Gong or Uighurs or Tibetans or the Chinese people. They are crimes against humanity. They are crimes against us all. If we expect only or specifically those with some connection to China to be concerned, the message of the universal nature of the crimes is lost.

A second reason is that those with connections to China are often all too easily intimidated or endangered. Nationals of China abroad have relatives at home under the thumb of the Chinese party-state. Those engaged in dealings with China run the risk of their affairs going off the rails if they displease its government.

A third reason is that the Government of China feels that it owns China and the Chinese. It sees itself as the voice of China and the Chinese people worldwide. Criticism from within the state or from within the Chinese community outside of China is belittled as political, whether it is or not. It is a lot harder to characterize external criticism that way when it comes from total outsiders.

Those who are most free to stand against Chinese human rights violations, those whose stance carries most graphically the universal human rights message, and, consequently, those whose opposition China finds hardest to ignore, are those with no connection to China whatsoever. When we stand against the killing of Falun Gong practitioners for their organs, we have nothing to gain, because we are not being paid and are not Falun Gong practitioners. We also have nothing to lose – unlike those inside China who are brutalized, or even those outside China who have or who, for their careers, would like to have positive dealings with China. As well, no one could plausibly suggest that we would have any political ambitions in China.

The Greek scientist Archimedes in the third century B.C. wrote: "Give me a lever long enough and a fulcrum on which to place it, and I shall move the world." In the corners of the planet farthest from China, the lever we have for moving China is long enough to do the job. With the fulcrum of human rights, we can move China more easily than those who are under threat of Chinese government retribution.

When we attempt to mobilize outsiders with no connection to China, we face another problem: indifference. When people themselves are victims or potential victims of human rights violations, it is easy to generate concern. Where the victims are others, all too many people just do nothing. It is easy to decry inaction in the face of human rights violations. But why does it happen? Who are the people who do nothing?

Some feel helpless, believing there is nothing they can do. Others are lazy, unable to muster the energy to act. A third group are self-centred, focusing on their own lives at the expense of the lives of others. A fourth are intimidated, fearing that the perpetrators will reach out to get them if they protest. All of these people accept that what is being done to the victims is wrong. They are just not prepared to do anything about it.

But by far the biggest obstacle to combating human rights violations is people who either do not know or do not care.

Those who do not care are either callous or conflicted. The callous are sadists. They share the cruelty of the perpetrators. Massive human rights violations go hand in hand with ideologies which first preach and then justify those violations. Many of the callous are believers, signing on to the ideology of human rights violations.

The conflicted have contrary interests. They are silent because they have family, social, career, financial or business interests, which would be jeopardized by confronting the perpetrators. The conflicted are morally compromised. They put their lesser personal interests above the prevention of grave wrongs.

By far the greatest number of the indifferent are those who do not know. But how can anyone not know? Massive human rights violations are widely publicized. They are the stuff of daily headlines. Reams of books, reports, articles and broadcasts bring the atrocities of this world into every living room.

The answer is the ideologies which accompany violations. Perpetrators do not just kill and torture and rape. They also incite to hate, propagandize, disinform, distort, evade and fabricate.

People are indifferent because they do not pay close enough attention to sort out truth from falsehood, the real from the unreal. The indifferent place the truth of the victims and the fabrications of the perpetrators and their apologists on the same level, dismissing the whole as a political dispute in a faraway land.

There are many eloquent remarks against indifference. One is that the worst place in hell is reserved for those who are indifferent. Another is that all that is necessary for evil to flourish is for the good to do nothing. William Butler Yeats wrote: "The best lack all conviction while the worst are full of passionate intensity." Elie Weisel said: "Indifference is always the friend of the enemy for it benefits the oppressor – never the victim."

Accusations of human rights violations are not always true and not always well-intentioned. Those politically opposed to any regime will easily resort to false accusations of human rights violations as a means of delegitimizing that regime.

The difference between imagined human rights violations invented for purposes of delegitimization and actual human rights violations denied by the perpetrators is reality. We cannot ignore reality and just consider charges and denials of human rights violations as so many words all of equal weight.

It would be irresponsible to feign neutrality between Holocaust deniers and Holocaust victims. Anyone concerned with truth and freedom and respect for human rights would disapprove strongly of those who treated Holocaust denial as a respectable opinion deserving the same weight and consideration as the tales of horror of Holocaust victims. But Holocaust denial, like the Holocaust itself, is not an isolated experience. It is, rather, the most extreme form of a whole spectrum of speech abuses. Every grave human rights violation has its deniers. Perpetrators everywhere have a whole litany of sorry excuses, but the first line of defence for them all is: "It did not happen."

Chinese repression in China of the Falun Gong is brutal, horrifying, gross, systematic, widespread. Yet that repression is not the whole story. When it comes to victimization of the innocent at home, China is much like many other tyrannies in the world. The chosen enemies vary from country to country, but, whatever the country, the story is much the same – innocents suffer so that despots can stay in power.

However, when it comes to action abroad, China is different. Only China has the political muscle and economic weight to conduct a global propaganda campaign against its chosen victims, who are primarily, but not only, the Falun Gong. Outside of China, Government agents do not have the power to kill, detain and torture. But, while keeping consistent with foreign law, they do what they can, and even violate foreign laws in ways that diplomatic immunity allows them to do.

This world has not seen the like of the Chinese party-state hatred of the Falun Gong since the Nazi Germany hatred of the Jews. Nazi Germany was not content to victimize its Jews in Germany. Anti-Semitism was a foreign policy – indeed the primary foreign policy goal – of Nazi Germany. Nazi Germany was intent on persecuting and killing Jews everywhere on the planet.

China has not gone as far as Nazi Germany. It does not invade foreign countries and murder Falun Gong practitioners there. But in its global sweep of repression against its chosen victims, it more resembles Nazi Germany than any other government since World War II.

This planetary attack against the Falun Gong takes a myriad of forms. First and foremost is incitement to hatred. The Government of China conducts a propaganda campaign against the Falun Gong wherever its agents operate. The propaganda takes advantage of whatever media outlets are available.

The Government of China utters foul slanders against the Falun Gong. Falun Gong practitioners respond with vigorous criticism of the Communist Party of China. To outsiders not paying much attention and unfamiliar with the Falun Gong, this dispute superficially looks like a foreign political slanging match. The tendency is not to get involved. For media, there is a tendency to report what each side says – as they would any dispute, attempting to be neutral.

Yet, the Communist Party of China has committed massive human rights violations against the Falun Gong. The Falun Gong are a group of innocents, a non-political, non-violent community.

The Communist Party of China, to justify its brutal hold on power, does what totalitarian parties have done everywhere – it admits nothing and denies everything. It manufactures phoney charges, concocts facts, and imagines quotes. To put its propaganda about the Falun Gong on the same level as evidence about the human rights violations perpetrated by the Communist Party of China, to create a false symmetry between them, ignores reality and turns a blind eye to the inhumanity staring us in the face.

There are, regrettably, all too many states inflicting massive human rights violations on their citizens. And there is never enough mobilization of concern to combat the violations. Yet at least elsewhere, there is a general consensus that what is happening is wrong and needs to stop. When it comes to human rights violations in Sudan or Iran or Burma or North Korea, the problems may seem intractable, but spreading awareness and appreciation of the problems is not.

In working on our report on organ-harvesting of Falun Gong practitioners in China, we have faced two formidable tasks. One was determining whether or not the allegations of organ-harvesting of Falun Gong practitioners in China were true. The second, once we determined that they were true, was mobilizing concern about this foul practice. As difficult as writing our report was, shaking the international community out of its indifference towards violations of human rights against the Falun Gong has been far more difficult.

It is not as if we were dealing with a slight or inconsequential problem. Why outside the Falun Gong community itself is there so little concern about the so numerous, so awful violations the Falun Gong suffer? One reason may be the very strangeness and newness of Falun Gong, discussed in Chapter Sixteen.

Another reason is the economic clout of China. Some people, unfortunately, measure the strength of their human rights commitment by its impact on their pocketbooks. China's economic weight by far surpasses that of other major human rights violators. But the most likely explanation of all is the global campaign of China against the Falun Gong set out in Chapter Eleven.

That chapter, long as it is, is just the tip of an iceberg. One can recount many more examples of these sorts of propagandizing, blocking and anticipatory actions. They are small matters compared to the torture and killings within China. But they stem from the same ideology and mentality which generate the graver abuses. And they have an impact on the persecution in China.

The struggle against human rights violations needs international solidarity to succeed. Chinese government efforts abroad against the Falun Gong eat away at that solidarity. This perpetual Chinese global campaign of incitement turns some against the Falun Gong. For many others, the result is immobilization. People do not have the time or the energy to pierce through the Chinese veil. They throw up their hands and walk away, leaving the Falun Gong to their fate. The end result is indifference.

How do we combat the indifference of those who do not know? By making our very best efforts to ensure they do know. For China, that means making every effort to proclaim the truth about what is happening there, not taking on faith anything coming from the Government of China about their victims, and not repeating anything they say against their victims unless and until it is verified. To do less means contributing to Chinese persecution.

Chapter Fifteen

Claim of difference

The Government of China and its apologists excuse human rights violations in China by claimed cultural differences between China and the Western world. The Chinese Communist Party has endorsed acceptance of human rights "in light of China's national realities".[166] The Government of China, so its representatives have said, works towards "Chinese-style democracy" rather than just democracy. The representatives have said: "It is natural for different countries to have different views on the question of human rights." Similarly, Derek Burney of the Canadian Defence and Foreign Policy Institute writes: "Canada has different values on human rights … from China's."[167]

For Westerners, the suggestion that human rights values are Western values has to make our heads spin. The greatest human rights violations of the past century have been committed in the West. The murder of six million Jews and the attempt to exterminate the whole Jewish population, as well as the Holocaust's associated genocides – the mass murder of the handicapped, Roma and homosexuals by the Nazis – were Western crimes. Nazism is Western. Fascism is Western. Communism is Western in origin. Colonialism is Western.

Even today, we have only to see how the West treats its refugee or aboriginal populations to see serious disregard for human rights. Refugee claimants and asylum seekers in the West are denied access to determination systems, subjected to racist attacks, deterred from making claims, and denied protection. One can as easily talk of a Western culture of human rights violations as a Western culture of respect for human rights.

There are elements of respect for human rights and violations of human rights which can be drawn from every culture, every belief, every region of the globe. Human rights standards are universal standards. They are not based on any one culture or belief. They do not come from any one region. It is a slur on any culture or belief or region to say it ignores human rights. It shows an exaggerated appreciation of any culture or belief or region to say that it is the source of human rights.

The principle of human rights rests on the dignity and inherent worth of the individual. Its foundation is the equality of all humanity. To talk of human rights based on a particular region or belief or culture is to use a contradiction in terms. Cultures and beliefs are varied. Human rights are uniform throughout the human family.

Indeed, to argue that human rights are universal is to indulge in a tautology. If human rights are relative, then they are not the rights of all humans, but only the rights of some humans.

To talk of human rights based on particular cultures or beliefs or regions can defeat the realization of human rights. At any given time, human rights violations are more prevalent in one part of the world more than another, within one culture more than another, with the adherents of one belief more than another. Apologists for those violations will often wrap themselves round with the protective cloak of their culture or belief or region and claim criticism of the violations is relativistic, based on some other culture, another belief, a different region.

To accept the notion of human rights based on a particular culture or belief or region is to accept the defence of violations based on a particular culture or belief or region. It would create a world of first- and second-class cultures or beliefs or regions. Members of some cultures, adherents of some beliefs, residents of some regions would be entitled to have their human rights respected. Members of other cultures, adherents of other beliefs, residents of other regions would not. Accepting the notion of human rights based on particular cultures or beliefs or regions is a step towards undermining the concept of equal human dignity for all.

The voice for cultural, belief or regional variations in human rights is always the voice of the perpetrators, never the voice of the victims. Victims never say, "It is my culture, my belief to be victimized." Victims and perpetrators often come from the same culture, live in the same area. When the perpetrators say that victimization is part of their culture, and the victims say the contrary, we suggest that the victims are the better indicator of ideals of the culture than the perpetrators are. Ultimately, it is the voice of the victims which must be decisive, not the voice of the perpetrators.

Admitting that human rights values are relative would mean not just tolerating some human rights violations in some places, but every human rights violation everywhere, or at the very least all prevalent human rights violations. An endorsement of cultural, belief and regional relativism leaves only isolated aberrations as human rights violations. With cultural, belief and regional relativism, the notion of a consistent pattern of human rights violations would become a contradiction in terms.

For Westerners to argue for cultural or regional or belief relativism of human rights value is a form of racism or neo-colonialism. It is inappropriate for Westerners to say that human rights violations are acceptable for "them" though not for "us", that human rights violations in other cultures – or in other regions or amongst believers in other faiths – are not true violations but "just the way things are".

One cause of relativism is post-colonial guilt. Because in the past the West imposed too much, there is a tendency now to have a totally hands-off attitude, to assert too little. We go from one extreme to another, from demanding everything – complete conformity to contemporary Western values – to demanding nothing, not even conformity to those values the West shares with the rest of the world. However, neither extreme is appropriate. The West's past overbearing attitudes should not become an inhibitor, preventing the West from asserting human rights values in places where colonialism once reigned.

In Britain, not that long ago, drawing, quartering and hanging were accepted forms of punishment. Those practices ended because of the revulsion they caused. A prevalent attitude that those practices were "just part of British culture" would not have allowed them to end when they did. On the contrary, the prevalence of such an attitude would have kept them around longer than they were kept.

Perpetrators deny. If they cannot deny, because the evidence is overwhelming, they then excuse. Human rights relativism is one of a feeble litany of excuses perpetrators manufacture in an effort to achieve immunity for their violations.

We have heard the suggestion that a posture of relativity is more likely to cajole violators into compliance than is confrontation and condemnation of wrongdoing. Our own view is that conceding relativity is a dangerous game, by giving legitimacy to an excuse for human rights violations. When we talk to violators to encourage compliance, our audience is not just the violators. It is victims as well, and the global community as a whole. To accede to the notion of relativity is an abandonment of the victims and a disparagement of human rights activism.

Human rights discourse can be abused by those with a particular agenda. That abuse should be seen for what it is, an attempt to corrupt human rights discourse. We should combat the attempt, not change the concept of human rights because of the attempt.

For perpetrators, relativism is an excuse for violations. For outsiders, it is an excuse for inaction. Human rights violations cry out for remedies. The wrongs today, regrettably, are still so numerous and so far-flung that there is a tendency for us to throw up our hands, to walk away, to say that nothing can be done. An argument of relativism is an admission of defeat, an acceptance of powerlessness in the face of violations. We need to combat the argument of relativism to combat our own tendencies to passivity, the temptation to feel that fighting human rights violations is futile.

Human rights activists who accept the regional relativity of human rights, even if they overcome the temptation to do nothing, end up either proselytizing or bargaining. Human dignity for all is not a religion. Human rights advocacy should not be a crusade. Yet, if we accept the relativity of human rights, then we turn human rights advocacy into missionary work.

Human rights advocacy, to be effective, should not be a pitch for others to be like us. It should be a statement of solidarity with the victims, an attempt to end the victimization of those people who, in many cases, come from the same culture and region as the perpetrators. The sort of human rights advocacy which takes for granted that human rights values are "our" values but not yet "yours" abandons one of the most persuasive arguments for respecting human rights, the need through practice to realize already accepted ideals.

Human rights advocacy is the mobilization of shame, the exposure of hypocrisy, the reminder that governments and armed opposition groups are violating in practice the principles they have accepted in theory. Relativism means abandoning this technique of human rights activism, hamstringing human rights work, even where it is not stopped altogether.

Once we accept an argument of relativism, human rights standards become subject to bargaining. If human rights values are "our" values, but not "theirs", and we want respect for human rights, then that means that we want others to be like us. Respect for human rights becomes something we want. The retort inevitably follows: "We will give you what you want if you give us what we want." Human rights values become bargaining chips in the global marketplace.

Human rights advocates have no authority to bargain away the rights of victims. The end of oppression is not a favour perpetrators grant to Western human rights advocates. Human rights are the rights of the people in the places where the perpetrators wreak their havoc, not the wishes of those outside who commiserate with the victims.

Accepting relativism can mean far worse than just ignoring violations or advocating their end for the wrong reasons. Accepting relativism can mean replicating the violations.

Cultural, belief and regional diversity, after all, should be respected. It is a matter of simple politeness – a case of "when in Rome, do as the Romans do". If we are to respect diversity, and if we accept that human rights values are diverse, then, when Westerners are abroad, in order to respect local cultures and beliefs, Westerners should engage in behaviour that would amount to human rights violations at home. Westerners abroad would join the ranks of perpetrators out of respect for local cultures and beliefs.

Relativism is more than a theoretical argument about the nature of human rights. It has practical everyday consequences for how Westerners behave abroad. If we accept relativism, we will not just tolerate human rights violations abroad. We will end up replicating the violations when we are abroad.

How can we possibly say that we believe in human rights and at the same time participate in human rights violations? Yet, once we move into a foreign region, an acceptance in the relativity of human rights leads to that participation. Relativity of human rights is not just one way of approaching human rights. It is the negation of human rights.

Although there were many surprises in the Chinese government responses to our report, one of them was the very rejection of the concept of human rights. The Universal Periodic Review is a new element of the United Nations Human Rights Council created in 2006 to replace the failed U.N. Human Rights Commission. Under the Universal Periodic Review, every state gets reviewed once during a four-year cycle. China's turn came up February 2009 in Geneva.

Only states can intervene in the Universal Periodic Review Working Group debate. But it can be any state; it does not have to be a state which is a member of the Human Rights Council. The debate is an interactive dialogue, meaning China has a right to respond.

David Matas went to Geneva and lobbied governments to raise the violations identified in our organ-harvesting report. He asked that states, at the very least, request China's compliance with foundational rights, the respect for which would have made the violations we identified impossible. Many delegates did speak out for these foundational rights during the two hours of the Universal Periodic Review Working Group allocated to these speeches – but to no avail. The Government of China rejected virtually all these rights.

The Universal Periodic Review Working Group came out with a report tabulating the recommendations of states which spoke during debate. The Government of China reaction, which followed immediately upon release of the report, gave us a clear idea of what its earlier words had meant. It accepted some recommendations, mostly from other gross violator states which commended the Government of China for its efforts and encouraged it to keep on doing what it was doing. It added that it would consider other recommendations. There was also a long list of recommendations the Government of China rejected out of hand.

Here is a partial list of the recommendations the Government of China rejected:[168]

1) Germany recommended that China guarantee all citizens of China the exercise of religious freedom, freedom of belief and freedom of worshipping in private. The Government of China said that it would not accept this recommendation.

2) Canada, the United Kingdom, Hungary, the Czech Republic, France, Sweden and New Zealand recommended that China abolish all forms of arbitrary detention, including re-education-through-labour camps. The Government of China said no to this recommendation.

3) Canada recommended that China implement the recommendations of the U.N. Committee against Torture. As we wrote in Chapter Eight, the Committee took cognizance of the fact that the U.N. Special Rapporteur on Torture had asked for a full explanation of the source of organ transplants to explain away, if possible, the fact that an increase in organ transplant operations had coincided with the beginning of the persecution of Falun Gong practitioners. Further, the Committee recommended that China conduct or commission an independent investigation into the claims that Falun Gong practitioners had been subjected to torture and used for organ transplants. As well, the Committee proposed that China take measures to

197

ensure that those responsible for such abuses were prosecuted and punished. The Government of China said no here, too.

4) Finland recommended that China take effective measures to ensure that lawyers can defend their clients without fear of harassment. One example we gave in Chapter Fourteen is the case of Gao Zhisheng. To this recommendation also, the Government of China said no.

So with the Government of China, we have more than just a denial of the facts. There is a rejection of the standards. The Government of China, relying on its own particularity, says:

- No to freedom of belief

- Yes to forced labour

- Yes to arbitrary detention

- No to an independent investigation into the allegations that Falun Gong practitioners are being killed for their organs

- No to explaining the discrepancy between sources of organs and volume of organ transplants

- No to bringing perpetrators of organ transplant abuse to justice

- No to allowing human rights lawyers to defend their clients without harassment

When the Government of China talks about acceptance of human rights "in light of China's national realities", working towards "Chinese-style democracy", having its own "different views on the question of human rights", the foregoing is what in practice it means. It is noteworthy that Sudan, Egypt and Algeria, all states with poor human rights records, commended China during the Universal Periodic Review interactive debate for implementing human rights in harmony with its national realities.[169] It seemed as if they were saying: "Good excuse, wish we had thought of it ourselves."

Some governments, media and individuals often do what the Chinese Communist Party wants – not necessarily because the Party has asked them to do it, and not really because of any relativity of human rights values, but in order to curry favour with the current government in Beijing. There was something similar in what happened with Nazi Germany.

Nazi Germany was characterized by initiatives from the bureaucracy and military in line with Hitler's broadly but dimly-defined and vaguely-worded goals, in an attempt to meet his perceived wishes. Ian Kershaw has argued that many of the steps that led to the Holocaust were undertaken by German officials without express orders from Hitler, on the expectation, which turned out to be correct, that such initiatives would find favour with him. This behaviour has been characterized as "working towards the Führer".[170]

We see something like this with the Chinese government and its persecution of the Falun Gong. Outside of China, the obsession of the government over the Falun Gong is apparent and the level of its intervention, both to propagandize against the Falun Gong and to block any attempts to expose their persecution, is quite detailed. Nonetheless, it would be going too far to say that every propaganda and blocking effort is action by the Government of China or compliance with specific requests from the Government. In some cases, individuals take their own initiatives in an attempt to meet the perceived wishes of the Government. These individuals work towards the Communist Party of China.

In both Wellington and Auckland, New Zealand, Falun Gong participation in the annual Santa Claus parades in 2007 became an issue. The Wellington City Council and the Auckland Santa Parade Trust both initially refused to allow the Falun Gong to participate in their parades.

Auckland Regional Council deputy chairman Michael Barnett opposed the participation of the Falun Gong in the Auckland parade because, according to him, the Falun Gong "attack a country that New Zealand has a relationship with".[171] The Falun Gong, of course, do nothing of the sort. They only protest their own persecution.

Wellington parade organizers eventually backed down and allowed the Falun Gong to participate. Auckland remained adamant. Wellington, nonetheless, banned the Falun Gong from its 2008 Chinese New Year's Parade. Peter Dunne, leader of the New Zealand political party United Future, believes that the two city councils are scared of upsetting the Chinese government while free trade talks with New Zealand enter the final stages.[172]

Had the Chinese embassy in New Zealand made specific requests to Auckland and Wellington not to allow the Falun Gong to participate in the parades? That is perfectly possible given the pattern of Chinese behaviour. But there is no public record of such a request and there is another explanation – that both the Wellington City Council and the Auckland Santa Parade Trust were working towards the Communist

Party of China, anticipating its wishes and taking their own initiatives to attempt to please the Party.

The Australian Minister of Foreign Affairs since March 2002 has been signing a certificate once a month banning Falun Gong adherents from displaying banners outside the Chinese embassy in Canberra. Australia is the only democratic country to impose such a restriction on the Falun Gong.[173]

Former Mayor Sam Sullivan of Vancouver in June 2006 issued an order that Falun Gong protests in front of the Chinese consulate, which by then had been going on for five years, must stop. Sullivan acknowledged that the Falun Gong display bothered the Chinese. He also said that he has heard from people in the Government of Canada who said the protest is not helpful to promoting closer links with China.[174]

The Government of Iceland in June 2002 denied entry to Iceland to Falun Gong practitioners who were planning to come (to protest Falun Gong persecution) during the state visit of Chinese president Jiang Zemin. The Government provided a list of these practitioners to Icelandair, which denied them boarding. Others, who arrived with other carriers, were deported on arrival or detained, at first, for deportation. After a media storm, those detained for deportation were released. The list came from the Government of China.[175] Iceland's Parliamentary ombudsman concluded in December 2005 that this denial of entry and deportation violated Icelandic law.[176]

French police arrested Falun Gong practitioners in January 2004 who were demonstrating in Paris during the visit of Chinese president Hu Jintao. The demonstrators were wearing yellow scarves. The only reason the police gave for the arrests was that "yellow scarves are illegal in France today". Those arrested were questioned for two hours and then released.[177]

Hong Kong police arrested and charged Falun Gong practitioners with obstruction for a protest outside the Chinese government liaison office in March 2002. The protesters were convicted in June 2002. Local human rights activists and opposition politicians called the case a political prosecution to appease Beijing.[178] The convictions were eventually overturned on appeal.[179]

The Singapore state prosecutor charged nine Falun Gong practitioners with assembling without a permit because the nine handed out flyers in the downtown area in October 2005, protesting persecution of the Falun Gong in China. The charges were issued in July 2006, nine months after the event, during the visit of Li Lanqing, a former head of the 610 Office. The Human Rights Law Foundation suggested that the charges were geared in part to prevent practitioners of Falun Gong from staging a protest during the visit of this official.[180] Judge Amy Tang in June 2007 found five of the accused guilty.[181]

Thai police rounded up ten Falun Gong practitioners and their families in December 2007, while the practitioners were holding a demonstration outside the Chinese embassy in Bangkok, protesting Chinese human rights violations. The protesters were charged with not carrying passports and were kept in a detention centre.

These practitioners were refugees, and recognized as such by the Office of the United Nations High Commissioner for Refugees. They did not have passports because of the Chinese government policy of denying passport renewal to Falun Gong. The *Bangkok Post* reported, "China has been known to put pressure on its close allies, such as Thailand, to suppress the group's (Falun Gong's) activities."[182]

If there is one thing you need to know to understand the Government of China, it is its treatment of the Falun Gong. When the Government of China treats the Falun Gong as its number one public enemy, when, to all appearances, it spends more staff time, money, and effort on the Falun Gong at its embassies and consulates around the world than on anything else, when it fills its prisons and labour camps with Falun Gong, this obsession tells us nothing about the Falun Gong. It tells us volumes about the Government of China. A focus on Chinese preoccupation with the Falun Gong gives us clearer insights into the mentality and dynamics of the Chinese party-state than any other focus.

Yet, in Chinese studies departments at universities around the world, almost without exception, there are no courses, no research projects, no publications, no guest lectures on the Falun Gong. China studies departments around the world are thunderingly silent about the persecution of the Falun Gong, despite the fact that the persecution tells us more about China than virtually anything else. In China studies departments, the Falun Gong is studiously ignored.

It is as if university physics departments were to ignore Einstein's theory of relativity, as if university English literature departments were to ignore Shakespeare. How could this happen?

When universities ignore something so central to China, and so obvious, it is not out of ignorance. It comes from a desire not to antagonize China's political elite. China scholars feel they need the co-operation of the Government of China, at the very least to get visas to enter

China, to pursue their work. In order to ensure that co-operation, they stay away from a subject the Government of China would not want them to consider. Scholars have enough integrity not to take the Chinese government line on the Falun Gong. But if they say anything else, Chinese officials hit the roof. To avoid that reaction, they say nothing.

In the face of the assertion of Chinese particularism, we must stand for universal human rights values. Freedom of belief is a right which must be respected everywhere. Forced labour and arbitrary detention must end everywhere. Human rights lawyers everywhere should be able to defend their clients in freedom and safety. Credible allegations of human rights violations should be independently investigated and perpetrators brought to justice everywhere. That is what universality means.

Chapter Sixteen

Ending the abuse

We do not consider this book to be the final word on this subject. There is much that, given the opportunity, we would rather have done before we wrote this book. But it would have meant pursuing avenues of investigation which were not open to us.

We would like to see Chinese hospital records of transplants. Are there consents on file? Are there records of sources of organs?

Donors can survive many forms of transplant operations. No one can survive a full liver or heart donation. But kidney donations are normally not fatal. Where are the surviving donors? We would like to do a random sampling of donations to see if we could locate the donors.

Family members of deceased donors should either know of the consents of the donors or have given the consents themselves. Here, too, we would like to do a random sampling of immediate family members of deceased donors to see if the families either consented themselves to the donations or were aware of the consent of the donor.

China has engaged in a major expansion of organ transplant facilities in recent years. This expansion likely would have been accompanied by feasibility studies indicating organ sources. We would like to see these feasibility studies.

It is easy enough to make a number of specific recommendations about ending the abuse. These are:

1) Organ-harvesting in China from all prisoners should cease.

2) All detention facilities, including forced labour camps, must be opened for international community inspection through the International Committee for the Red Cross or some other human rights or humanitarian organization.

3) Gao Zhisheng should be freed. His right to practise his profession should be restored.

4) The military in China should get out of the organ transplant business.

5) Foreign states should enact extra-territorial legislation, penalizing participation in organ-harvesting without consent.

6) State medical funding systems should deny reimbursement for commercial organ transplants abroad and aftercare funding for those benefiting from such transplants.

7) Any person known to be involved in trafficking in the organs of prisoners in China should be barred entry by all foreign countries.

8) Until China stops harvesting organs from prisoners of any sort,
   i) foreign governments should not issue visas to doctors from China seeking to travel abroad for the purpose of training in organ or bodily tissue transplantation,
   ii) foreign medical transplant personnel should not travel to China for training or collaboration in transplant surgery,
   iii) contributions to scholarly journals on transplant research drawn from the Chinese experience should be rejected,
   iv) medical professionals abroad should actively discourage their patients from travelling to China for transplant surgery,
   v) pharmaceutical companies should not export anti-rejection drugs or any other drugs solely used in transplantation surgery to China,
   vi) foreign states should ban the export of anti-rejection drugs or any other drugs solely used in transplantation surgery to China.

9) The onus should be on foreign professionals to determine beyond any reasonable doubt that the source of organ donation in China is voluntary before there is any referral to China or any co-operation with China relating to organ transplants.

10) The medical profession in every foreign country should set up a voluntary reporting system to accumulate aggregate data about patients who have travelled to China for transplants.

11) Chinese hospitals should keep records of the source of every transplant. These records should be available for inspection by international human rights officials.

12) Every organ transplant donor should consent to the donation in writing. These consents should be available for inspection by international human rights officials.

13) The Government of China should promote voluntary organ donation from its own population.

14) Foreign states should issue travel advisories warning their populations that organ transplants in China are sourced almost entirely from unconsenting prisoners, whether sentenced to death or Falun Gong practitioners.

15) The repression, imprisonment and mistreatment of Falun Gong practitioners should stop.

16) The Government of China should explain the discrepancy in the number of transplants and the numbers from identifiable sources of organs.

17) Governmental, non-governmental and intergovernmental human rights organizations should take seriously the charges this report addresses and make their own determinations as to whether or not they are true.

18) The Government of China should conduct or commission an independent investigation into the claims that some Falun Gong practitioners have been subjected to torture and used for organ transplants and take measures, as appropriate, to ensure that those responsible for such abuses are prosecuted and punished.

19) China and every other state now party to the Convention against Torture should accede to the Optional Protocol to the Convention against Torture.

20) The current form of international dialogue with the Government of China over human rights should cease. In hindsight, governments erred in agreeing to the talk fests in exchange for abandoning the yearly motion criticizing China's government at the then U.N. Human Rights Commission.

To accept these recommendations does not require accepting that the allegations about organ-harvesting of Falun Gong practitioners are true. We suggest adoption of these recommendations in any case. The recommendations make sense and could be implemented whether the allegations are true or false. Several recommendations are addressed to the international community, asking the community to promote respect within China of international standards about organ transplants.

We are well aware that the Government of China denies the allegations. We suggest that the most credible and effective way for it to assert that denial is to implement the recommendations addressed to it, which could be implemented whether the allegations are true or false. If these recommendations were implemented, the allegations considered here could no longer be made.

To those who are sceptical about the allegations, we ask you to ask yourself what you would suggest to prevent, in any state, allegations like these from becoming true. The commonsensical precautions to prevent the sort of activity here alleged have pretty much all been missing in China.

Every state, and not just China, needs to lay in defences in order to prevent the harvesting of organs from the unwilling, the marginalized, the defenceless. Whatever one thinks of the allegations – and we reiterate we believe them to be true – China is remarkably undefended to prevent the sorts of activities here discussed from happening. Until the recent legislation was in force, many basic precautions to prevent the abuses here discussed from happening were not in place. That legislation does not fill the gap unless and until it is comprehensively implemented. We urge the government of China, whatever they think of our conclusions about organ-harvesting from Falun Gong practitioners, to build up their defences against even the possibility of the harvesting of organs from the unwilling.

Recommending specific changes begs a basic question. Is reform possible? Are we dealing with just a regrettable lapse or a behaviour intrinsic to the current regime?

To answer that question, we have to answer a prior question. Why are Chinese Communists persecuting Falun Gong practitioners?

The Communist Party of China represses every belief system it does not control. The repression of the Falun Gong in 1999 just seemed Party business as usual. When the Communist Party is repressing every other community of belief it does not control, it is hardly surprising that it also banned the practice of Falun Gong.

What is striking about the repression of the Falun Gong is not so much the fact of repression as the extent of repression. Practitioners of Falun Gong are persecuted far more, far worse than adherents of any other belief system.

Falun Gong has the ignominious honour of leading by far the parade of human rights victims in China. They represent two-thirds of the torture victims and half the people in detention in re-education-through-labour camps.

Falun Gong practitioners and prisoners sentenced to death are the sole groups systematically targeted for organ-harvesting. We know that this is so because only Falun Gong practitioners and prisoners sentenced to death are systematically blood tested and organ examined, a necessary precondition for organ sourcing.

The extremes of language the Chinese regime uses against Falun Gong are unparalleled, unmatched by the comparatively mild criticisms China has of the victims the West is used to defending. The documented yearly arbitrary killings and disappearances of Falun Gong exceed by far the totals for any other victim group.

The question which arises from all this is not so much why the Falun Gong is being persecuted. To believe in anything the Party does not control, if you live in China, means you run the risk of persecution. The question, rather, is: Why is the Party persecuting Falun Gong practitioners so much worse, so much more than adherents of other beliefs? Why is Falun Gong, alone of all the belief systems which the Communist Party represses, the victim of organ-harvesting?

There are two obvious answers for organ-harvesting: the large numbers and the grotesque incitement. Only the Falun Gong are a large enough number in the Chinese detention system to constitute, on their own, a captive organ donor bank throughout the country. Only the Falun Gong are dehumanized so viciously that their jailers and the hospitals who pay them off do not even think of them as human.

But that does not get us very far. Why are the Falun Gong jailed in such large numbers? Why are they so dehumanized? We have a number of suggested explanations.

1. One is simply the numbers. Falun Gong before it was banned had, according to a 1999 Government estimate, 70 million adherents. That year, the Communist Party of China membership was an estimated 60 million. In Beijing alone, before the banning, there were more than 2,000 Falun Gong practice sites. Practitioners were found everywhere, at all levels of society and government and within the inner reaches of the Communist Party.

    A group that size, no matter what its belief, attracts the attention of a repressive government. The Falun Gong, before their banning, were not anti-Communist. But they weren't Communist either. For the Communists, that was a matter of concern. These were people who had no particular fealty to the Communist Party of China.

2. When it comes to victimization of the innocent at home, the Chinese Communist government is much like other tyrannies. The chosen enemies vary from country to country, but, whatever the country, the story is much the same – innocents suffer so that despots can stay in power.

    At one level, the Chinese Communist Party repression of Falun Gong is sheer totalitarian nuttiness, the manufacturing of an enemy out of thin air, a form of paranoia to which the followers of Joseph Stalin and Mao Tse Tung are prone. The Communist Party needs enemies in order to justify their continuing hold on power, and the Falun Gong had the bad luck to be around in sufficient numbers and available to fill the enemy slot.

    For a communist regime, far worse than having bitter enemies is having no enemies at all. Without anyone to demonize, communists are left speechless when justifying their hold on power.

3. Another trait of the Falun Gong community which led to their being singled out is their principles. In brief, the Falun Gong stand for three basic beliefs – compassion, tolerance and truth. Anyone who believes in any one of these principles spells trouble for the Communist Party government – a cruel, repressive, dishonest regime. Tens of millions of Chinese believing in all three principles had to give the Party chills.

    The worst nightmare of a gangster is an honest person. The nemesis of the corrupt are those who will not take a bribe. The venal speak a common language with the unscrupulous. With the principled, dialogue is impossible. All that is left is force.

4. The collapse of the Soviet Union and Communism in Central and Eastern Europe haunts the Chinese Communist Party. The practice of Falun Gong went from a standing start in 1992 to numbers greater than the membership of the Party within the space of seven years, spreading rapidly throughout China immediately after the Tiananmen Square massacre, the collapse of the Soviet Union and the loss of Communist Party control in Central Asia and Eastern and Central Europe. The Party in China feared a similar collapse, a similar loss of control.

When the Party saw its own Chinese nationals in the tens of millions engaging publicly in a form of exercise which had an underlying belief system completely divorced from communism, its leaders fantasized the Falun Gong as the engine of their destruction. They turned a group of innocents into an enemy and launched a persecution to combat an imaginary foe.

5.   Lack of structure is a factor. Falun Gong is neither a movement nor an organization; it is not even people. Rather, it is a set of exercises with a spiritual foundation. The exercises can be done by anyone, anywhere, at any time, though commonly they are done once daily in groups. Those who are interested can begin the exercises whenever they want and stop whenever they want. A person need not register with anyone or join anything to practise the exercises. All information about how to do the exercises is publicly available.

Those who practise Falun Gong have no organizational leadership. Li Hongzhi got things going. He has written books and given public lectures, widely available in print and on the Internet, which have inspired individual Falun Gong practitioners. He is the founder of the practice, its first teacher, a spiritual leader, but not an organization leader.

There are some Falun Gong practitioners who have formed and joined support organizations, Falun Dafa associations. Falun Dafa associations are local or national. There is no one international Falun Dafa Association.

These associations encompass only a portion of Falun Gong practitioners. They may facilitate some Falun Gong activities, but they do not represent or lead or organize all Falun Gong practitioners.

These associations make representations to government on behalf of Falun Gong practitioners. In formulating these representations, they operate by consensus of all and any of the practitioners who volunteer to participate in the discussion about what those representations should be.

The amorphous nature of Falun Gong meant that it was impossible for the Communist Party to control it. Because other beliefs are organized, the Government of China has responded in part by attempting to take over the organizations.

There is a Chinese-government-appointed Buddhist Panchen Lama, Chinese-government-selected Roman Catholic bishops,

Chinese-government-chosen Muslim imams. These designations mitigate the attacks the Government of China launches against these beliefs, since it does not want to undermine its own appointees.

If Falun Gong had a leadership, the Party, as it had done with the major religions, would have appointed some of its cronies and said that they were the leadership of the Falun Gong. But Falun Gong does not lend itself to this sort of usurpation.

For Falun Gong, since there is no organization and no leadership, there is no one the Government of China can appoint to head the Falun Gong. Not being inhibited by undermining its own appointees, the Government's attacks on the Falun Gong know no bounds.

6. The mobilization capacity of Falun Gong practitioners alarmed and frightened the Communist Party. Before Falun Gong was banned in July, 1999, its adherents gathered regularly throughout China to do their exercises.

The April 25, 1999 event (the Falun Gong gathering to appeal the beating and arrest of their fellow practitioners in Tianjin two days earlier) was the largest gathering in Beijing since the Tiananmen Square massacre. Many of the leadership in the Party had no advance warning of this event and were startled.

It is worth remembering here the April 25, 1999 letter from President Jiang to standing members of the Political Bureau of Central Committee of the Chinese Communist Party about that gathering. The text of the letter is in Chapter Two of this book. To recap, Jiang wrote in part:

"Without being noticed by humans or ghosts, more than 10,000 people gathered around the gate of the centre of the Party and State Power Centre, for a whole day ... However, our relevant departments had found nothing at all beforehand, even though from the Internet one can quickly find the local contacts of the Falun Gong organization ... This incident has been the one that has the most participants among many other events since the 89's incident. I have repeatedly stressed the need to prevent the small from becoming large, and to report all major events to us. Since 1992, Falun Gong became involved in the activities of a considerable number of social groups of party members and cadres, intellectuals, servicemen, workers and peasants, yet it has not aroused our vigilance. I am deeply ashamed ..."

7. The Falun Gong community was the first in China to take advantage of modern technology to gather in large numbers. The growth of the practice of Falun Gong and mobilization of its practitioners is directly attributable to the advent of the Internet and cellphones. Through cellphones and the Internet, it is possible for large numbers of people to do the same thing at the same time, be at the same place at the same time, without organization or leadership. For Falun Gong practitioners, one can say: "Make publicly available the exercises and beliefs, spread the technology of cellphones and the Internet and they will come, without organization or leadership." This phenomenon was unknown in China before it was manifested through the Falun Gong.

    Again we can turn to the words of then President Jiang. He wrote:

    "Its [Falun Gong's] transmission of information is so rapid. It is indeed rare ... The rapid development of information technology is posing new subjects of studies. Our various departments have quite many computers. Has anyone noticed these new social trends?"

8. Mirror imaging worked against the Falun Gong community. Though the Falun Gong is not an organization with a leadership, the Communist Party of China is. When you are a hammer, everything looks like a nail. The Communist Party of China saw the Falun Gong community as a mirror of itself, organizationally similar but ideologically different.

    The absence of organization and leadership of Falun Gong has not stopped the Government of China from believing such things exist. Chinese officials just think the structure is hidden. The very lack of visibility of leadership and organization has led the Government of China to greater suspicion, greater fears.

    President Jiang in his April 25 letter wrote:

"Its organization is so strictly disciplined ... Is there a behind-the-scene 'master' in the planning command?"

Calling an uncoordinated mass of individuals engaged in parallel activities an organization with a leadership may on its own just be an innocent mistake. But once one starts attributing anti-state activity to this imagined organization, the mistake ceases to be innocent. The error becomes paranoic, a conspiracy fantasy.

When the Communist Party leadership saw a group of people doing the same thing at the same time, they were intellectually incapable of attributing this spontaneous activity to cellphones and the Internet. Many in the leadership of the Party simply had no idea of modern mobilization capacity. What they saw instead is what they knew – an organization, a hierarchy, a leadership, a plan, rather than what was in fact staring them in the face.

The Party projected onto others, a disparate group of Falun Gong practitioners, its own manner of operation. The persecution of the Falun Gong began and continues with a simple mischaracterization.

9. A large measure of the persecution against Falun Gong can be attributed to petty personal jealousy of then-President Jiang Zemin. Initially, it was Jiang alone in the central leadership of the Party who wanted Falun Gong banned. Others eventually fell into line because he was insistent and because he was the person in charge.

One can see this jealousy in the language he used. He wrote on April 25, 1999:

"Can't the Marxism our communists have, the materialism, atheism we believe in really win over that suit of stuff aired by Falun Gong? If that were not the case, would it not be a thumping joke?"[183]

He was concerned that he personally would be seen as a "thumping joke".

Jiang attempted to provide a cover for the continuation in power of the Communist Party of China, after the end of communism elsewhere, with his own ideological speeches and writings. Yet, outside of the factotums of the Communist Party who had to pay attention to what Jiang wrote for the sake of their own careers, Jiang's excursions into communist post-modern philosophy developed no following. Jiang was envious that something proposed by an outsider, Li Hongzhi, could become so popular while his own writings languished in obscurity.

10. Falun Gong detainees are more vulnerable than other detainees because of their refusal to self-identify, described in Chapter Three. Though this refusal was done to protect family, friends and relatives, it left them remarkably undefended.

11. Repressed democracy activists, journalists, human rights defenders, Tibetan and Christian activists generate more sympathy than the Falun Gong because they are more familiar to the West, more in tune with Western sensibilities. The Falun Gong are recent (started in 1992), foreign, without an obvious link to global traditions.

To outsiders, there is the immediate, albeit superficial, strangeness of the name Falun Gong. The words "Falun" and "Gong" in Western languages mean nothing.

For the Communists, victimizing the Falun Gong is a crime which is easier to get away with than victimizing other, better-known groups. Falun Gong victims are often people without Western connections or Western languages. It is much easier for outsiders to relate to victims who have universal labels – journalists, human rights defenders, democracy activists – than a group with a name which means nothing to most ears.

It is also harder to misrepresent the known than the unknown. When the Communists slur Tibetan Buddhists or the Christian house churches, we know that they are talking nonsense. When the Communists slur the Falun Gong, many people are not sure whether there is any basis for the charges.

The incitement to hatred against the Falun Gong, like all incitement to bigotry, has an impact. The place with the most ferocious impact is China, where the propaganda is uncontradicted. But the incitement has an insidious effect everywhere.

Even in democratic states, people may know enough not to swallow Chinese propaganda whole. But there is often a tendency to think that where there is smoke, there is fire. The Chinese noise about the practice of Falun Gong confuses and obscures. Many of those who do not accept Chinese propaganda in its entirety nonetheless hold the view that there must be something improper about Falun Gong behind all the Chinese government charges. Outsiders do not have either the acquired knowledge or the time and energy to do the research to contradict Chinese Communist propaganda.

12. The Communist Party fright from the rise of the Falun Gong came from content as well as form. Falun Gong is authentically Chinese, rooted in and blended from ancient Chinese spiritual and exercise traditions.

As exercise, it is a form of qi gong, a set of Chinese exercise practices. The form most familiar to Westerners is Tai Chi. But there are many such Chinese exercise practices.

Nor does Falun Gong have just any spiritual foundation. Its spiritual formulation has direct links with Taoist and Buddhist disciplines, ancient Chinese beliefs.

The global TV network run in the main by Falun Gong practitioners is called NTD TV. NTD stands for New Tang Dynasty. The old Tang Dynasty, which ran from 618 to 907 A.D., was a particularly glorious period of Chinese history, a period to which Chinese look back with pride.

The Falun Gong, then, are an outgrowth from ancient Chinese traditions; they are its modern form. They are the face of the real China, the grassroots China, the China of the people, in Marxist terms the China of the proletariat.

It is no coincidence that the Falun Gong emerged in 1992 at the time of the collapse of the Iron Curtain and the disintegration of the Soviet Union. What was to fill the ideological gap left by the global breakdown of communism? For China, it seemed, the answer was Falun Gong.

Once the Communist state of China renounced its own socialist ideology, many beliefs sprang up to take its place. Once Communism ceased to stand for anything, the number of people believing in something other than Communism increased dramatically. But the predominance was Falun Gong, an updating and intertwining of the ancient Chinese exercise and spiritual traditions.

The threat the Communist Party of China saw from the Falun Gong in 1999, when repression was decreed, was not political; but it was and is ideological. To the Chinese Communist Party, Falun Gong was a regression, a huge leap backward, back to where China was before the Party took over. For Falun Gong to prevail would mean a China that would continue as if the Chinese Communist Party never existed, aside from the scars the Party left behind.

The problem for the Communists was not just that Falun Gong is so authentically Chinese. It is also that Communism is so patently foreign, being a Western ideological import into China. Communists saw a widespread, popular Chinese-based ideology as cutting out from under them the very ground on which they stood.

Tolerating the Falun Gong would not have meant, at least in the short run, the collapse of the current regime. But it would have meant the disappearance of whatever ideological presence the Communist Party still had in the hearts and minds of the Chinese people. Once there was no one left to believe in Communism, even within the Communist Party, the loosening of the Party's grip on power could not be far behind.

The rise of Falun Gong exposed a fault line in Communist rule of China. Is the only real and practical way to end the abuses against the Falun Gong ending the Chinese Communist Party's hold on China?

The Chinese constitution states: "The State respects and preserves human rights."[184] But it does not. The problem is not just hypocrisy. Nor is it the inevitable failure, that we all face, to achieve the ideal. The problem is embedded in the constitution itself.

The Chinese state, according to the Chinese constitution, is a "democratic dictatorship".[185] The notion of a democratic dictatorship is a contradiction in terms. "Democracy" means rule of the people. "Dictatorship" means that someone is being told what to do, dictated to, by someone else. In a dictatorship there are those who give orders and those who are expected to follow them.

The Chinese constitution defines democracy. It states: "The state organs of the People's Republic of China apply the principle of democratic centralism."[186] Again that is a contradiction in terms. "Centralism" means rule of the centre, and not of the people, who are everywhere and not just in the centre.

The preamble to the constitution refers to a system of multi-party co-operation and political consultation system under the leadership of the Communist Party of China. So the "centre" of democratic centralism in China is the Communist Party. Democratic dictatorship means Communist Party dictatorship.

What is Communism today? Karl Marx in 1875 defined Communism succinctly with this slogan: "From each according to his means; to each according to his needs."

However, Communist states which tried to realize this ideal failed. When the state took away the wealth of those with means, no one had an incentive to accumulate means. When the state catered to claimed needs, needs expanded without limit. The work ethic collapsed. Communist states became aggregations of whining malingerers, doing nothing but asserting needs and waiting for the state to meet them.

Chinese Communist Party leader Deng Xiao Ping anticipated the collapse of Communism and shifted ideologies. He said in 1984, shortly before the disappearance of Communism from Eastern and Central Europe: "To get rich is glorious." What he did not say is that there are some ways of getting rich which are shameful. He introduced a system of carnivore capitalism without the rule of law. The arbitrary power of the state became the arbitrary licence to do whatever became necessary to make a buck.

But what was left of Communism when its ideological core was gutted? More or less nothing except the desire of those already in power to remain in power. The new Communist slogan became: From each according to their distance from the people in power; to each according to their proximity to the people in power.

The fact that the Communists in China had gutted their own ideology did not change their old bad habit of repression. On the contrary, the reflex of repression became ever more dangerous.

Communism today in China is an ideology of repression for those who object to the rule of the Party, of immunity for those in power, and of wealth accumulation for the ruling elite. For those out of power, there is nothing in which to believe. But the people who will succeed those in power are out of power today. When they come to power, Communism in China will be finished.

We can be more specific. One can think of ethical systems in either positive or negative terms, what they stand for or what they reject. Ethical systems are both religious and secular. For both, there is a connection between the standards and the environments in which they emerge.

The connection is most obvious for secular ethical systems. The most clear-cut are the international war crimes tribunals – the International Military Tribunal, the International Criminal Tribunal for the Former Yugoslavia and the International Criminal Tribunal for Rwanda. The standards set out in the instruments governing these tribunals existed before the crimes were committed; otherwise to prosecute the crimes would violate the principle against retroactive punishment. Regardless, the fact of the articulation of the standards at the times and places they were set out is directly linked to immediate past events. The tribunals are a reaction to the war crimes which preceded them.

One can say that more generally about the present international human rights structure. Though the concept of human rights and its standards existed well before the Holocaust, its centrality to international discourse today and its detailed evolution are a statement in positive form of revulsion to the Holocaust.

One can say something similar of historical human rights standards such as the British Magna Carta, the American Bill of Rights in the U.S. constitution, or the French Declaration of the Rights of Man. None of these sets of standards descended out of the blue. They state rights in reaction to wrongs. Though the phrase "never again" has been associated in particular with the Holocaust, it is a philosophical underpinning to all human rights standards. Human rights standards have differed over time in detail and emphasis because what they were reacting to, what they wanted through the standards to prevent from happening, differed.

While the link between secular wrongs and secular standards is more straightforward, one can draw the same link between secular wrongs and spiritually-based ethical standards. When a spiritual system emerges, there is more going on than just a rejection of surrounding wrongs. The rejection is not the whole genesis, but it is part of it.

There is a connection between Jewish slavery in Egypt and the ethical standards of the Jewish religion. A refrain embedded in Jewish liturgy is: "Remember that we were slaves in the land of Egypt." One can think of Jewish ethical standards, at least in part, as a rejection of the treatment Jews received in Egypt and a commitment never themselves to behave that way.

Similarly, one can think of Christianity as a reaction to the brutality of the Roman Empire. The cross, the symbol of the Christian religion, is a reminder and transfiguration of Roman cruelty.

The rapid growth of the Falun Gong in China in the early 90s can be explained in these terms as well, although it is not the whole explanation. It would be natural, once China was suffering from an ideological void brought about by the worldwide collapse of Communism and its gutting of ideological content within China, for a spiritual system grounded in ancient Chinese beliefs to fill the void. With the growth of the Falun Gong, there was more going on than that. There was also a reaction to Communist Chinese wrongs.

When one reads today the ten commandments, they may seem trite. Who argues today for, say, the right to kill? One way to appreciate their significance is to consider the murderous environment from which they emerged.

As noted earlier, Falun Gong is based on three simple ethical principles – compassion, truthfulness and tolerance. These principles too, in isolation, may seem trite. One way of appreciating their significance is considering the wrongs of Chinese Communism. If one had to describe the Communist regime in China in three words, cruel, dishonest and intolerant would pretty much sum it up. The Falun Gong is a reaction to this cruelty, dishonesty, and intolerance, a statement that these wrongs should be inflicted never again. The Falun Gong are an assertion of differentiation, a statement that the Falun Gong do not want to be like the Chinese Communists.

What does all this have to do with the future of China? Friedrich Hegel explained the evolution of history as the evolution of thought. Hegel explained that thought developed as a conceptual hierarchy. Each level of the hierarchy is more sophisticated than the one before. Each level grows out of the one before. The engine for development of this hierarchy is the dialectic. The dialectic is a process of thesis, antithesis, synthesis.

Karl Marx adopted this dialectical analysis but shifted it to the economic sphere. World history, to Marx, could be explained as the working of a sequence of economic theses, antitheses and syntheses.

We can think of Communism in China as a thesis, or a sequence of theses – spiritual, political and economic. Economically, the thesis of socialism has already been replaced by its antithesis, unbridled capitalism. But Communist China is still stuck in the thesis stage of its history for political and spiritual thought.

What is the spiritual antithesis of Chinese Communism? It is surely Falun Gong. By asserting the values of compassion, truthfulness and tolerance, the Falun Gong have presented to China the complete opposite of what Chinese Communism has meant in practice for the people of China. Chinese Communists do not assert the values of cruelty, dishonesty and intolerance. But they have practised them. In the everyday reality of China, that is what Communism has meant; that is what Communism has brought.

Communist rule in China was founded on an economic concept, socialism, which it has abandoned. The current regime believes in nothing, has little popular support and stays in power through corruption, propaganda, incitement to hatred and brute force. A regime which has no ideological justification is fragile. But what would replace it? China is at the edge of a chasm. It may well fall into the abyss. But if it gets to the other side, what is to be found there?

The Falun Gong, despite the fears they aroused in then-President Jiang Zemin, who bore primary responsibility for their repression, are not the candidate one might think of first as replacing Communism in China. Falun Gong has no political ideology nor political platform. If a revolution in China were to happen tomorrow and someone wished to hand over power to the Falun Gong, it would be hard to figure out who should be given the power, since there is no leadership amongst the group. Moreover, if one were arbitrarily to pick a few Falun Gong practitioners and make them the Government of China, it would be hard to guess what they might do – aside from ending human rights violations – since there is no Falun Gong political agenda.

Nonetheless, one cannot ignore the significance of belief systems as organizing principles. A parallel is the adoption of Christianity as the official religion of the Roman Empire. Even though Christianity began, at least from one perspective, at least in part, as a reaction to the brutality of the Roman Empire, even though the Roman Empire persecuted Christians most cruelly, even though Christianity had no political agenda and urged its followers to "render unto Caesar that which is Caesar's", eventually the Roman Empire became Christian.

Emperor Constantine converted to Christianity in 312 A.D. Emperor Theodosius made Christianity the official religion of the empire in 391 A.D. Belief in Christianity had grown so strong and belief in traditional Roman values had grown so weak that Christianity became a better organizing idiom for the empire than the old Roman values.

Religious conversion is not only or even primarily practical. Yet when the leaders of an empire convert from one belief system to another, there is a measure of practicality in what they are doing.

One can see the same happening in China. Communism today is incapable of holding China together. At some time the leadership will realize that they need a better set of principles than they have got if they are going to maintain China as a going concern. The successors of

Mao, each in their own way, have been attempting to identify those principles, without any success.

The person who got it right was Li Hongzhi. Though his writings had no political content or intent, he managed to articulate a set of beliefs which reverberates with the Chinese people, the Chinese soul. At some point, the leadership of China will realize this.

Repressive regimes sometimes are dislodged. But when they are not, they rot from within. With repressive regimes, insiders victimize outsiders. But the insiders of tomorrow are the outsiders of today. Nepotism forestalls this phenomenon since the leadership does not victimize its own children. But a country as large as China cannot be ruled by nepotism alone.

When the victims get to power, they abandon the ideology which victimized them and cast about for a new one. It is just a matter of time before they alight on the Falun Gong, the most compelling belief system to come out of China since the fall of the Iron Curtain.

The Chinese leadership today treats the Falun Gong as their worst enemy, imprisoning and torturing them more than any other group, killing only them and prisoners sentenced to death for their organs. At some point, they will realize that the Falun Gong are their best friends, an authentic Chinese belief system that is capable of keeping China united, capable of keeping China – to use the catchword of the muddled ideology of current Chinese President Hu Jintao – harmonious.

China one day will be predominantly Falun Gong not because the current set of Falun Gong practitioners will one day take over the leadership of China, but because the leadership of China will one day become Falun Gong practitioners. In the wings of the stage of Chinese history stands a Constantine.

Endnotes

Chapter One

1   Human Rights Watch, "Organ Procurement and Judicial Execution in China", August 1994.

Chapter Two

2   *The Black Book of Communism,* Harvard University Press, 1999; Jung Chand and Jon Halliday, *Mao: The Unknown Story,* Knopf, 2005.

3   See Amnesty International and Human Rights Watch annual reports for China.

4   U.N. Commission on Human Rights: Report of the Special Rapporteur on torture and other cruel, inhuman or degrading treatment or punishment, Manfred Nowak, on his Mission to China from November 20 to December 2, 2005, E/CN.4/2006/6/Add.6, March 10, 2006.

5   Ibid, paragraph 42.

6   Danny Schechter, *Falun Gong's Challenge to China,* Akashic Books, 2000, pages 44 to 46.

7   We found this letter in Chinese on the Beijing Spring website <beijingspring.com>. Website addresses of specific items are constantly changing as webmasters reorganize websites. Also, website addresses within China often disappear as the Government of China/ Communist Party of China shifts its views on what should be publicly accessible. At our own website, www.organharvestinvestigation.net, we keep website addresses up to date. As well, we have archived all material coming from within China and provided links to the archived material when the original source disappears. Rather than provide in this book Internet links valid as of the date of the writing of the book, we refer the reader to our website, which has up-to-date links.

8-11   See endnote 7 above.

12   China. Chinese Central Politburo Meeting. Directive from Comrade Jiang Zemin, regarding an urgent and fast way to solve the Falun Gong problem 7 Jun. 1999. For website reference, see endnote 7 above.

13   This information comes from an interview with Li Baigen who attended the meeting. He was then assistant director of the Beijing Municipal Planning office. He is now resident in the United States. The U.S. Department of State Country Report for China for 1999 refers to the meeting, but not the quote.

14   See endnote 7 above.

15   See www.organharvestinvestigation.net Report Appendix 8. Despite the police recommendation, the Attorney General decided not to prosecute on freedom of speech grounds. This decision was challenged in court unsuccessfully. The Court ruled it would not interfere with the exercise of discretion of the Attorney General.

16   Article 58.

17   U.S. Department of State 2005 Country Reports on Human Rights Practices - China, March 8, 2006. Website reference is available at www.organharvestinvestigation.net

18   2008 Report on International Religious Freedom: China. Website reference is available at www.organharvestinvestigation.net

Chapter Three

19   International Convention for the Protection of All Persons from Enforced Disappearance, Article 2.

Chapter Four

20   "I Had Blood Forcibly Drawn During Physical Exam at a Beijing Forced Labour Camp". Website reference is available at www.organharvestinvestigation.net

21   "Falun Gong Practitioners Forced to Go Through Medical Examinations in Sanshui Women's Labour Camp in 2003". Website reference is available at www.organharvestinvestigation.net

22   See endnote 7 in Chapter Two.

23   The authorities in charge at the time of Yang's death include:

Yu Minghuan, instructor at the Jiangong Police Department, Yanji City, 86-433-2824004 (office), 86-433-2754022 (home), 86-13844335577 (cell); Cui Songguo, head of Jiangong Police Department, Yanji City, 86-433-2834145 (office), 86433- 2857752 (home), 86-13904435380 (cell); Li Dongzhu, deputy head of Yanji City Police Department, in charge of persecuting Falun Gong, 86-433-2514600 (office), 86-433-2525232 (home), 86-13804487858 (cell).

24-26   See endnote 7 in Chapter Two.

27   Suizhu's 610 Office leader: Zhang Shujun, home telephone number: 86-516-8323943.

Yang Shuguang: 86-516-8381755, 86-516-8382317

Xuzhou Police Station: 86-516-3745000 Suining County is governed under Xuzhou City Suining County Police Department: 86-516-8331804.

28   See endnote 7 in Chapter Two.

Chapter Five
29-32   See endnote 7 in Chapter Two.

Chapter Six
33   "The high price of illness in China", Louisa Lim, BBC News, Beijing, 2006/03/02.

34   "Public Health in China: Organization, Financing and Delivery of Services", Jeffrey P. Koplan, July 27, 2005.

35   "Implementation of the International Covenant on Economic Social and Cultural Rights in the People's Republic of China", April 14, 2005, paragraph 69, page 24.

36-40   See endnote 7 in Chapter Two.

41   Canadian Organ Replacement Register, Canadian Institute for Health Information. Website reference is available at www.organharvestinvestigation.net

42   Donor Matching System, The Organ Procurement and Transplantation Network (OPTN). Website reference is available at www.organharvestinvestigation.net

43-57   See endnote 7 in Chapter Two.

Chapter Eight
58-60   See endnote 7 in Chapter Two.

61   "China to 'tidy up' trade in executed prisoners' organs", *The Times*, December 03, 2005. Website reference is available at www.organharvestinvestigation.net

62   Index of AI Annual reports.Website reference is available at www.organharvestinvestigation.net

63   Article 211.

64   See endnote 7 in Chapter Two.

65   "The Number of Renal Transplants (Asia & the Middle and Near East)1989-2000", Medical Net (Japan). Website reference is available at www.organharvestinvestigation.net

66   See endnote 7 in Chapter Two.

67   "CURRENT SITUATION OF ORGAN DONATION IN CHINA FROM STIGMA TO STIGMATA", Abstract, The World Transplant Congress.

      Zhonghua K Chen, Fanjun Zeng, Changsheng Ming, Junjie Ma, Jipin Jiang, Institute of Organ Transplantation,

      Tongji Hospital, Tongji Medical College, HUST, Wuhan, China.

      Website references are available at www.organharvestinvestigation.net

68-70 See endnote 7 in Chapter Two.

71   Please see Case 7 in Chapter Five.

72   Please see Call (4) in Chapter Seven.

73-76 See endnote 7 in Chapter Two.

77   According to Deputy Minister of Health, Mr. Huang Jiefu. Website reference is available a www.organharvestinvestigation.net

78-85 See endnote 7 in Chapter Two.

86   Human Rights Watch, "Organ Procurement and Judicial Execution in China", August 1994.

87   Report of the Special Rapporteur on torture and other cruel, inhuman or degrading treatment or punishment, Addendum, Manfred Nowak U.N. Document A/HRC/4/33/Add.1, 20 March 2007, paragraph 40; Report of the Special Rapporteur on freedom of religion or belief Addendum, Asma Jahangir, U.N. Document A/HRC/4/21/Add.1, 8 March 2007, paragraphs 107 to 111.

88   Report of the Special Rapporteur on torture and other cruel, inhuman or degrading treatment or punishment, Addendum, Manfred Nowak, U.N. Document, A/HRC/7/3/Add.1, 19 February 2008, paragraph 36; Report of the Special Rapporteur on freedom of religion or belief, Addendum, Asma Jahangir, U.N. Document A/HRC/7/10/Add.1, 28 February 2008, paragraphs 40 and 41.

89   U.N. Document A/HRC/7/3/Add.1.

90-91 See endnote 7 in Chapter Two.

92   Concluding observations of the U.N. Committee against Torture on China U.N. Document number CAT/C/CHN/CO/4, 21 November 2008, paragraph 18(C).

Chapter Nine

93   "Going Public about Communist Concentration Camps" by Gary Feuerberg, *Epoch Times* April 21, 2006.

94-98   See endnote 7 in Chapter Two.

Chapter Ten
Notes for Treasure Article

99   *Journal of the Royal Society of Medicine,* Volume 100, March 2007, Pages 119-121, reproduced with permission of the author.

100   China International Transplantation Network Assistance Centre: The Cost of the Transplantation. Website reference is available at www.organharvestinvestigation.net

101   Zhang Feng, "New Rule to Regulate Organ Transplants", *China Daily,* May 2006. Website reference is available at www.organharvestinvestigation.net

102   Matas D, Kilgour D., "Report Into Allegations of Organ Harvesting of Falun Gong Practitioners". Website reference is available at www.organharvestinvestigation.net

103   Chinese Embassy. Website reference is available at www.organharvestinvestigation.net

104   Lifton, R. J., *The Nazi Doctors,* New York, Basic Books, 2000.

105   Reproduced with permission of the author.

Notes for Allison Statement

106   The suppression of Falun Gong was organized under the so called "610 Office" whose charge is to "eradicate Falun Gong". The formula, reportedly of 610 Office head Li Lanquing during a mass meeting in the Great Hall of the People in 1999, comprises "defaming their reputations, bankrupting them financially and destroying them physically". Reported by Li Biagen, assistant director of the Beijing Municipal Planning Office. In Matas and Kilgour Report (note 2), p. 9. China is a signatory to the Convention Against Torture and Other Cruel Inhuman or Degrading Treatment or Punishment (ratified 12/12/1986) but excuses itself from Article 20 (investigation of alleged violations) and Article 30, paragraph 1, arbitration between states.

107   Convention Against Torture and Other Cruel Inhuman or Degrading Treatment or Punishment, Article 12 (1) and Article 15 (1)(a), respectively.

     According to the Congressional Executive Commission on China Annual Report 2006, in 2005 alone 4.62 million pieces of Falun Gong publications were seized. Website reference is available at www.organharvestinvestigation.net

108   International Covenant of Economic, Social and Cultural Rights. Website reference is available at www.organharvestinvestigation.net

109   Report of the Special Rapporteur on Torture and Other Cruel, Inhuman or Degrading Treatment or Punishment, Manfred Nowak, on his Mission to China (20 November to 2 December 2005), E/CN.4/2006/6/Add.6, p.2.

110   Ibid, p. 13. See Table 1: Victims of alleged torture.

Percentages: Falun Gong 66; Uighurs [a Muslim separatist minority] 11; sex workers 8; Tibetans 6; Human rights defenders 5; political dissenters 2; others (HIV/AIDS infected; religious groups) 2.

111   Congressional Executive Commission on China Annual Report 2006, p. 59, note 224, p.201: "Organ Transplants: A Zone of Accelerated Regulation" [Qiguan yizhi: jiakuai guizhi de didai], *Caijing Magazine* (Online), 28 November 05, reporting that over 95 percent of organs transplanted in China come from executed prisoners.

112   Circa 65% of capital offenses were for nonviolent crime.

Congressional Executive Commission on China Annual Report 2006, note 210, p. 200.

113   Congressional Executive Commission on China Annual Report 2006, note 212, p.200.

114   Amnesty International, "People's Republic of China. Executed 'according to law'? The Death Penalty in China.", 22 March 2004.

Also "Death, Yunnan style." *Beijing Today,* 7 March, 2003. Website references are available at www.organharvestinvestigation.net

115   Calum MacLeod, "China makes ultimate punishment mobile", *USA Today,* 15 June 2006, 8A [with photo].

116   Organs for sale: China's growing trade and ultimate violation of prisoners' rights: hearing before the Subcommittee on International Operations and Human Rights of the Committee on International Relations, House of Representatives, One Hundred Seventh Congress, first session, June 27, 2001. 57-61.

Website reference is available at www.organharvestinvestigation.net

117   World Medical Association Resolution on Physician's Conduct Concerning Human Organ Transplantation (1994). Adopted by the 46th WMA General Assembly, Stockholm, Sweden, September 1994. Website reference is available at www.organharvestinvestigation.net

118   World Medical Association, "World Medical Association demands China stops using prisoners for organ transplants", 22 May 2006.

Website reference is available at www.organharvestinvestigation.net

119   "Facts of Chinese Transplantation." China International Transplant Center

        Website reference is available at www.organharvestinvestigation.net

120   See Erik Baard, Rebecca Cooney. "China's Execution, Inc.", *The Village Voice*, 8 May 2001, 36 and 38-40.

121   Organs for sale: China's growing trade and ultimate violation of prisoners' rights: hearing before the Subcommittee on International Operations and Human Rights of the Committee on International Relations, House of Representatives, One Hundred Seventh Congress, first session, June 27, 2001.

        Website reference is available at www.organharvestinvestigation.net

122   Zhen Feng, "New rule to regulate organ transplantations", *China Daily*, 05/05/06, p.1.

        Website reference is available at www.organharvestinvestigation.net

123   "Organ sales 'thriving' in China", BBC News, 9/27/06.

        Website reference is available at www.organharvestinvestigation.net

124   "China bans transplant organ sales", BBC News, 3/28/06.

        Website reference is available at www.organharvestinvestigation.net

125   Take for example United Nations General Assembly Resolution 59/156 of 20 December, 2004, Preventing, combating and punishing trafficking in human organs: "34. To be able to give valid consent, the competent donor must be thoroughly informed about the purpose and nature of the removal, as well as its consequences and risks.

        In addition, the consent must be voluntary, free from coercion and undue pressure."

126   See Matas and Kilgour Report, pp. 18-19. Website reference is available at www.organharvestinvestigation.net

127   The meeting took place on June 9, 2006 in Minneapolis, Minnesota.

128   Kirk C. Allison, "Mounting Evidence of Falun Gong Practitioners used as Organ Sources in China and Related Ethical Responsibilities", reprinted in *The Epoch Times*, 8/7/06.

        Website reference is available at www.organharvestinvestigation.net

129   An interview with a physician, a Dr. Lu, at Nanning City Minzu Hospital in Guangxi Autonomous Region (22 May, 2006) indicates physicians select the prisoners to be used for organ sources at the point of demand. See Matas and Kilgour Report Appendix 14, p. 3-4. Website reference is available at www.organharvestinvestigation.net

130   www.organharvestinvestigation.net

Chapter Eleven

131-132 See endnote 7 in Chapter Two.

133 Kevin Steel, "Sowing Confusion; Embarrassed by reports of live organ harvesting, China's sympathizers launch a high-tech disinformation campaign", *Western Standard,* April 9, 2007.

134 "La régime chinois prend le contrôle d'un journal montréalais", *La Presse Cinoise,* July 10, 2007.

135 Jason Loftus, "Chinese Regime Tries to Crush Cultural Show in Canada", *Epoch Times,* January 18, 2007.

136 See David Kilgour and David Matas "Bloody Harvest: Organ Harvesting of Falun Gong Practitioners in China" Appendix 8, at www.organharvestinvestigation.net

The Attorney-General of Canada refused to consent to the prosecution. The complainants challenged the refusal in the Alberta courts, unsuccessfully.

137 Broadcasting Public Notice CRTC 2006-166, paragraphs 95 to 107.

138 Ibid, paragraphs 112 and 113.

139 *Taipei Times,* AFP "Australia gives Chinese ex-cop a protection visa", August 2, 2005; BBC News, "China Defector Accuses Australia", June 6, 2005.

140 See endnote 7 in Chapter Two.

141 Michael Chase and James C. Mulvenon, "You've Got Dissent!: Chinese Dissident Use of the Internet and Beijing's Counter-Strategies", Santa Monica, Rand Corporation, 2002.

142 Jason Loftus, "TV Network Calls on Canada to Expel High-Ranking Chinese Official Over Interference", *Epoch Times,* April 22, 2007.

143 Jason Loftus, "Chinese Embassy Tried to Silence TV Network in Canada, Leaked Document Shows", *Epoch Times,* April 4, 2007.

144 Broadcasting Public Notice CRTC 2005-105, November 24, 2005.

145 Ofra Edelman, "TAU exhibit on Falun Gong meditation shuttered over Chinese pressure, students charge", *Haaretz,* 11/03/2008.

146 See endnote 7 in Chapter Two.

147 "Divine Performing Arts Debuts in South Korea", *Epoch Times,* Apr 25, 2007.

148 Yang Sun, "Chinese Embassy Interferes with DPA in South Korea Again", *Epoch Times,* January 15, 2008.

149 John Turley-Ewart, "Falun Gong persecution spreads to Canada", *National Post,* March 20, 2004.

150   Jan Wong, "Feeling the long arm of China", *The Globe and Mail,* August 6, 2005.

151   *Huang v. 1233065 Ontario Inc. (Ottawa Senior Chinese Cultural Association),* 2006 HRTO 1. The decision was set aside on procedural grounds, inadequate service. See *1233065 Ontario Inc. (Ottawa Senior Chinese Cultural Association) v. Ontario Human Rights Commission,* 2007 CanLII 44345.

152   Universal Declaration of Human Rights, Article 15(1).

153   "Government revokes visas for two television reporters seeking to accompany Canadian prime minister on visit to China", International Freedom of Expression eXchange January 17, 2005. (At time of publication of this book, the website address of the International Freedom of Expression eXchange is http://www.ifex.org.)

154   California Assembly Bill number 2612, Chapter 228, amending section 19.8 to add section 490.7 to the Penal Code.

155   "Governor signs bill providing fines stealing newspapers", Associated Press, September 11, 2006.

156   John Nania, "A Strange Chinese Export", Association for Asian Research, December 26, 2005.

Chapter Twelve
157   Constitution of the People's Republic of China, Article III(2).

158   Ibid, Article III(1).

159   Ibid, Article IV(1).

160   "New rule to regulation organ transplants", *China Daily,* May 5, 2006.

161   "Success Leads to More Liver Transplants", *China Daily,* August 15, 2007.

162   Jim Warren, "China moving rapidly to change transplant system", *Transplant News,* September 2007.

163   Concluding observations of the U.N. Committee against Torture on China, U.N. Document number CAT/C/CHN/CO/4, 21 November 2008, paragraph 18(C).

164   Canadian Export and Import Permits Act, Section 13.

Chapter Thirteen
165   Robin Munro, "The Soviet Case: Prelude to a Global Consensus on Psychiatry and Human Rights", *Columbia Journal of Asian Law,* vol. 14, no. 1 (2000), January 2001.

Chapter Fifteen

166   National report submitted in accordance with paragraph 15(a) of the annex to Human Rights Council resolution 5/1, China, United Nations Document A/HRC/WG.6/4/CHN/1, 10 November 2008.

167   "Canada must outgrow its juvenile relationship with China", *Globe and Mail,* 11 April, 2009.

168   Human Rights Without Frontiers International, "United Nations: China says NO to democracy and human rights", 16 February, 2009.

169   Human Rights Council Eleventh session Agenda item 6, Universal Periodic Review Report of the Working Group on the Universal Periodic Review China, U.N. Document A/HRC/11/25, 3 March, 2009.

170   Kershaw, Ian, *Hitler 1889–1936 Hubris,* W.W. Norton, New York, 1998, pages 529-531.

171   Brian Rudman, "Victory for Falun Gong", *New Zealand Herald,* November 16, 2007.

172   "United Future's leader Peter Dunne is critical of a decision to ban the Falun Gong from Wellington's Chinese New Year parade", Radio New Zealand, February 8, 2008.

173   Mike Steketee, "Kowtowing to China", *The Australian,* March 12, 2005.

174   Brian Hutchinson, "Falun Gong Must Go", *National Post,* June 16, 2006.

175   United States Department of State International Religious Freedom Report 2002, "Iceland".

176   "Government broke law in denying Falun Gong entry says Ombudsman", Iceland Review Online, December 12, 2005.

177   "Taiwanese Falun Gong slams Police", AFP, January 30, 2004.

178   Dirk Beveridge, AP, August 21, 2002, "As Hong Kong court prepares arrest warrants, convicted Falun Gong say someone stepping in to pay their fines".

179   United States Department of States Country Reports on Human Rights, 2006, China, Hong Kong and Macau.

180   Statement of Human Rights Law Foundation November 30, 2006.

181   Singapore Democratic Party, "Singapore Subordinate Court", January 22, 2007.

182   "Falun Gong detainees find Norway home", January 27, 2006.

Chapter Sixteen

183   Jiang, Zemin, Comrade, to standing members of the Political Bureau of the CCCCP, 25 Apr. 1999. Website reference is available at www.organharvestinvestigation.net

184   Constitution of the People's Republic of China, Article 33.

185   Ibid, Article 1.

186   Ibid, Article 3.

Suggestions for further reading

Chang, Jung, *Wild Swans,* New York, Anchor Books, 1992

Chang, Jung and Halliday, Jon, *Mao – The Unknown Story,* New York, Anchor Books, 2006

Gao, Zhisheng, *A China More Just,* Broad Press U.S.A., 2007

Gutmann, Ethan, *Losing the New China,* San Francisco, Encounter Books, 2004

Hattaway, Paul and Brother Yun, *The Heavenly Man,* Dereham (U.K.), Monarch Books, 2003

Hutton, Will, *The Writing on the Wall – China and the West in the 21st Century,* London, Little Brown, 2006

Kynge, James, *China Shakes the World,* London, Phoenix, 2006

Monk, Paul, *Thunder from the Silent Zone – Rethinking China,* Victoria (Australia), Scribe Publications, 2005

Navarro, Peter, *The Coming China Wars – Where They Will Be Fought and How They Can Be Won,* New York, Financial Times Press, 2008

Terrill, Ross, *The New Chinese Empire,* Sydney, UNSW Press, 2003

Worden, Minky, *China's Great Leap – The Beijing Games and the Olympian Human Rights Challenges,* New York, Seven Stories Press, 2008

Zeng, Jennifer, *Witnessing History – One Woman's Fight for Freedom and Falun Gong,* Sydney, Allen and Unwin, 2005